COPYFRAUD
and OTHER ABUSES
of INTELLECTUAL
PROPERTY LAW

COPYFRAUD
and OTHER ABUSES
of INTELLECTUAL
PROPERTY LAW

Jason Mazzone

Stanford Law Books
An Imprint of Stanford University Press
Stanford, California

Printed in the United States of America on acid-free, archival-quality paper

Library of Congress Cataloging-in-Publication Data

Mazzone, Jason, author.
 Copyfraud and other abuses of intellectual property law / Jason Mazzone.
 pages cm.
 Includes bibliographical references and index.
 ISBN 978-0-8047-6006-5 (cloth : alk. paper)
 1. Copyright—United States. 2. Fair use (Copyright)—United States. 3. Intellectual property—United States. I. Title.

KF2994.M399 2011
346.7304'82—dc22

                                                      2011008078

Typeset at Stanford University Press in 10.5/15 Adobe Garamond

For updates and further information, visit the author's website
www.copyfraud.com

CONTENTS

PREFACE

CALIFORNIA HAS 3,427 miles of shoreline.[1] Under the state's constitution, the shoreline is available, up to the mean high-tide line, for the public to use. Owners of beach-front homes, however, would prefer to keep the whole beach abutting their properties to themselves. In Malibu, homeowners place phony "No Trespassing" signs on the public beach, and they deploy security guards on all-terrain vehicles to chase away beachgoers. In Malibu's Broad Beach neighborhood, residents have bulldozed wet sand from the shoreline up to the high-tide mark to create a giant access barrier. At Carbon Beach, gated homes spanning multiple lots form a wall that blocks access to the shoreline from the Pacific Coast Highway. Whenever public interest groups have sought to open up pathways to the beach so that the state's constitution may be honored, homeowners have vigorously fought back. In 2005, DreamWorks co-founder David Geffen's decision to give up the keys to locked wooden gates next to his Malibu home, allowing the public to enter a stretch of beach, was headline news because it followed years of litigation and daily fines imposed upon Geffen for unlawfully blocking beach access. Battles over beaches occur in other states as well. In most states, the wet sand area of a beach is held by law in public trust, meaning it exists for the use and benefit of the population as a whole, even when the adjacent property is privately owned. Yet property owners routinely attempt to make their rights go farther than they actually do by interfering with people's ability to access beaches. On the New Jersey shore, homeowners have obstructed public entry points near their properties by erecting fences, and private beach clubs have set up entrance gates that admit only paying members onto public lands. On the island of Oahu, in Hawaii, gated subdivisions have turned public beaches into private sands. And in certain New York municipalities, local voters have passed ordinances limiting the use of the beach to town residents, notwithstanding the fact they have no legal right to do so. Increasingly, the beach—the public's playground—is subject to private claims.

Like the owners of beachfront property, owners of intellectual property regularly claim more than the law gives them. Intellectual property law gives private parties rights in the works they create while also protecting the public's interests in accessing and using information. To achieve this laudable balance between public and private interests, intellectual property rights are limited. The law imposes various requirements that a creative work must meet to merit protection in the first place, and it specifies the kind and scope of rights that may be asserted. For example, copyrights and patents exist for limited terms; when the term of protection expires, the work falls into the public domain, where anybody is free to copy and use it. Increasingly, however, creators and content providers do not adhere to the distinction that intellectual property law draws between what belongs to them and what belongs to the public. They attach illegitimate ownership notices to works that are in the public domain. They wall off public works behind technological barriers. Their lawyers issue threats against individuals who have not infringed any actual property rights. They overreach.

While there are many other books on intellectual property, this is the first to examine overreaching as a distinct problem and to show how to solve it. Intellectual property law in the United States does not work well, and it needs to be reformed—but not for the reasons given by most critics. The principal defect of intellectual property law is not, as many observers have maintained, that intellectual property rights are too easily obtained, too broad in scope, and too long in duration. Rather, the primary problem is the gap that exists between the rights that the law confers and the rights that are asserted in practice. Overly broad claims to intellectual property rights are a widespread phenomenon. Such claims interfere with legitimate uses and reproductions of a wide variety of works, impose enormous social and economic costs, and undermine creative endeavors. The solution is not to change the scope or content of intellectual property rights, but to create mechanisms to prevent people and organizations from asserting legal protections beyond those they legitimately possess.

This book does three things. First, it shows the astonishing extent to which overreaching occurs and the effects of overreaching on the balance between private rights and public interests. Although the book focuses largely on copyrights, because copyright law is, of all the different kinds of intellectual property law, the one that ordinary people confront most regularly, we will see many examples of overreaching in a variety of sectors and media, including the music, movie, and software industries, and by a variety of actors, including owners of trademarks in children's toys and television characters and, most surprising, nonprofit entities such as academic presses, museums, and archives.

Second, the book explains why creators and content providers overreach. In some instances, overreaching is simply about making money. Creators and content providers who can claim they own more than they actually do sell licenses to people who believe their claims. In other cases, overreaching is designed to inhibit competition. Profit is not, however, the only motivation. Overreaching also occurs when creators and content providers seek to control who gets to use creative works and for what purposes. For example, sometimes overreaching is intended to stifle criticism, promote a political agenda, or otherwise interfere with free speech.

Third, the book shows how to remedy overreaching. It presents a series of proposals by which government, organizations, and private actors can stand up to creators and content providers when they seek to grab more than the law gives them. We will see ways in which intellectual property law needs to be changed to prevent overreaching as well as how existing laws can be deployed to combat it. In identifying these remedies, we will draw lessons from other countries that have taken firm steps to keep intellectual property rights within their proper bounds. We will learn also how ordinary people can prevent and respond to overreaching claims. The public can and should take back its metaphorical beach. This book shows how to do that.

The book uses a typology to classify different kinds of overreaching along with the factors inherent in our intellectual property system that contribute to its occurrence. The typology allows the reader to recognize and understand overreaching when it occurs, as well as to identify the best remedy for the particular problem at hand. The typology distinguishes between two principal kinds of overreaching. False claims to intellectual property involve an assertion of ownership (and the accompanying ownership rights) when there is no basis for the claim. Claiming copyright in a work after the copyright has expired is one kind of false claim. The second general kind of overreaching, overzealous assertions of intellectual property rights, involves owners of intellectual property asserting their rights in ways that, while not dishonest, are of dubious validity. For example, threatening a lawsuit for copyright or trademark infringement when there is little likelihood of such a lawsuit prevailing (and thus little likelihood the case will ever be brought) entails an overzealous assertion of rights.

As to factors that contribute to overreaching, we will encounter laws that enable overreaching to occur. For example, copyright law does not punish very severely false claims of copyright. As a result, false copyright claims are common. In other cases, overreaching occurs because content providers are able to take advantage of the fact that the boundaries between private rights and public access are not always visible to the public. Just as the tide line can shift and cause confusion about where private property ends and the public beach begins, intellectual property is not always clearly demarcated. In such circumstances, private parties are able to extend their rights to the maximum degree possible by denying that the public owns anything at all. One example of this phenomenon is the vagueness of the fair use provision of copyright law: intended to facilitate certain uses of copyrighted works without the permission of the copyright owner, fair use law ends up enabling copyright owners to claim that *all* proposed uses require their permission. The book thus explores how intellectual property law itself provides, perversely, the basis for creators and content providers to claim rights far beyond those they actually possess.

Confronted with these extravagant ownership claims, people make conservative uses of existing intellectual property. Rather than risk a lawsuit, people alter or abandon their own creative projects. So too will we see how risk-averse gatekeepers such as publishers, distributors, and insurers prevent legitimate uses of intellectual property by the creators they represent. Conservative uses and the role of gatekeepers enable overreaching to occur.

Throughout the book, we will see gaps between norms and laws. In a variety of contexts, people behave according to norms that are more protective of the rights of intellectual property owners than is the relevant law. These norms sustain a culture of licensing in which all uses of intellectual property, even in ways the law permits, require permission and payment of a fee. The gap between norms and laws relates to the problem of misinformation. Confronted with inaccurate information about intellectual property law, content providers claim more than they have and users do less than the law allows them, on the basis of misunderstandings of the scope of legal protections. Misinformation thereby buttresses the phenomenon of overreaching.

As this discussion already suggests, as we explore these elements of the typology, we will see also how they interact. For example, misinformation leads to false claims, which nervous gatekeepers do not confront. Laws that enable rights holders to make overzealous assertions result in conservative uses of intellectual property law, which in turn embolden rights holders to overreach in the future. The gap between laws and norms makes gatekeepers cautious. And so on. Understanding these interactions helps in curing the disease.

Current debates about the proper role and reach of intellectual property rights in the modern information society have reached an impasse. On one side of the gulf stand creators and their representatives. They see widespread infringement of their intellectual property rights—helped along by new technologies—and declining sales in their traditional markets. Their position, one that has reached sympathetic ears in Congress in recent years, is that intellectual property rights need greater protection, including increased penalties for infringement. On the other side of the divide are individuals and organizations that believe that corporations have profited too long from hardworking artists, and that intellectual property rights stifle creative endeavors that build upon preexisting works. From this perspective, intellectual property law is too severe, it serves those who don't deserve the law's protections, and it undermines the public domain.

There has been little hope of closing the divide between these two positions. Since I began writing this book, I have attended, moderated, and participated in numerous conferences and other discussions bringing together industry representatives who are in favor of strong intellectual property laws and those who advocate loosening intellectual property rights. These conversations have never approached any agreement because the participants have such different views on what the problem is. Content providers believe they are under threat; their critics contend that content providers themselves are the threat.

This book takes a different approach and offers a way out of the impasse. I believe in both strong intellectual property rights and a strong public domain. The way to enhance the public domain is not by limiting the scope and duration of intellectual property rights. Instead, the focus should be on developing mechanisms to keep those rights within their designated limits. Rather than choose between the rights of creators and the interests of the public, it is essential to protect both. This book shows how to achieve that goal.

COPYFRAUD
and OTHER ABUSES
of INTELLECTUAL
PROPERTY LAW

CHAPTER I

COPYFRAUD

A POCKET VERSION of the U.S. Constitution popular among law students contains a copyright notice along with this warning: "No part of this publication may be reproduced or transmitted in any form or by any means . . . without permission in writing from the publisher."[1] The notice and warning are obviously absurd. Whatever the Constitution's framers and ratifiers had in mind when they authorized Congress to create laws protecting copyright, they did not expect that somebody would one day claim a copyright in the Constitution itself. Imagine for a moment, though, a world in which the U.S. Constitution *is* copyrighted. Lawyers would need permission to quote the provisions of the Constitution that help their clients' causes. Newspaper columnists discussing freedom of speech would need to license the text of the First Amendment. Lawsuits would be filed to remove unauthorized copies of the Constitution from high school classrooms. Reproducing the text of the Constitution in a book or on a website would require advance clearance. Government agents would raid warehouses and stores and seize unauthorized "We the People" coffee mugs, tote bags, and T-shirts.

There is a good reason nobody owns a copyright in the U.S. Constitution. The Constitution belongs to everyone. Along with millions of other works, the Constitution is part of the public domain. The public domain is the collection of works that are not protected by copyrights. A work becomes part of the public domain when the copyright on it expires, because the work did not qualify for copyright protection in the first place, or because the creator of the work has given the work to the public. Public domain works are free for anybody to use and reproduce because nobody has the right to control their use.

Under the law, the word *fraud* is used to describe a false claim by one person to another. *Copyfraud* is therefore the term I use to refer to the act of falsely claiming a copyright in a public domain work. In the typology I use in this book to classify forms of overreaching, copyfraud entails a false claim to intellectual property where none exists.

Examples of copyfraud abound. In general, copyright belongs to the author of a published work and expires seventy years after the author's death. Yet copyright notices appear on modern reprints of poems by William Cullen Bryant (who died in 1878) and on the piano scores of Ludwig van Beethoven (who died in 1827). There is no basis for claiming copyright in reproductions of two-dimensional public domain artworks. Yet modern publishers hawk greeting card versions of Monet's water lilies, Van Gogh's sunflowers, and Cézanne's apples—each bearing a copyright mark. Poster-sized reproductions of works by Vermeer and Da Vinci, each embossed with a false copyright notice, brighten the walls of college dorm rooms across the country. Archives claim blanket copyrights in everything in their collections, including historical works as to which copyright, which probably never belonged to the archive in the first place, has long expired. The publishers of school textbooks do not explain that their copyright notices apply only to the authors' own words and original arrangements and not to the books' reproductions of the Declaration of Independence, the Gettysburg Address, Supreme Court cases, or *George Washington Crossing the Delaware*. Corporate websites include blanket copyright notices even when they feature the U.S. flag, list stock reports, contain a calendar, or rely on other materials squarely in the public domain.

Copyfraud has serious consequences. In addition to enriching publishers who assert false copyright claims at the expense of legitimate users, copyfraud stifles valid forms of reproduction and creativity and undermines free speech. False copyright claims, which are often accompanied by the threat of litigation for reproduction of a work without the putative owner's permission, result in users seeking licenses and paying fees to reproduce works that are free for everyone to use, or altering their creative projects to excise the un-copyrighted material. Copyfraud also fosters misunderstanding concerning the scope of intellectual property law, which further emboldens publishers and other content providers to claim rights beyond those they actually possess.

SOME COPYRIGHT LAW BASICS

The point of copyright is to promote creativity. Under the Constitution, Congress has power "[t]o promote the progress of science and useful arts, by securing for limited times to authors and inventors the exclusive right to their respective writings and discoveries."[2] The Constitution therefore empowers Congress to create copyright protections in order to encourage creative production by allowing authors to monopolize, for a limited period, revenues from their own works. As the Supreme Court has explained, copyright law is thus instrumental. The monopoly that a copyright confers "is intended to motivate the creative activity of authors."[3] The ultimate goal is an enrichment of publicly accessible works: "[P]rivate motivation must ultimately serve the cause of promoting broad public availability of literature, music, and the other arts."[4]

Congress enacted the first federal copyright statute in 1790. Our modern copyright statute is the Copyright Act of 1976, which took effect in 1978, and which itself has subsequently been revised and updated. Its granting of monopolistic rights to authors gives copyright an uneasy relationship with the First Amendment, which, in general, prohibits government from conferring exclusive rights in speech. The Constitution strikes a delicate balance between supporting authorship and suppressing speech by permitting copyrights only "for limited times." Accordingly, under federal statutory law, the term of copyright protection is limited. Once a copyright expires, the work falls into the public domain, where anybody is free to use it.

The Copyright Act provides that for works created on or after January 1, 1978, the copyright in the work lasts until seventy years following the author's death. For works with multiple authors, the term is seventy years after the death of the last surviving author. The duration of copyright protection for pre-1978 works is more complicated; other writers have usefully summarized the various rules.[5] For present purposes it suffices to note four major categories of works that are no longer protected by copyright and are therefore in the public domain: (1) any work published in the United States before 1923, (2) any work published in the United States between 1923 and 1963 for which copyright was not renewed, (3) unpublished works by authors who died more than seventy years ago, and (4) all works published outside the United States before July 1, 1909.

Congress has also limited the kinds of works that may be copyrighted. Under the Copyright Act, a copyright belongs to the author of a work if the work meets three requirements. The first requirement is *fixation*. To enjoy copyright protection, a work must be fixed in a "tangible medium of expression."[6] This means that the work must be in some concrete form, such as occurs when a work is typed on a page, posted to a website, or painted on a canvas. Works that are not fixed—for example, a speech that is not recorded or written down—are not eligible for copyright. The second requirement to merit copyright protection is *originality*. The work must be the author's own work in that the author must have created it. If a work contains some original elements and some elements the author has copied from somewhere else, only the original elements of the work are eligible for new copyright protection. The originality requirement does not mean that the work has to be novel. If I draw a squiggle on a page, the squiggle is original so long as I independently created it. It doesn't matter that thousands of people before me have created the same squiggle: so long as in drawing my squiggle I didn't copy somebody else's, the squiggle is deemed original. The third requirement a work must meet in order to be eligible for copyright protection is that the work must entail *minimal creativity*. This is a separate requirement from that of originality. A work can be original without being creative. The standard for creativity is not very high. One need not be a Mozart to produce a creative work within the meaning of the copyright law. However, some works do not satisfy the requirement. For example, while my squiggle might be my own work, and thus original, a court might determine that drawing the squiggle did not entail sufficient creativity on my part and thus the squiggle is not protected by a copyright. Making use of somebody else's work does not preclude a finding of minimal creativity, which can lie in how the prior work has been reworked or arranged. If I copy the *Mona Lisa*, for example, but I give her blonde hair, earrings, and a frown, my work is minimally creative.

An implication of the minimal creativity requirement is that copyright protection does not depend on the degree of effort that goes into producing a work. It may take years to produce a particular work, and the work might be fixed in a tangible form and original, but if the work is not also minimally creative, it is not eligible for protection. Mere exertion—sweat of the brow—does not a copyright confer. An important Supreme Court decision illustrates the principle. In 1991, in *Feist Publications v. Rural Telephone Service Company*, the Supreme Court held that there can be no copyright in a telephone directory that merely compiles names, towns, and telephone numbers.[7] Names, towns, and telephone numbers are all facts. Facts, the Court said, cannot be copyrighted because no author created them.[8] The directory of facts could also not be copyrighted. Despite the effort involved in compiling the information in the directory, an alphabetical listing of names, locations, and telephone numbers did not entail original creativity. Anybody preparing a directory of telephone numbers would arrange the information in the same way. Invoking the language of the Constitution, the Court stated, "The primary objective of copyright is not to reward the labor of authors, but 'to promote the Progress of Science and useful Arts.'"[9] Similarly, databases that merely compile information or works by others are not protected by copyright unless the compilation involves creativity in the selection or arrangement.[10]

An important corollary to these three requirements for copyright eligibility is that copyright law does not protect facts, ideas, theories, or discoveries but only protects the way in which those things are expressed.[11] If, for example, I conduct research on the habits of bumblebees and write a book in which I report my findings, copyright law does not prevent somebody else from writing about my findings. Only my expression of the research findings is eligible for copyright protection. As the Supreme Court has stated, "every idea, theory, and fact in a copyrighted work becomes instantly available for public exploitation at the moment of publication."[12]

COPYRIGHTING THE PUBLIC DOMAIN

Copyrights are limited in scope and duration. The public domain comprises works that are not protected. Why, then, does copyfraud occur? One important explanation is that the law itself enables this form of overreaching. A basic defect of modern copyright law is that statutory protections for copyright are not balanced with affirmative protections for the public domain. Congress has enumerated the rights of copyright holders but has left protections for the public domain largely dependent upon holders respecting the limits on those enumerated rights. Under these conditions, copyfraud flourishes.

Remedies for infringement of copyright are severe. A copyright owner can seek a court order to prevent publication of an infringing work; impounding and disposition of infringing articles; actual damages and profits earned by the infringing party or statutory damages up to $30,000 per work and $150,000 per work in the case of willful infringement (meaning that the defendant knew that it was infringing the plaintiff's copyright);[13] and, at the discretion of a court, costs in bringing the lawsuit and associated attorneys' fees. Under rules of secondary liability, those who facilitate copyright infringement by others may also be held liable. In addition to civil remedies, section 506(a) of the Copyright Act contains a criminal infringement provision, with the possibility of prison time and substantial monetary penalties. Further, section 506(d) of the Copyright Act criminalizes fraudulent removal of copyright notices from works. Beyond the Copyright Act itself, other federal statutes provide civil and criminal remedies for specific kinds of copyright violations.

By contrast, the Copyright Act provides no civil remedy against publishers who improperly claim copyright over materials that are part of the public domain. Just two provisions of the Copyright Act deal in any manner at all with improper assertions of ownership to public domain materials. Section 506(c) criminalizes fraudulent uses of copyright notices. It states, "Any person who, with fraudulent intent, places on any article a notice of copyright or words of the same purport that such person knows to be false, or who, with fraudulent intent, publicly distributes or imports for public distribution any article bearing such notice or words that such person knows to be false, shall be fined not more than $2,500."[14] Section 506(e) also punishes, by the same amount, knowingly making a false representation of a material fact in the application for copyright registration. Yet these criminal provisions are all bark and no bite. In requiring knowledge and intent, the provisions impose a higher level of proof than is needed to show copyright infringement in a civil action. In addition, false assertions of copyright carry much smaller penalties than those for copyright infringement. Most seriously—and in contrast to the general pattern of copyright law—the provisions do not create a private cause of action; that is, they do not allow for individuals to bring a claim in court to enforce the law. Left to the government, these provisions are almost never enforced. During 2008, the most recent year for which comprehensive statistics are available, not a single defendant was prosecuted for fraudulent uses of a copyright notice under section 506(c) or for making false representations in registering a copyright under 506(e). During the entire period from 1994 to 2008, just four cases were filed under section 506(c) and eight cases were filed under 506(e).[15]

Other features of our system of copyrights reflect a similar imbalance between affirmative protections that exist for copyright and for the public domain. The federal Copyright Office registers copyrighted works, but there exists no federally supported Public Domain Office to catalog publicly owned materials. While the symbol © designates what is copyrighted, there is no corresponding mark to indicate public domain works. A variety of federal agencies, including the FBI and the Department of Justice, are charged with protecting copyrights. However, no federal agency is specially charged with safeguarding the public domain.

The end result is that copyright law itself creates an irresistible urge for publishers and other content providers to claim ownership, however spurious, in everything. Facing no threat of civil action under the Copyright Act for copyfraud, and little risk of criminal penalty, publishers and other content providers are free to put copyright notices on everything and to assert the strongest possible claims to ownership. Copyright law itself enables overreaching. Like a "For Sale" sign attached to the Brooklyn Bridge, the upside to attaching a false copyright notice is potentially huge—some naive soul might actually pay up. The only downside is that the false copyright notice will be ignored by savvy individuals who understand the legal rules and call the bluff. Under these conditions, content providers have every incentive to try to sell off pieces of the public domain. Indeed, that is exactly what many content providers have done.

FROM THE FEDERALIST TO "JESUS LOVES ME":
COPYFRAUD IS EVERYWHERE

Browse any bookstore, buy a poster or a greeting card, open up sheet music for choir or orchestra practice, or flip through a high school history text: copyfraud is everywhere. Despite the fact that copyrights are limited by time and original authorship, modern publishers routinely affix copyright notices to reprints of historical works in which copyright has expired. The publisher making the reprint is not the creator of the original work; absent a transfer by the creator of the work, the publisher would not be entitled to claim copyright in the first place. And since the copyright on the original work has expired—indeed, that is the very thing that allows the modern reprint to be made and sold—the work is in the public domain.

Copyright notices appear on modern reprints of William Shakespeare's plays even though the new publisher had nothing to do with their creation and Shakespeare's writings are squarely in the public domain.[16] Reprints of *The Federalist* carry copyright notices even though the words of James Madison, Alexander Hamilton, and John Jay cannot be copyrighted by anyone.[17] Similar misuse of copyright exists with respect to reprints of works by Charles Dickens,[18] Jane Austen,[19] and Benjamin Franklin,[20] none of which are copyrightable. Not every modern publisher of historical works is an offender, but publishers who make proper use of copyright symbols are few and far between.[21]

Books compiling public domain documents also improperly carry blanket copyright notices. For example, a copyright symbol appears on the copyright page of Richard D. Heffner's *A Documentary History of the United States* even though the book consists entirely of reproductions of historical documents ranging from the Declaration of Independence to the Supreme Court's decision in *Roe v. Wade.*[22] Nick Ragone's *The Everything American Government Book* carries a copyright notice and states that "[t]his book, or parts thereof, may not be reproduced in any form" even though parts of this book are reproductions of the Constitution and the Declaration of Independence.[23] Dictionaries of famous quotations bear blanket copyright notices and admonitions against reproducing their contents—even though these books themselves just reproduce the words of others.[24] Law school casebooks, written by people who should know better, bear copyright notices that do not distinguish between the copyrightable editorial comments and the public domain cases reproduced.[25]

Sheet music commonly bears false copyright notices. Nobody has to pay to reproduce, or for that matter to perform, Chopin's nocturnes, Bach's cantatas, Handel's *Messiah*, or "The Star-Spangled Banner."[26] Yet publishers selling sheet versions of these works assert copyright ownership over them, with the result that orchestras, choirs, and other users purchase additional sets rather than simply making a legitimate photocopy.[27] One publisher claims a blanket copyright in J. S. Bach's *The Well-Tempered Clavier* even while it states the source is "J. S. Bach's own hand."[28] Likewise, opera scores often carry improper copyright notices. Online retailer Sheet Music Archive, which bills itself as "the most popular classical sheet music web site," makes available public domain sheet music with this claim: "PDF files made by the SMA are copyrighted by SheetMusicArchive.net, and may not be sold, re-distributed, or used to derive other PDF files, without express written authorization."[29] Even church songs are not safe: Christian Copyright Licensing International, which sells licenses to songs for congregational use, offers 102 versions of "Jesus Loves Me," with just one properly marked as falling within the public domain.

To be sure, a new arrangement or adaptation of a public domain musical work qualifies for copyright if it is sufficiently original. There might also be a copyright in a selection and compilation of music scores. One federal appellate court found that arrangements of "When the Red, Red, Robin Comes Bob, Bob, Bobbin' Along" were insufficiently original to merit copyright protection but, the court explained, new arrangements can be copyrighted if "something of substance" is added so that the earlier work becomes "to some extent a new work with the old song embedded in it."[30] Yet few modern publishers of public domain sheet music adhere to this standard.[31]

The digital explosion of the past years has increased the incidence of copyfraud. Providers of digitally repackaged public domain materials take the position that because they have digitized or otherwise made available a public domain work, they own the copyright in it. Not so. Scanning an old newspaper or broadside is not an act of creation. It is copying, pure and simple. Copyright is not renewed just because somebody puts the work on film or a CD-ROM or posts it online and sells it to researchers. Yet compilers of public domain works frequently claim copyrights in those works. For example, ProQuest offers a subscription-based service containing digital versions of newspapers from the nineteenth century to the present.[32] Every single newspaper page reproduced in the database includes ProQuest's own copyright notice. These notices are false. As the U.S. Copyright Office states, "digitization . . . does not result in a new work of authorship," and therefore there is no copyright.[33] A publisher that selects and arranges non-copyrightable works in a particular way might own a copyright with respect to the original selection and arrangement. The computer search mechanisms a publisher develops to retrieve materials from a database of non-copyrightable works might also be protected. However, there is no copyright obtained in the underlying works, which remain in the public domain.

Publications of the U.S. government are in the public domain.[34] Yet many publishers falsely claim copyright ownership when they reproduce and distribute government documents and other materials. For example, Barnes & Noble has issued the 1964 Warren Commission report in book form. It states that, in addition to the two-page editor's note being copyrighted, "[n]o part of this book may be used or reproduced in any manner whatsoever without written permission of the Publisher."[35] Since the whole book is just a photocopy of the original government report, Barnes & Noble owns no copyright in it. So too do websites that market e-book versions of government publications falsely assert copyright. One such site, Fictionwise, sells the 9/11 Commission Report at $1.99 and claims a copyright in the report. The e-book comes with the following notice:

Copyright © 2004 by Fictionwise.com
    NOTICE: This ebook is licensed to the original purchaser only.
Duplication or distribution to any person via email, floppy disk, network,
print out, or any other means is a violation of International copyright law
and subjects the violator to severe fines and/or imprisonment. . . . This book
cannot be legally lent or given to others.[36]

The statement is nonsense. Making a copy of the 9/11 Commission Report will not lead to prison time. Fictionwise does not obtain a copyright in a government report simply by distributing it in electronic form (and even if it did, copyright does not prohibit lending). From Fictionwise's perspective, though, the extravagant warning makes perfect sense. Some people who see the notice will believe it and buy a second version of the report (Fictionwise encourages buyers to purchase additional copies for friends) rather than recognize the bluff.

Congress included in the Copyright Act a penalty for claiming copyright in U.S. governmental materials, but the effectiveness of this penalty is very limited. The penalty applies only with respect to works that include copyrighted material along with federal governmental material. For such works, a failure to distinguish in a copyright notice the copyrighted portions from the public domain portions can lead to a court awarding reduced damages in the case of infringement of the copyrighted material. The penalty operates in the following way: in all copyright infringement cases, when a defendant is found liable, a court has discretion to reduce the damages owed to the copyright owner if the infringer can show the infringement was "innocent" because he or she "was not aware and had no reason to believe that his or her acts constituted an infringement of copyright."[37] For obvious reasons, a defendant cannot make this argument if the copyrighted work contained a copyright notice.[38] However, there is an exception to that rule which is the basis for penalizing copyright claims in federal governmental materials. Section 403 states that for works consisting "predominantly of one or more works of the United States Government," use of a copyright notice defeats an innocent infringement claim only if the notice "includes a statement identifying, either affirmatively or negatively," which portions are actually copyrighted.[39] In other words, a work covered by section 403 must carry a copyright notice that distinguishes the original material from federal governmental works or the copyright owner risks receiving reduced damages in the event of infringement of the copyrighted portions.

It is not difficult to see why this section 403 penalty does little to stop copyright claims in governmental works. The penalty is only imposed when a copyright owner brings a copyright infringement action in court. It does not, therefore, address the fact that the mere use of a false copyright notice and the simple threat of a lawsuit are often enough to deter legitimate uses of public domain works. The penalty does nothing to prevent Barnes & Noble, Fictionwise, and others from publishing their own versions of government documents with phony copyright notices. In addition, the penalty only applies with respect to works that consist predominantly of federal governmental material. It does not, therefore, prevent anyone from using a blanket copyright notice on a work in which governmental materials are included but do not predominate. In light of the limited reach of the penalty, copyright notices on governmental material are common.

THE CURIOUS CASE OF THE COPYRIGHTED
PYRAMIDS: COPYFRAUD AND ART

In December 2007, the Egyptian Parliament took up a bill that would copyright its pyramids, the Sphinx, and various museum pieces. Under the proposed law, which would apply worldwide, anyone seeking to make an exact replica of a copyrighted artifact would need Egypt's permission and would have to pay royalties. Funds generated would be used to help pay for the upkeep of Egypt's historic sites.[40] Explaining the proposed law, Zahi Hawass, the head of Egypt's Supreme Council of Antiquities, stated, "It is Egypt's right to be the only copyright owner for these monuments in order to benefit financially so we can restore, preserve and protect Egyptian monuments." He added, "The new law will completely prohibit the duplication of historic Egyptian monuments which the Supreme Council of Antiquities considers 100-percent copies."[41]

While commentators in the United States mocked the Egyptian plan, copyrighting the pyramids seems less bizarre when we consider some of our own practices with respect to public domain artwork. Commercial services claim copyright in images of public domain paintings they market to the public. There is, however, no copyright in a perfect reproduction—what courts refer to as a "slavish" copy—of a painting (or other two-dimensional work) that is in the public domain, because, by definition, the reproduction does not entail original creativity. In *Bridgeman Art Library v. Corel*, the Bridgeman Art Library, a British company operating in the United States, marketed reproductions of old paintings on color transparencies. The defendant, the Corel Corporation, published a CD-ROM containing reproductions of old paintings made from images from the Bridgeman transparencies. When Bridgeman sued Corel for copyright infringement, the federal court correctly held that under U.S. and British law, Bridgeman owned no copyright in its transparencies because "a photograph which is no more than a copy of the work of another as exact as science and technology permit lacks originality."[42] This was not a case of a court failing to appreciate the art of photography. The court recognized that "there is little doubt that many photographs, probably the overwhelming majority, reflect at least the modest amount of originality required for copyright protection. Elements of originality . . . may include posing the subjects, lighting, angle, selection of film and camera, evoking the desired expression, and almost any other variant involved."[43] However, the court explained, in accordance with the Supreme Court's decision in the *Feist* case, "slavish copying, although doubtless requiring technical skill and effort, does not qualify" for copyright protection.[44]

As the *Bridgeman* case itself makes clear, this is not to deny that some photographs of other works may entail sufficient originality to merit copyright protection. For example, one court found that photographs of fabrics involved significant creative decisions by the photographer and therefore the photographs constituted original works.[45] But originality remains the touchstone of copyright law. So too was the court in *Bridgeman* careful to note that it was dealing with photographs of two-dimensional works. A photograph of a three-dimensional work, because of the different photographic techniques involved, may entail sufficient originality to merit copyright protection.

Seemingly undeterred by its loss in court, the Bridgeman Art Library continues to assert copyright in reproductions of the *Mona Lisa* and other public domain works. On its website, where users can purchase digital copies of images, Bridgeman states, "All images supplied by the Bridgeman Art Library are copyrighted photographs. The Bridgeman Art Library either owns the copyright in the photograph or acts as the authorized agent of the copyright holder. A license must be obtained from the Library before any reproduction is made or this will constitute an infringement of copyright."[46] Further, under its terms and conditions, Bridgeman asserts, "The Reproduction of the Photographs is strictly forbidden without . . . specific written consent."[47]

The Bridgeman Art Library is not alone in claiming copyrights in digital reproductions of public domain art. Corbis, founded by Bill Gates, is a digital archive of art and photography. It makes available through licensing for professional and private use more than one hundred million images, including many images of two-dimensional public domain works. Corbis's license agreement requires users to "include a copyright notice and credit adjacent to each Image (in the format: '© photographer's name/Corbis' or as specified on the Specific Content Web Page) with each publicly distributed Image."[48] In a similar way, ARTstor and Art Resource, major digital libraries of public domain art, claim copyright in the images they supply and impose restrictions on how the images may be used.[49]

GATEKEEPERS TO OUR CULTURAL HERITAGE

Owning a physical copy of a work does not by itself give rise to ownership of a copyright in the work. Yet many archives and museums claim to hold a copyright in a work merely because they possess a physical copy of the work. For example, the American Antiquarian Society in Worcester, Massachusetts, is one of the largest archives of early American materials, including early broadsides, pamphlets, newspapers, and almanacs. The vast majority of these materials, dating as they do from the seventeenth, eighteenth, and nineteenth centuries, are in the public domain. Yet the society states on its website that "[a]ll uses . . . of images from the collection . . . must be licensed by the Society in consequence of its proprietary rights."[50] The society licenses images at a rate of $100 each for reproduction in a commercial work. In the society's license agreement, "the Licensee [must] acknowledge . . . that the copyrights and all other proprietary rights in and to the Licensed Material are exclusively owned by and reserved to the Society."[51] The American Antiquarian Society is not alone in making these kinds of false copyright assertions. Many other archives assert broad copyright ownership with respect to materials in their physical possession. To access an online collection of nineteenth- and early twentieth-century photographs from the New York State Historical Association's Fenimore Art Museum in Cooperstown, New York, users must accept a click-through agreement that provides, "Images are copyright © New York State Historical Association, which reserves all rights. I will obtain written permission for the use of any image."[52] Individual images come with their own notices: "Prior written permission is required for any reproduction, redistribution, publication, or other use of the images in any media, . . . [including, but] not limited to, printed or electronic media."

Museums are also immersed in a culture of licensing. Museums claim rights in reproductions and charge fees for their use, they require that a copyright notice accompany reproductions used in publications, and (as we will see in Chapter 5) they oblige users to accept strict licensing terms that track or exceed protections available to copyright owners even though the museums have no copyright interest whatsoever. Digital imaging vastly increases access to works of art, but it has also resulted in museums exercising increased control over those works. For example, the Museum of Fine Arts in Boston offers for a licensing fee thousands of images of works in its collection, including such public domain works as Monet's *Valley of the Creuse (Gray Day)* (1889), Degas' *Landscape* (1890), and Boughton's *Sea Breeze* (ca. 1880). The museum claims, wrongly, that these images are copyrighted.[53]

An archive or museum *might* own both the physical copy of a work and the copyright in the work. The most common case is when the creator of the work or some other owner of the copyright—for example, the author's heir—has transferred the copyright to the archive or museum, which then becomes the copyright owner.[54] Yet this only holds true if the work is in fact protected by copyright in the first place. If there is no copyright because it has expired, then there is nothing to transfer. Nonetheless, archives and museums regularly assert copyright ownership where none exists. As the former president of the Society of American Archivists has remarked, "[m]any repositories would like to maintain a kind of quasi-copyright-like control over the further use of materials in their holdings, comparable to the monopoly granted to the copyright owner," and "[o]ne strategy . . . is based on their ownership of the physical manifestation of a once-copyrighted work."[55] The trend is fueled by the ever-growing number of books and seminars marketed to archivists and curators about the minefield of copyright laws and the need to assume everything is protected.

Copyfraud by archives, museums, and other not-for-profit institutions is especially troubling. These entities are publicly supported through tax benefits, and often government grants, because their collections benefit the public. We should be able to expect in return that public domain works be left in the public domain. It should be noted, however, that not all publicly supported institutions are guilty of copyfraud. The Library of Congress, for example, appropriately makes clear that it does *not* own copyrights in the materials in its collections.[56] With respect to specific materials, the library provides information about whether any copyright exists and the identity of the copyright owner. Unfortunately, the Library of Congress's accurate use of copyright notices is rare among repositories of public domain works.

COPYFRAUD'S CREATIVE COSTS

Copyfraud stifles creativity and imposes financial costs upon consumers. False copyright claims lead individuals to pay unnecessarily for licenses and to forgo entirely projects that make legitimate uses of public domain materials. Copyfraud is a land grab. It represents private control over the public domain. Copyfraud upsets the balance that the law has struck between private rights and the interests of the public in creative works.

For example, as a result of copyfraud, documentary filmmakers find it difficult to make use of public domain works in their productions. Owners of the physical copies of public domain footage often impose copyright-like restrictions on the footage: charging licensing fees for reproduction, limiting the ways in which the footage can be used, and prohibiting future sublicensing. Filmmaker Gordon Quinn of Kartemquin Films in Chicago states that a director of footage that he once wished to use asserted copyright and insisted upon payment even though the footage in question had been produced by the federal government and was therefore in the public domain.[57] When filmmaker and Stanford professor Jan Krawitz sought to include an excerpt from

an early public domain instructional film in one of her films, the archive
that owned the reel told her it made no distinction between copyrighted
and public domain works in its collection. To use the film, Krawitz
would have to pay the archive a substantial licensing fee just as if the
film were copyrighted.[58]

Filmmakers confront a licensing culture in which there is an
entrenched norm against using any prior work without authorization.
Entertainment lawyer Michael C. Donaldson emphasizes that the
various gatekeepers working with a filmmaker—insurers, studios,
distributors, and these parties' lawyers—are often the ones responsible
for unnecessary permissions and fees.[59] Even when represented by
counsel, filmmakers who use public domain footage are told by studios to obtain permission and pay a licensing fee—sometimes many
thousands of dollars—to the original creator or owner of the master reel.
Clearance fees often constitute a substantial portion of a film's budget.
Rather than persuade these gatekeepers that a license is not necessary,
the filmmaker must normally comply with the request or else eliminate
the material from the film. Distributors and broadcasters impose strict
clearance procedures on filmmakers. Broadcasters have required them to
obtain permission to include public domain movie trailers in a film, and
studios have been known to prohibit use of such trailers altogether.[60]
All this has created an industry standard based on a false premise.
"Don't ever assume that any film clip is in the public domain," warns
MovieMaker magazine.[61] Similarly, "[i]t is always safest to clear," states
Donaldson in his handbook on clearance and copyright for independent
filmmakers.[62] A popular guide written by three entertainment lawyers
advises against using *any* kind of prior footage because of the inherent
"clearance nightmare."[63] Distributors advise filmmakers that if there is
any doubt about something, they should eliminate it from the film:
"The Filmmaker should continually monitor the Film at all stages, from
inception to final cut, with the objective of eliminating material that
could give rise to a claim."[64] The industry motto is "When in doubt, cut

it out."[65] Distributors also typically require filmmakers to indemnify them for any liability resulting from the use of anyone else's work. Insurers issuing the universally required errors-and-omissions insurance impose very high clearance standards and expect to see authorization for every prior work included in the film.[66] A recent analysis notes that "[w]hile many filmmakers are willing to take risks on using images . . . their distributors and producers are not."[67] Norms governing use do not reflect the distinction the law draws between copyrighted works and works that are in the public domain and free for any filmmaker to use.

Filmmakers who face what one commentator has termed the "pay-or-cut dilemma"[68] often avoid certain types of projects altogether rather than deal with the hassles and expense of licensing. In interviews with documentary filmmakers, Patricia Aufderheide and Peter Jaszi found that filmmakers "shape their film projects to avoid the problem of rights clearance, omitting significant details," and that "the avoidance of clearance problems may help to dictate filmmakers' choices of subject-matter, influencing them (for example) to avoid projects involving current events or modern history—which tend to be minefields . . . because strict compliance through licensing is required."[69] One popular journal for filmmakers concludes that with so many filmmakers "abandoning projects because of cost or self-censoring materials," the "sense in the [independent filmmaker] community [is] that the problem [of clearance] has reached a crisis point."[70] In Chapter 10 we will see how some filmmakers have fought back against overreaching intellectual property claims; their story represents a rare victory.

In many other creative industries as well, those seeking to make lawful uses of existing works routinely confront false copyright notices and other forms of interference with lawful reproductions. Nonfiction authors often face challenges in reproducing public domain images in their books. For example, authors who seek to reproduce an image from a museum's collection may well understand that the museum's claim of copyright in a public domain reproduction is invalid. Yet in order to obtain access to the reproduction, and to satisfy their publishers and other gatekeepers, authors regularly accept the terms of the deal. Michael Krondl wanted to include in *The Taste of Conquest: The Rise and Fall of the Three Great Cities of Spice,* his 2007 book on the history of the spice trade, images of public domain works: paintings, prints, and codices from 1300 through 1700. Krondl's publisher, Random House, required him to locate and pay for those images in addition to obtaining permission to use any copyrighted material in his book. When Krondl contacted the museums and libraries in the United States that held the original works that would illustrate the book's text, these institutions told him that in order to use images of the works, he would have to pay a substantial reproduction fee and a copyright licensing fee and comply with various conditions of use. Some institutions refused him permission entirely on the ground that the proposed use was "inappropriate" or "commercial."[71]

Krondl's experience will be familiar to many authors who have sought to use images from museums. As we have seen, museums limit who can use reproductions of works in their collections, restricting access to those who accept their claim of copyright and abide by other conditions. Images of public domain works are therefore published with a notice that this or that institution owns a copyright and has granted permission. As University of Chicago Press editor Susan Bielstein reports in her book on securing permissions from museums and other entities, "[s]ome institutions have the idea that if they just say they own the copyright to reproductions of public-domain works and consistently put forth claims that not only go unchallenged but are acknowledged by writers who agree to use exact credit lines in exchange for rights to publish images, then it will eventually be accepted as so."[72]

Like the clearance requirements imposed on filmmakers, the licensing culture of museums inhibits expression. Authors modify their projects because they are denied permission to use an image or it comes with a hefty price tag. Some works are not published at all. At a panel discussion at the Association of the Bar of the City of New York in 2008, one publisher explained that securing rights for an art book can run to as much as $30,000, making such books unpublishable. As a result, this publisher observed, publishing is distorted: art books that are published tend to be those that are financed or supported by people with a professional or financial stake in the success of the publication. Rather than serving as authoritative guides to art, books become promotional vehicles for art exhibits and sales.

COPYFRAUD'S FINANCIAL IMPACT ON EDUCATION

Copyfraud also affects the cost of higher education. In the 1990s, publishers began targeting the common practice in universities of photocopying, without permission or payment, portions of copyrighted works to distribute to students. High-profile lawsuits were brought against Kinko's in connection with its preparation of course packets for students at New York schools and against a copy shop that served students at the University of Michigan. The defendants in these cases asserted that inclusion of copyrighted materials in course packets fell within the fair use provision of the Copyright Act, but the courts rejected this argument and found that without permission from the copyright owners, the course packets constituted copyright infringement.[73]

We will take up fair use in the next chapter. For now, the general point to be made is that as a result of these cases, universities adopted stringent policies with respect to course packets. They now make conservative uses of intellectual property law. Many professors and universities pay licensing fees for everything they reproduce and distribute to their students, even when it is a public domain work that is being copied. Schools shift responsibility for resolving copyright issues to individual faculty members and tell their professors they must avoid any risk of litigation and therefore use only licensed works. Licensing is often excessively expensive, and as a result, students pay hefty fees, often several hundred dollars per semester, for their course packets—which, unlike real books, cannot easily be resold.

Typically, universities obtain reproduction permissions through the Copyright Clearance Center, a not-for-profit entity that offers online processing and payment for licenses to millions of works. This system conveniently connects professors with publishers. However, by failing to distinguish copyrighted from public domain works, the system encourages publishers to overreach, and it encourages professors to overpay for materials they distribute to students. Many of the licenses for sale through the Copyright Clearance Center are to public domain works. My own search turned up more than two dozen editions of *The Federalist*, with licenses priced at between ten cents and $1 per page for each copy. Other public domain works being licensed at the Copyright Clearance Center are Joseph Story's *Commentaries on the Constitution*, Blackstone's *Commentaries*, and Madison's notes from the Constitutional Convention, all available at fifteen cents per page per copy; numerous plays by Shakespeare at various prices; and Thomas Paine's *Common Sense* at eleven cents per page per copy. Even at these prices, not all uses are authorized. When I requested through the Copyright Clearance Center permission to reproduce a portion of *The Federalist* in a textbook, permission was denied because, the center told me, the publisher does not license *The Federalist* for this purpose.

Some modern versions of public domain works, including versions available for licensing from the Copyright Clearance Center, contain introductory essays, editorial comments, and other original material that can be copyrighted. For instance, the edition of *The Federalist* edited by Jacob Ernest Cooke contains Cooke's own introduction, which is subject to copyright protection, even though the words of Hamilton, Jay, and Madison are not.[74] But you wouldn't know it by visiting the Copyright Clearance Center's website, where *every* page of Cooke's reprint of *The Federalist* is available for licensing at twenty cents per page per copy in academic course packets. Twenty cents to copy a page of *The Federalist* may not sound like much, but it can add up to a pile of easy cash for the overreaching publisher who enlists the center's services. A professor unnecessarily purchasing a license to copy Madison's *Federalist No. 10*, which runs ten pages in the Cooke edition, incurs $2 in fees per course packet. For each class of one hundred undergraduates, the publisher—in this case, Wesleyan University Press—receives $200 in undeserved licensing payments. One hundred college professors teaching one course per year in which *Federalist No. 10* is assigned create an annual publisher's windfall of $20,000.

The savvy professor might of course know that the publisher does not own a copyright in Madison's work. Yet knowledge does not necessarily translate into power because gatekeepers enforce restrictions. The professor's department or university has almost certainly told the professor to obtain licenses for all course packet materials—perhaps with a reminder that if infringement is later found, the professor will personally be held responsible for any resulting liability and will be subject to internal disciplinary action. The copy shop to which the professor delivers the originals for reproduction will be under similar instructions if it is part of the university or otherwise wary if it is a commercial copier. For example, FedEx Office has a strict requirement that customers obtain "written permission from the copyright owner before reproducing or modifying any copyrighted material,"[75] and it requires customers to indemnify the business and pay lawyers' fees if it is sued for infringement.[76] It is often easier for a professor simply to pay the fees than to explain to the average copy shop employee that Jacob Cooke and Wesleyan do not really own the copyright in *Federalist No. 10*. In the course of my research for this book, I tested FedEx Office's policy by asking my local branch to make ten copies of *The Merchant of Venice*. The clerk told me that first I needed signed authorization from the copyright holder. (William Shakespeare?) In the case of *Federalist No. 10*, passing along $2 to each student, still cheaper than buying the entire book, is easier than dealing with an administrative hassle.

Paying a fee is especially attractive when the university copying center requires a professor submitting course packets for copying to sign a broad indemnification agreement. Here too false copyright claims by publishers combine with pressures from one's own institution to force professors to obtain permission.

THE LOST PUBLIC DOMAIN

From the U.S. Constitution to old newspapers, from the paintings of old masters to the national anthem, the public domain has been copyrighted. Several factors conspire to allow copyfraud to flourish. Economic considerations provide an incentive for copyrighting the public domain, and copyright law imposes no punishment for doing so. Content providers adhere to and replicate norms that require licensing of public domain works—even though the law says those works are free for anybody to use. Gatekeepers block legitimate uses of the public domain, frustrating lawful efforts to draw upon it. By fostering confusion about the scope of intellectual property rights, copyfraud facilitates ever more claims of ownership in public domain materials.

Copyfraud is the most outrageous type of overreaching in intellectual property law because it involves claims to a copyright where none at all exist; however, overreaching also occurs when holders of valid copyrights extend their legitimate rights beyond their lawful limits. The next chapter takes up the first example of copyright owners claiming stronger rights than the law gives them: copyright owners interfering with fair use.

CHAPTER 2

VANISHING FAIR USE

Many new creative works build upon, borrow from, and react to earlier works. Fair use permits these kinds of activities. A movie critic often desires to quote language from the script. News broadcasters convey statements made by others. Historians enrich their works by reproducing the words and works of their subjects. Humorists draw on preexisting writings and images to poke fun at them. If these things could not be done without the permission of—and payment to—the copyright owner, the loss to the public would be enormous.

The basic idea of fair use goes back to the constitutional purpose behind copyright: to promote creative progress. Society benefits from allowing people to make certain uses of a work even though the work is protected by copyright. Fair use is copyright law's safety valve. It promotes the overall flow of creative works by authorizing some copying without the copyright owner's permission. A person sued for copyright infringement can assert that the use of the copyrighted material was fair. If the court agrees that the use falls within the scope of fair use, there is no liability.

However, copyright owners routinely interfere with fair uses of copyrighted works by overzealously asserting their rights. Copyright owners often deny there is even such a thing as fair use, insisting that their permission is needed for anybody to use, in any manner, their copyrighted works. Publishers and other content providers treat fair use as something akin to a legal technicality that allows criminals to go free. The *Boston Globe* claims, for example, that its "prior written permission" is required to "copy, reproduce, distribute, [or] publish any of the newspaper's content."[1] That is not the law. Fair use requires nobody's permission. So too do distributors of DVDs overreach when they attach to their products false notices prohibiting all copying.[2] In addition to their outright denials of fair use, copyright owners also take a highly restrictive view of what fair use law allows. The Associated Press tells bloggers they may reproduce four words from its articles free of charge. Reproducing five to twenty-five words costs $12.50, and the cost goes up from there. Fair use law easily allows five-word excerpts—and often passages of even twenty-five or more words—without payment. Major League Baseball announces before its televised games, "This copyrighted telecast is presented by authority of the Office of the Commissioner of Baseball. It may not be reproduced or retransmitted in any form, and the accounts and descriptions of this game may not be disseminated, without express written consent." Fair use protects many forms of reproduction and transmission (and no law prevents anyone from describing what happened in a baseball game). As we will see in this chapter, however, because the law of fair use does not easily allow individuals to determine definitively how much copying would be fair, copyright owners like Major League Baseball claim that all copying is unlawful. And faced with the prospect of being sued, individuals refrain from making fair uses of copyrighted works.

Copyright owners have several motivations to interfere with fair use. One is financial. Copyright owners who can persuade others that a proposed use requires permission can extract a fee for their permission.

Copyright owners also interfere with fair use because they believe that fair use gives their competitors a leg up. They reason, "My competitor should not be able to get ahead by using what I have created." Other copyright owners desire to maintain strict control over how their work is used, sometimes as part of an overall effort to control their public image. For instance, the recording artist Prince vigorously polices all uses of his work and has threatened fans with legal action for using his work or likeness on fan sites or for other purposes.[3] This is of particular concern with respect to works that criticize or ridicule earlier works: in a world in which permission is needed for any use, the flatterer is more likely to receive the necessary authorization than the critic, and it is indeed the case that copyright owners often interfere with fair use in order to silence critics or to punish those who have caused offense. More generally, there is no downside to interfering with fair use. The Copyright Act provides no remedy against copyright holders who prevent fair use of their works by others.

Interference with fair use imposes costs when creators of new works pay for permissions they don't need. It also impedes expression when, threatened with lawsuits, creators modify or abandon their projects rather than rely upon the fair use provision of the Copyright Act. There are numerous examples of the consequences of interference with fair use. *Sing Faster: The Stagehands' Ring Cycle* is a 1999 documentary film directed by filmmaker Jon Else. The film captures the backstage activity of union stagehands during the San Francisco Opera's production of Richard Wagner's *Ring* cycle. One scene shows two stagehands playing checkers backstage during the performance of the opera. In filming the scene, Else captured four seconds of a television in the background playing an episode of *The Simpsons*. Fox Broadcasting Company, which owns the copyright in *The Simpsons*, demanded a licensing fee of $10,000 for the four-second background use of the show. While Else's use almost certainly fell within the bounds of fair use, he did not want to risk litigation. Nor could he pay the sum Fox wanted. Else therefore digitally replaced the image of *The Simpsons* on the television set with four seconds from a film he owned.[4] Else's decision to alter part of his documentary—to fictionalize it—rather than invoke fair use is not unusual. Filmmaker Katy Chevigny says, "Many documentary filmmakers (myself included) feel obligated to alter their footage to avoid copyright disputes—an act akin to self-censorship."[5] Without fair use, there is no guarantee that a documentary can show what actually occurred.

SOME FAIR USE BASICS: FROM JUDGE-MADE
DOCTRINE TO THE COPYRIGHT ACT

The law of fair use began as a judge-made doctrine in the mid-nineteenth century. In 1841 in *Folsom v. Marsh*, Justice Joseph Story, sitting on the federal circuit court in Massachusetts, faced what he called an "intricate and embarrassing question" in a copyright piracy case.[6] The plaintiff in the case was Folsom, Wells, and Thurston, the publisher of Jared Sparks's twelve-volume work *The Writings of George Washington; being his Correspondence, Addresses, Messages, and other Papers, Official and Private, Selected and published from the Original Manuscripts, with a Life of the Author, Notes, and Illustrations.* Sparks had received permission from Washington's estate to reproduce Washington's writings. Defendant Marsh, Capen and Lyon, a Boston publishing house, had published the Reverend Charles W. Upham's two-volume *The Life of Washington in the form of an Autobiography; the Narrative being, to a great extent, conducted by himself, in Extracts and Selections from His Own Writings, with Portraits and other Engravings,* which reproduced 319 letters from Sparks's publication.[7] After finding the letters copyrighted, Justice Story went on to ask whether Upham's work was "a justifiable use of the original materials, such as the law recognizes as no infringement of the copyright of the plaintiffs."[8] Here, Story thought, there were no hard-and-fast rules, and the resolution of the controversy required application of multiple criteria to the particular facts of the case. Drawing upon earlier court decisions in this area, Story considered "the nature and objects of the selections made" and "the quantity and value of the materials used," as well as whether the use would affect sales of the original work or replace it in the market.[9] Applying these factors, Story concluded that Upham's use of the letters was unjustified.[10]

In the ensuing years, judges used similar multifactor tests to determine whether limited copying from a copyrighted work could be deemed not to infringe the copyright. In this manner, fair use operated as a judge-made doctrine until Congress codified fair use in the 1976 Copyright Act.[11] Section 107 of the Copyright Act provides for fair use and sets out the circumstances under which it applies. Section 107 is a limitation on the exclusive rights that the statute otherwise grants to copyright owners. It states first that "fair use of a copyrighted work, including such use by reproduction in copies . . . for purposes such as criticism, comment, news reporting, teaching (including multiple copies for classroom use), scholarship, or research, is not an infringement of copyright."[12] Recalling Justice Story's approach in the *Folsom* case, section 107 then lists factors relevant to determining whether any particular use is fair. It says,

In determining whether the use made of a work in any particular case is a fair use the factors to be considered shall include—

(1) the purpose and character of the use, including whether such use is of a commercial nature or is for nonprofit educational purposes;

(2) the nature of the copyrighted work;

(3) the amount and substantiality of the portion used in relation to the copyrighted work as a whole; and

(4) the effect of the use upon the potential market for or value of the copyrighted work.[13]

Section 107 is deliberately flexible in defining fair use and setting out the test for determining whether fair use exists. Notably, section 107 does not list *all* the types of uses that can constitute fair use; instead, it provides some examples. Section 107 also does not define once and for all the conditions that must be met for fair use to be found; rather, it lists factors that, among others, should be taken into account.

It is not hard to see why Congress opted for flexible terminology in codifying fair use. People seek to reproduce copyrighted works in a wide variety of ways and for many different purposes. No statute could possibly list all those uses, and a statute that purported to do so would quickly become obsolete because it could not predict new uses of copyrighted works that people would seek to make in the future. Congress therefore opted to describe fair use with general standards and examples rather than provide a definitive list of acceptable uses or criteria.[14]

Although this flexible approach had obvious appeal, it has produced a serious problem. Because the fair use provision of the Copyright Act is written in general terms, it is hard to tell from reading the statute whether any proposed use of a copyrighted work is a fair use and therefore does not infringe the copyright. The statute does not provide precise guidance to the law-abiding person who wants to use a copyrighted work in a lawful manner. While the statute tells us that fair use includes comment, news reporting, and teaching, among several other purposes, this list is of limited value because the statute does not say that these purposes *always* make a use fair, or that uses for other purposes that are not listed cannot be fair use. The four-factor test also generates confusion in that the specified factors are themselves vague. For example, which "purpose[s] and character[s]" suggest fair use? What does the "nature" of a copyrighted work refer to, and when does the nature suggest a use is fair or not? When does the "amount and substantiality" of the portion used become an unfair use? What sort of impact on the potential market and value of the copyrighted work determines that a use is no longer fair? These and other questions can make it hard to know with certainty whether a proposed use of a copyrighted work is permissible. Determining whether or not a use of a copyrighted material is fair can be a high-stakes game. Fair use is a complete defense to a claim of infringement, allowing the defendant to avoid the substantial remedies available under the Copyright Act to a copyright owner.[15] The uncertainty about the meaning of the fair use law, combined with the possibility of a large penalty for guessing wrong, makes fair use hazardous terrain.

JUDGES AND THE FOUR FAIR USE FACTORS

Into all this wades the judge charged with applying section 107 and determining whether a use is fair. Now the problem is the exact opposite. Whereas Congress refused to think in terms of specific cases and so gave us general rules, judges necessarily issue rulings closely tied to the facts of individual cases. The question a judge is asked to resolve is whether a particular individual's copying of a specified excerpt of a given work for a certain purpose falls within the protections of fair use. Judicial decisions therefore also fail to provide much *general* guidance about when a proposed use is fair, making future determinations difficult. Judges themselves have recognized this problem. As one federal judge has put it, court decisions "reflect widely differing notions of the meaning of fair use" and "[e]arlier decisions provide little basis for predicting later ones"; therefore parties "can only guess and pray" as to whether a court will find any particular use fair.[16] Fair use law, then, exists at one extreme as a body of vague statutory language, and at the other extreme as a set of narrow, fact-specific judicial decisions. A helpful middle ground does not exist. In addition to the inherent difficulty of weighing the four factors against each other to determine whether a use is fair, each individual fair use factor presents its own interpretive challenges.

The first of the four fair use factors asks courts to consider the purpose and character of the use, including whether such use is of a commercial nature or is for nonprofit educational purposes. In 1984, the Supreme Court suggested that a commercial use was presumptively unfair use.[17] The next year, the Court softened the approach and said that a commercial use "tends to weigh against a finding of fair use" in the multifactor analysis.[18] In 1994, the Court retreated further, saying that the "force of that tendency" depends very much on context.[19]

Recognizing that a large number of uses of copyrighted material have a commercial component, some courts have given this factor little weight.[20] Most courts, however, take the position that while a work that is being used for a commercial rather than nonprofit purpose is less likely to qualify as fair use, the inquiry does not end at that point. In accordance with instructions from the Supreme Court, many courts examine the degree to which the new work is transformative: a work, even one for commercial purposes, that alters or adds to the copyrighted work can qualify as a fair use.[21] For example, in one case a search engine displayed search results as thumbnail pictures of copyrighted images from websites. The search engine operator argued that the use of the images was fair, and the court agreed. With respect to the first fair use factor, the court reasoned that although the use was commercial, it was transformative because the website operator used the images not for their original aesthetic purposes but to index and improve access to images on the Internet.[22] Similarly, the fact that a use is for nonprofit educational purposes does not automatically mean that the use is fair. Context matters.

In applying the second statutory factor, the nature of the copyrighted works, courts have distinguished between informational works such as news reports and works of entertainment such as movies and plays. On the theory that the law should lend stronger protection to disseminations of factual works, copying is more likely to be fair use if the underlying work is informational than if it is a creative work. Yet here the divide quickly becomes hazy. Many informational works contain a high degree of creativity: a television advertisement, for example, conveys information, but it is also often highly creative. So too are many creative works informational. In one case, a filmmaker sought to incorporate copyrighted footage, photographs, and music into a biography about Elvis Presley. While ultimately finding that the second factor tipped in favor of the copyright owner, the court explained that the footage presented "a close call."[23] On one hand, Elvis's television appearances and concerts were creative in nature. On the other hand, the footage was of such historical significance that it was also newsworthy or informational. The photographs and the musical compositions were more clearly creative.[24]

The third fair use factor asks a court to consider the amount and substantiality of the portion that is taken from the copyrighted work. The analysis is therefore both quantitative and qualitative. Here again there are no hard-and-fast rules. Instead, courts determine whether the specific amount and the particular substance in the case at hand weigh in favor of or against a fair use claim. Thus, for example, one court found the fair use defense available where a defendant quoted between 5 and 6 percent of twelve works and 8 percent of eleven other works.[25] Another court found that a biographer's copying of one-third of seventeen letters and 10 percent of forty-two letters by J. D. Salinger was not fair use.[26] One court found that this factor favored a defendant who copied a fifteen-second excerpt of John Lennon's "Imagine," a song that runs three minutes in total.[27] None of these decisions tell us, however, whether different uses of these same works would be fair or whether the same uses of different works would be permissible.

Because the third factor involves both qualitative and quantitative inquiry, courts have rejected fair use defenses when the defendant has taken what the court has deemed a small but critical portion of a copyrighted work. For example, in one case, Harper & Row had acquired the rights to publish President Gerald Ford's memoirs. As the result of a leak, the *Nation* obtained Ford's unpublished manuscript and published a 2,250-word article with several hundred words' worth of verbatim quotes from the manuscript. This pre-publication scooped *Time*, which had received a license from Harper & Row to publish advance excerpts. Sued for copyright infringement, the *Nation* asserted that its reproduction of portions of Ford's manuscript constituted fair use. The Supreme Court held there was no fair use: although the amount copied was only a small portion of the manuscript, the copied portions were central elements of the memoirs and constituted the "heart" of the copyrighted work.[28] Fair use did not permit the copying of a small but qualitatively significant portion of the copyrighted work.

On the other hand, because determining fair use involves a multifactor test, even the use of an *entire* work does not bar a finding of fair use. One famous example is the Supreme Court's first decision on the meaning of fair use in 1984 in *Sony Corporation of America v. Universal City Studios*. The case involved a claim by Universal Studios that Sony was liable for contributory copyright infringement by manufacturing and selling the Betamax VCR. Although the VCR clearly could be used to infringe copyright, the Court held that that was not enough to make Sony liable. Instead, the Court explained, "the sale of copying equipment, like the sale of other articles of commerce, does not constitute contributory infringement if the product is widely used for legitimate, unobjectionable purposes. Indeed, it need merely be capable of substantial noninfringing uses."[29] Sony argued that the Betamax allowed people to record copyrighted programs broadcast on television in order to watch the programs at a later time, and that this practice was a fair use that did not infringe the movie studio's copyrights. The Supreme Court agreed with Sony that recording for time-shifting was fair. Although entire copyrighted works were being reproduced, on balance, copying television programs for the purpose of watching them at a later time was fair. Since the Betamax was therefore used in ways that did not infringe copyright, Sony was not liable to the studio.

Before we turn to the fourth of the fair use factors, the doctrine of de minimis copying, which applies to many of the examples of overreaching in this chapter, bears mentioning. The basic idea of this doctrine is that some forms of copying are so trivial that it is not even necessary to ask whether the use is fair. *De minimis non curat lex*: the law does not concern itself with trifles.[30] While fair use requires an analysis under the statutory factors, de minimis is a defense based solely on the *amount* of copying. For example, in one case, a court found that a hip-hop group's use of a three-note sequence from a musical composition was de minimis copying and did not infringe the copyright in the composition.[31] In another case, several photographs by the plaintiff appeared very briefly in the defendant's film. The court found that the copying was de minimis, and therefore there was no infringement of the plaintiff's copyright.[32] Like fair use, de minimis copying is a defense: it can be raised by a party sued for infringement. And as with fair use, whether the defense will succeed depends on the particular circumstances of the case.

The fourth fair use factor asks courts to consider the effect of the use upon the potential market for or value of the copyrighted work. Relying upon language from the Supreme Court's decisions in the *Sony* and *Harper & Row* cases, courts at one time took the position that if a use is commercial, market harm to the copyright holder may be presumed. In 1994, however, in *Campbell v. Acuff-Rose Music*, the Supreme Court made clear that there should be no such presumption, at least in cases not involving simple duplication of an existing work for commercial purposes.[33] *Campbell* involved a commercial parody of Roy Orbison's song "Oh, Pretty Woman" by the rap group 2 Live Crew. Rejecting the argument that market harm could be presumed, the Court reasoned that the rap version was not likely to displace sales of the original work because the markets for the two works were different.[34] *Campbell* was significant as well because it resolved a difficulty that stemmed from *Harper & Row*. In seeming disregard of the statutory language, the Court in *Harper & Row* had announced that the fourth of the fair use factors was "undoubtedly the single most important element of fair use."[35] *Campbell*, however, made clear that "all [four factors] are to be explored, and the results weighed together, in light of the purposes of copyright."[36]

Not surprisingly, the four factors do not always all point in the same direction. A court therefore has to try to balance factors against each other. The difficulty in this task is that attendant to any balancing test: the factors ask different things and so cannot easily be measured against each other. Recall also that the fair use analysis is not limited to the four enumerated factors, which are presented as *among those* that should be considered. Courts have therefore taken into account other factors in determining whether a use is fair. For example, courts often consider whether a defendant has acted in good faith in making use of a copyrighted work. Not knowing exactly what a court will consider also makes predicting the outcome in many cases difficult.

Compounding these difficulties is the fact that courts resolve only a small fraction of fair use disputes. Most fair use disputes are settled by the parties rather than decided by a judge determining whether the use in question is fair. While settlement conserves the resources of the judicial system and allows parties to avoid the risks of going to trial, it also means we lack a more comprehensive body of fair use decisions that would allow us to discern reliable rules. Indeed, the cases that courts do decide are probably not typical of the fair use disputes that arise. Litigated cases are likely to be cases in which the question of whether infringement has occurred is a close one so that each side believes it can prevail; in which the circumstances are so unusual that it is hard to predict an outcome at all; or in which one of the parties is determined to have its day in court. Some legal scholars have offered conclusions about the meaning of fair use based on a close reading of judicial opinions in fair use disputes. However, because the cases that judges decide often involve atypical problems, it is hazardous to try to generate from judicial opinions fair use rules that can be applied in other contexts.

HOW UNCERTAINTY LEADS TO OVERREACHING

The end result is considerable uncertainty as to whether any particular use is a fair use. On the one hand, by aiming for flexibility when it wrote the fair use provision of the Copyright Act, Congress did not provide clear guidance as to how the provision would apply. On the other hand, it is often hard to generalize from the courts' decisions in specific cases in order to make future determinations with confidence.

There is widespread consensus that fair use is not a coherent doctrine and that it is often difficult to predict how a future case will turn out. Even when copyright scholars and lawyers may agree that a particular use is fair, ordinary members of the public find it hard to make sense of the statutory factors and the cases interpreting them. As one commentator rightly notes, copyright law is increasingly important to the general population, but fair use has become "so vague and abstract as to preclude its effective use by the vast majority of users."[37]

For copyright owners, however, the confusing state of fair use is an unexpected gift. The vagueness of the fair use doctrine allows copyright owners to interfere with fair uses of copyrighted works. The law therefore enables overreaching. When ordinary users cannot themselves determine whether a proposed use would be fair, copyright owners are able to assert that *any use* would constitute infringement. When experts have difficulty making sense of fair use, nobody can guarantee that litigation will not ensue or, if there is a lawsuit, that a court will find a particular use to be fair. Under these circumstances, fair use, designed to enable speech and creativity, vanishes.

When the law does not regulate or does not regulate with sufficient predictability, markets can, of course, supply the rules. Somebody who wants to make use of a copyrighted work without facing a legal penalty can therefore license the use from the copyright owner. A valid license removes the use from the vagaries of fair use doctrine. Contract law can produce the certainty that copyright law, as written by Congress and applied by the courts, fails to supply. Yet leaving fair use to the market is far from desirable. Fair use is not meant to be something that is sold and bought like other market goods. Fair use is free use. Nobody is meant to pay for the privilege of using a copyrighted work in a manner that the law already deems *not* to infringe the copyright. Fair use is a use that does not require permission because it is not infringement. Fair use also permits uses that copyright owners find objectionable—uses that cannot be licensed. More generally, fair use does not merely benefit

private parties. Society also benefits when people are able to make use
of a copyrighted work without seeking permission from the copyright
owner.

VANISHING FAIR USE IN
THE PUBLISHING INDUSTRY

The copyright notices carried by books published nowadays suggest that fair use does not exist. Typical of these notices, one work of
fiction claims, "[N]o part of this publication may be reproduced . . . in
any form, or by any means . . . without the prior written permission of
both the copyright owner and the . . . publisher."[38] That is not the law.
Fair use and the doctrine of de minimis copying permit some forms of
reproduction and use even without a copyright owner's permission.

These bluffs are rarely called. As a result, books routinely contain
statements that permission has been obtained (unnecessarily) to quote
small excerpts from copyrighted works—the very thing the de minimis
doctrine permits and fair use encourages. The author of one book, for
example, acknowledges permission received to reprint brief excerpts
from four songs.[39] Another thanks copyright owners for authorizing
quotations of a few lines from seven show tunes, and a third acknowledges
permission to quote four lines from a poem.[40]

Book publishers operate in a licensing culture that puts them at odds
with their own authors, who may strongly support fair use because it is
beneficial to them, and who do not prepare the overreaching notices that
become attached to their works. In addition to requiring permission to
quote from their books, many publishers create substantial hurdles for
their own authors who wish to reproduce, quote from, or otherwise draw
upon works by others. They impose on their authors the responsibility
for seeking permissions and paying fees, and when these permissions
cannot be obtained, they often edit out quotations from manuscripts
to avoid legal liability. For example, a publisher of college textbooks
provides the following instructions to its authors: "[E]very publisher

has its own set of guidelines" and "copyright holders (and, if a serious dispute arises, the courts) decide what is fair use and what is not," "you are . . . responsible for obtaining permission for any quoted or borrowed material that you utilize to illustrate or amplify your own arguments," and "[i]f you want to quote or reproduce what someone else has written, said, sung, or otherwise originated, you must apply to the holder of the copyright for written permission to do so."[41] This situation is not unique to trade publishers; university presses impose similar requirements.[42]

Overzealous claims by copyright owners lead to conservative reliance upon fair use in the publishing industry. *The Chicago Manual of Style*, a widely used author handbook, notes that "many publishers tend to seek permission if they have the slightest doubt whether a particular use is fair" and that "[p]ublishing agreements place on the author the responsibility to request any permission needed" for the use of any such material and "stipulate that any fees to be paid will be the author's responsibility."[43] In all this, the norm of licensing is reinforced and reproduced, with publishers obtaining permissions from each other for uses that would be fair.

As a recent incident illustrates, fair use tends to be invoked only when somebody messes up. Penguin states on its website that authors wishing to quote from any Penguin book must seek permission from the publisher and offers a number of examples in which such permission would be required: "a short quotation from one book used in another book, a poem to be used in another book of poetry, a chart from a book to be used in a corporate newsletter, a short story to be photocopied for classroom use, etc."[44] Despite its seeming denial of fair use in this instance, the company itself invoked fair use in 2008 when bloggers claimed that passages of Signet author Cassie Edwards's romance novels were lifted from other sources. In response to the allegations, Signet, a Penguin imprint, announced, "[C]opyright fair-use doctrine permits reasonable borrowing and paraphrasing of another author's words especially for the purpose of creating something new and original."[45] Penguin's statement, undoubtedly correct, represented a rare embrace of fair use but came about only because Penguin had seemingly flouted the publishing industry's licensing norms.

The gap between what the law of fair use permits and what industry norms dictate means that many uses that are legally permissible are not made. But there is an even more insidious way in which norms and resulting practices undermine fair use. Recall that the fourth fair use factor asks about "[t]he effect of the use upon the potential market for or value of the copyrighted work."[46] James Gibson shows how norms and practices have a feedback effect on the legal application of this factor.[47] According to Gibson, when individuals license materials rather than rely upon fair use, they create "licensing markets": markets for buying and selling the right to use a copyrighted work.[48] When, in turn, courts apply the fourth fair use factor, they invoke the existence of these licensing markets as evidence that an unlicensed use affects the market value of the work.[49] Because of this interaction between licensing practices and the legal determination of what constitutes fair use, "[o]ver time, fair use naturally shrinks and the scope of copyright expands."[50] More generally, because fair use is about fairness, ultimately a normative concept, industry practices may subtly inform a court as to what should be deemed permissible. If most people expect a use to be licensed, and industry practices point to licensing, it is not an unreasonable assumption that a failure to license is unfair. To the extent that the gap between the law and norms of fair use closes, then, it is because the law—as reflected in court decisions—becomes more restrictive of users' rights. Norms do not just lead users to give up on fair use. Norms also change what fair use law itself permits.

FAIR USE IN SCHOOLS: THE CLASSROOM GUIDELINES

Congress meant for educators to be able to take advantage of the fair use provision of the Copyright Act in teaching students, conducting research, and producing scholarship. During the drafting of what would become the 1976 Copyright Act, Congress encouraged industry representatives to develop guidelines that would specify fair use of copyrighted works in the educational context. Representatives of the Authors League of America, the Association of American Publishers, and the Ad Hoc Committee of Educational Institutions and Organizations on Copyright Law Revision agreed to the Classroom Guidelines, which were incorporated into the legislative history to the 1976 act.[51] The Classroom Guidelines are intended to "state the minimum and not the maximum standards of educational fair use."[52] Among other things, the guidelines allow teachers to make a single copy of a copyrighted book chapter or a newspaper article; the teacher may also copy and distribute to each student 250 words of a copyrighted poem, a complete article if it runs fewer than 2,500 words, an excerpt of 1,000 words from a work of prose (or 10 percent of the work, whichever is less), and up to 10 percent of a copyrighted piece of sheet music. The Classroom Guidelines have not been adopted by Congress and therefore they do not have the force of law. However, many educational institutions follow the Classroom Guidelines. Courts have also deferred to them, with one federal appellate court saying that the Classroom Guidelines "evoke a general idea, at least, of the type of educational copying Congress had in mind," and another recognizing the guidelines as "persuasive authority" in determining whether an educational use is fair.[53]

Nonetheless, educators still face difficulties in making fair use of copyrighted works. The Classroom Guidelines have had a perverse effect. While intending to state a *minimum* amount of copying that is permitted by fair use, the guidelines tend to be treated as establishing a fair use ceiling; rather than encourage the fair use of copyrighted materials, they end up constraining it. An important cause of this is the outcome of a closely watched copyright infringement lawsuit that a group of publishers filed against New York University in connection with its preparation of student course readers. In settling the lawsuit, NYU agreed to be bound by the Classroom Guidelines as setting forth the *maximum* amount of permissible copying.[54] While some courts have shown a willingness to permit greater copying than the guidelines specify,[55] the case against NYU has had a tremendous impact on educational institutions, and many schools now consider the guidelines to constitute a fair use ceiling.[56] Even though many observers have criticized the Classroom Guidelines as embodying a cramped version of fair use, schools take the view that the lawfulness of copying that exceeds the Classroom Guidelines is untested and such copying may trigger a lawsuit. These fears are not unfounded. In April 2008, three publishers sued Georgia State University for copyright infringement when professors posted course reading materials online. The publishers alleged in their complaint that fair use rules the university had developed for its own faculty members (which deemed copying up to 20 percent of a work fair use) "plainly exceed legal boundaries."[57]

Despite these efforts to formulate general guidelines to fair use for educational purposes, some schools rely on faculty members to make their own fair use determinations. However, this returns us to the original problem of the uncertainty of fair use law. When legal professionals are not easily able to determine whether a proposed use of a copyrighted work is fair, teachers cannot be expected to make fair use determinations even if they are given some basic tools to do so. Exemplifying this problem is the online "Fair Use Checklist" provided by Columbia University's Copyright Advisory Office to help professors and researchers determine whether a proposed use would be fair. The checklist breaks down each of the four statutory factors into elements that favor or oppose a finding of fair use. For example, in the category "amount," the elements favoring fair use are "Small quantity," "Portion used is not central or significant to entire work," and "Amount is appropriate for favored educational purpose." The elements that disfavor fair use are "Large portion or whole work used" and "Portion used is central to work or 'heart of the work.'" The instructions state, "As you use the checklist and apply it to your situation, you are likely to check more than one box in each column and even check boxes across columns. Some checked boxes will favor fair use and others may oppose fair use. A key concern is whether you are acting reasonably in checking any given box; the ultimate concern is whether the cumulative 'weight' of the factors favors or opposes fair use. Because you are most familiar with your project, you are probably best positioned to make that decision."[58] The problem is that it is hard to know whether to check a box (how much is a "small quantity," for instance?), and harder still, in the absence of a formula for doing so, to weigh the checked boxes that favor fair use against those that disfavor fair use to reach a reliable conclusion.

Many educational institutions caution their faculty members against making any fair use of copyrighted works. The University of Minnesota tells its faculty members that "although this exemption [for fair use] can prove invaluable for educational purposes, any adaptation or reproduction of copyrighted works without consent is a risk and caution should be used when claiming fair use."[59] Some schools warn faculty members about personal liability if a copyright owner sues.[60] Still other schools state that the problem in relying on fair use is that educators in particular have an ethical duty to avoid any possible copyright infringement.[61] Even schools that emphasize the availability of fair use present it as a risky enterprise. While Stanford University, for example, gives detailed guidance to faculty members about how to avail themselves of the fair use doctrine, it also tells them that the risk of litigation may outweigh the benefits of fair use.[62]

If there is any place for robust fair use, it is in education. The Copyright Act lists teaching, scholarship, and research among the ends fair use serves; the first of the four statutory fair use factors asks specifically whether the use of copyrighted material is for an educational purpose. Fair use should be alive and well in schools. However, uncertainty about the meaning of fair use law makes it difficult for educators to know whether any use of a copyrighted work is lawful; warnings from their institutions about the risk of liability additionally pressure educators to seek permission rather than invoke fair use. By acting conservatively, educators impede rather than facilitate lawful uses of copyrighted works. Educational institutions should be concerned about keeping down costs for their students and invested in the free exchange of ideas. However, under the current regime of unclear standards for fair use, educators join the race to the bottom.

UNIVERSITIES AS COPYRIGHT OWNERS

Beyond wanting to avoid lawsuits, universities also have a more specific institutional interest in promoting a culture of licensing that denies the availability of fair use. Universities are both users of copyrighted works and copyright owners. Universities hold copyrights in works produced by their employees, which may include faculty members. Many universities operate their own presses, which have an interest in protecting the copyrights in the books and journals that they produce. University campuses are also home to archives and museums that seek to control uses of materials within their collections.

When universities, as users, experience restrictive fair use practices by others, they, as copyright owners, will seek in the same manner to limit fair use of the copyrighted works that they own. Rather than act as advocates for fair use in ways that would benefit their own employees, students, and authors, universities end up as gatekeepers, making fair use of copyrighted works more difficult. "As we get serious about protecting everyone else's copyrights," the University of Texas tells its professors, "we'd better get serious about our own copyrights and begin to manage them more effectively."[63]

By taking a hard line when it comes to their own intellectual property, educational institutions cannot effectively promote robust fair use of works that are copyrighted by others. Educational institutions therefore reproduce a licensing culture, unwittingly making fair use law more restrictive even though it undermines their core mission of expanding knowledge.

DEATH AND FAIR USE: ESTATES AS GATEKEEPERS

Another example of interference with fair use comes from the
practices of authors' estates, which gain control of the copyright in an
author's works following his or her death and frequently block fair use
of the deceased author's works. Sometimes this is for financial gain. In
many instances, however, the estate simply wishes to maintain control
over the deceased author's reputation. Stanford University English
professor Carol Loeb Shloss spent a decade researching and writing her
book *Lucia Joyce: To Dance in the Wake*, published in 2005. The book
centers on the life of James Joyce's mentally ill daughter, Lucia, and her
influence on Joyce's writings. Shloss's original manuscript reproduced
excerpts from Lucia's memoirs, medical records, correspondence, and
other documentary evidence to support her thesis. However, when
Shloss was preparing the manuscript for publication, the estate of James
Joyce, which objected to Shloss's depiction of Lucia, threatened to sue
her for copyright infringement if she reproduced materials the estate
found objectionable. The estate owned a copyright in some, but not all,
of these materials. When a lawyer for Shloss's publisher informed the
estate that the inclusion of the copyrighted materials in the book was
protected by fair use, Joyce's grandson, Stephen James Joyce, responded
that such a claim "sounds like a bad joke or wishful thinking" and
threatened that "there are more ways than one to skin a cat."[64] Unwilling
to risk litigation, Shloss's publisher excised the copyrighted materials
from the book. Following its publication, reviewers criticized the book
on the ground that it did not include sufficient supporting evidence
for its claims. Shloss therefore decided to create an online password-
protected supplement to her book containing the materials deleted
from the printed version. The Joyce estate again threatened litigation.
Represented by Lawrence Lessig, then a professor at Stanford Law School,
Shloss filed a lawsuit against the estate and Stephen James Joyce. In the
lawsuit, Shloss sought a ruling that the electronic supplement would be

fair use and therefore not infringe any of the copyrights the Joyce estate owned, as well as a ruling that the estate had misused its copyrights by interfering with Shloss's use of materials in which the estate did not in fact own an interest. The case settled with an agreement that allowed Shloss to publish the material electronically and also publish a printed supplement to her book.[65] Shloss's online supplement shows the material omitted next to the book page where she intended it to appear; viewers can see that from page after page of Shloss's manuscript supporting evidence was deleted.[66] The supplement provides striking evidence of how overreaching copyright owners collude with fearful publishers to interfere with fair use, and of the resulting damage to creative works.

Joyce's heirs are not unique in interfering with fair use. The estate of Martin Luther King, Jr., which generates substantial licensing revenues for King's heirs, aggressively polices uses of the civil rights leader's writings. According to King biographer David J. Garrow, "The behavior of the King estate . . . has created a climate of fear and intimidation among people interested in quoting King's words."[67] The estate of Sylvia Plath has refused to allow biographers critical of her husband, Ted Hughes, to quote from Plath's copyrighted works.[68] According to Frederick Nolan, biographer of Lorenz Hart (of Rodgers and Hart), Hart's estate refused him permission to quote from Hart's lyrics because, years earlier, Nolan had shared his research with other authors who wrote that Hart was gay.[69] The estate of photographer Diane Arbus also maintains tight control over uses of her work. When the art criticism and theory journal *October* published an article by Carol Armstrong about Arbus's work, the journal editors appended a statement that no images could be included in the article because "[a]s a condition of granting permission to reproduce the requested photographs, the estate wished to exercise censorship over the contents of the article."[70]

Creativity belongs to the living. Death does not seal off an author's work from new creative projects that use the work in ways the Copyright Act deems permissible. If a copyright survives the death of an author, so does fair use. Just as future generations will draw upon works created today, we today are entitled to draw upon works from the past. Estates are wrong to interfere with fair use and wrong to seek to use copyright law to preserve an author's works and reputation from ongoing evaluation.

TEACHING KIDS TO JUST SAY NO TO FAIR USE

Adding to the problem of interference with fair use are pro-publisher organizations posing as public interest groups that disseminate misinformation about copyright and fair use. The Friends of Active Copyright Education—an initiative of the Copyright Society of the USA—is no friend to de minimis copying or to fair use. The organization makes the following pro-publisher statements on its website: "[C]onsent is required from the copyright owner to use clips or photographs in a motion picture, no matter [how] de minimis or short," and "Use of any copyrighted music . . . no matter how short (even if only a few notes) . . . must be cleared with the copyright owner."[71] Further, the Friends advise, since "relying on the doctrine of 'fair use' . . . is risky[,] . . . [t]he best course of action is simply to seek permission for all copied material you intend to use."[72] In addition, "[i]f you intend to quote or even paraphrase the words of another author, you should obtain that author's permission before doing so."[73] These statements virtually deny any possibility of de minimis copying or fair use of copyrighted works. Other organizations deliver similarly restrictive messages. The Music Publishers Association of the United States includes among its frequently asked questions the following: "[Q.] What do I do if I want permission to reprint portions of a work in my thesis, book, or journal article? [A.] Permission from the copyright holder must be granted prior to use. Contact the publisher to first find the copyright holder."[74]

In recent years, industry representatives have embarked on ambitious campaigns to teach their restrictive views of fair use to children. In conjunction with a pro-publisher outfit called the Copyright Alliance Education Foundation, a variety of industry organizations disseminate slick multimedia curricula materials for teachers to use to instruct their students on copyright.[75] These materials exaggerate the rights of copyright owners and fail to teach children about the availability of fair use. A classroom poster that is included in the Recording Industry Association of America's "Music Rules!" curriculum reads, "Never copy someone else's creative work without permission from the copyright holder."[76] Students are instructed, "Books, poems, pictures, movies, computer software, websites, and many other creative works are also protected by copyright. In fact, your own drawings and writings are protected by copyright. They are your intellectual property—made up out of your ideas—and no one has the right to make copies without your permission."[77] The activity sheet uses rap lyrics to reinforce the point—"'Cause songlifting's wrong, and it's got to stop, see?"[78] Another activity sheet on the subject of "songlifting" tells elementary school students to "interview" family members and friends "about where they get their music" and to bring the reports back to class so they can be used to "figure out how much songlifting occurs among the people you know."[79] Perhaps because this sounds like something out of pre-1990s East Germany, an accompanying teacher manual advises teachers that the students should not collect names.[80] The Business Software Alliance offers a "B4UCopy" educational program for teachers to help their students become "copy smart." The program instructs, "Computers make it easy to make copies of computer software, pictures, words, movies and songs. But copyright laws make it illegal to copy the creative work without the owner's permission. Making copies of a work protected by copyright is just like stealing."[81] And in teaching materials developed by the Motion Picture Association of America, students meet Lucky and Flo, "the world's first-ever DVD-sniffing dogs," and learn that "anyone who sells, acquires, copies or distributes copyrighted materials without permission is called a pirate."[82] Fair use is not part of the curriculum.[83]

WHEN COPYRIGHT OWNERS CONTROL FAIR USE

Designed to allow authors and creators to draw freely upon copyrighted works without facing liability, fair use has fallen under the control of copyright owners themselves. Some copyright owners deny there is fair use, while others exploit the uncertainty of legal doctrine to assert highly restrictive views of what fair use law allows. Industry norms impose licensing requirements even for uses of copyrighted works that the law would permit. Nervous gatekeepers prevent authors from relying on fair use in many circumstances. Misinformation about fair use reinforces norms, emboldens copyright owners, and deters invocation of the fair use law. Fair use is failing when it requires permission and payment.

The legitimacy of our copyright system depends upon robust fair use. The ability to make fair use of a copyrighted work is the condition for granting copyright owners substantial control over their works for extended periods. When fair use vanishes and licensing takes its place, a copyright becomes a powerful tool to shut down expression and quell criticism. Interference with fair use also undermines creativity. This effect is especially pronounced when it comes to making music, the subject of the next chapter.

CHAPTER 3

SAMPLES AND MASH-UPS

MUSICIANS HAVE LONG borrowed from each
other. Classical music, folk music, jazz, and rock
all incorporate and rework elements from prior musical works. Bach
and Handel borrowed from other composers. Béla Bartók made use of
Hungarian folk songs. Elvis Presley's music was heavily influenced by
African American blues and gospel sounds. Led Zeppelin borrowed
from Bukka White. The songs of the Beatles incorporate falsetto calls
from Little Richard, two-part harmonies from the Everly Brothers, and
the influences of Buddy Holly, early Motown, and Elvis. Bob Dylan
derived the melody for "Blowin' in the Wind" from the old spiritual
"No More Auction Block."

Digital technology has turned musical borrowing into a new form of
art. Musicians using digital technology (producers, as they often prefer
to be called) isolate portions—samples—of existing sound recordings
and manipulate and combine those samples, often in unrecognizable
forms, and include them in their compositions or use the samples to
create entirely new recordings. Hip-hop, the musical genre pioneered
by Jamaican immigrants in the South Bronx in the 1970s, began as

live performance using two turntables connected by a cross fader to combine sounds from records. Beginning in the early 1980s, hip-hop artists commonly used digital samplers to create their works. By the time the Beastie Boys released their 1989 album *Paul's Boutique*, which sampled from more than one hundred individual songs, hip-hop artists were using digital technology to turn out dense combinations of beats, loops, and vocals. Today, digital sampling technology is cheaply available. Anybody can sample using a stand-alone sampler or software on a computer. While the hip-hop artists of the 1970s performed at block parties, the Internet enables today's producers to share their works with the entire world. Sampling has spread well beyond its hip-hop roots and features in many musical styles and in songs that top today's charts.

The same technological developments that facilitate sampling have also contributed to the diminished fortunes of the recording industry, by way of illegal online sharing of music and the emergence of independent labels and other new distribution mechanisms that give the public access to a vast catalog of music unconnected to the large labels. The recording industry's response to these developments has been to aggressively enforce its copyrights through, among other things, lawsuits against file sharers and lobbying of Congress for enhanced protections for copyright owners and increased penalties for infringers. The industry has also sought out new revenue streams.

The recording industry's twin desires to control its copyrights and to increase its revenues have resulted in record labels demanding that *all* samples from copyrighted works they control be licensed. In other words, the industry takes the false position that there is no fair use in the music world. Today, anybody can sample past recordings and create new songs. But according to the music industry, everybody who does so without permission is breaking the law.

FROM THE SOUTH BRONX TO THE COURTHOUSE

Assuming the other requirements for copyright eligibility are met, a sound recording is protected by a copyright because the recording is a fixation of the performance of a composition. The copyright in the sound recording is usually assigned by the artist to the record label. There is a separate copyright in the musical composition (unless it is in the public domain) that is the basis of the recording. That copyright is typically held by a music publisher. When elements of an existing sound recording are used in a new work, there are, therefore, two copyright owners who may have a claim that the new work is infringing.

During the 1980s, when hip-hop entered its heyday, the legal status of digital sampling was uncertain. The technology for digital sampling only became available after the enactment of the Copyright Act in 1976, so the statute does not deal specifically with sampling. At first, artists and record companies acted with little regard to whether sampling was lawful. Artists did not typically ask for permission to sample, and record labels did not object when they sampled. The labels did not see much at stake—what was the big deal in using a short snippet of a track that was no longer popular?—and they had their own artists who were doing the same thing, so it was better not to rock the boat. When artists did ask permission to sample, it was generally given for a few hundred dollars.

The landscape began to change in the late 1980s. Record companies had seen the commercial success of hip-hop albums and began seeking fees for samples. Initially, these took the form of buyouts: the copyright owner would grant a license to use the sample for a one-time fee. Buyout fees started at $1,500 but soon crept higher. Copyright owners also began insisting on additional payments once album sales exceeded a specified number. Further, record companies demanded back payments for samples in recordings that had already been released.

Public Enemy's 1988 album, *It Takes a Nation of Millions to Hold Us*

Back, is one of the most successful and influential hip-hop albums of all time. The album's densely packed samples include trumpet squeaks from a James Brown recording, a drum loop from the Commodores, Bob Marley vocals, and a speech by Malcolm X. According to Public Enemy's front man, Chuck D, when in the late 1980s hip-hop albums were generating substantial revenues, the labels clamped down on unauthorized uses of their recordings.[1] This led to a system of reciprocal enforcement among the major labels. Chuck D says, "All the rap artists were on the big six record companies, so you might have some lawyers from Sony looking at some lawyers from BMG and some lawyers from BMG saying, 'Your artist is doing this,' so it was a tit for tat that usually made money for the lawyers, garnering money for the company."[2]

A 1991 decision by a federal district court in New York gave an important boost to the argument by copyright owners that they were entitled to payment for *all* samples. The court held that rapper Biz Markie had infringed the copyright in Raymond "Gilbert" O'Sullivan's "Alone Again (Naturally)," which Markie had sampled for his single "Alone Again" on his album *I Need a Haircut.* For his version of "Alone Again," Markie took a ten-second sample from O'Sullivan's recording and repeated or "looped" it to create the background to the song. Markie also used the title of O'Sullivan's song as his chorus. Markie's label, Warner Brothers Records, had asked O'Sullivan's representatives for permission to use these elements, but Warner released the album before receiving a response. In deciding the ensuing copyright infringement suit against Warner and Markie, the court began its opinion as follows: " 'Thou shalt not steal.' has been an admonition followed since the dawn of civilization. Unfortunately, in the modern world of business this admonition is not always followed. Indeed, the defendants in this action for copyright infringement would have this court believe that stealing is rampant in the music business and, for that reason, their conduct here should be excused. The conduct of the defendants herein, however, violates not only the Seventh Commandment, but also the copyright laws of this country."[3] In addition to barring distribution of Markie's album, the court referred the case to the U.S. attorney for criminal prosecution.

The district court's opinion in this case was remarkably short on analysis. It cited not a single case or statutory provision in support of its conclusion that Markie's sampling infringed the copyright in the plaintiff's song. Biz Markie was not prosecuted; nonetheless, the case had a profound effect on sampling, particularly by hip-hop artists. The case, and a wave of copyright infringement actions brought following it, signaled to copyright holders that they could claim infringement for any unauthorized sampling and therefore had a right to insist that all samples be licensed and paid for. The decision was also a warning to record companies that they could be sued if samples were not licensed. In short order, the major labels refused to release recordings unless samples were cleared, and they developed among themselves a practice of licensing.

THE DAY THE MUSIC DIED

De minimis copying and fair use of sound recordings were soon dealt a more targeted blow. Bridgeport Music, Inc., is a one-person corporation owned by former music producer Armen Boladian. Bridgeport does not actually produce any music; instead, its business is acquiring music copyrights and then enforcing them. In the 1970s, according to Bridgeport, it obtained the copyrights to most of the works of funk pioneer George Clinton and his band Funkadelic. (Clinton has disputed Bridgeport's ownership claims.) Along with the music of James Brown, Clinton's music was the most frequently sampled by rap artists in the 1990s. In 2001, Bridgeport brought in federal court in Nashville, Tennessee, some five hundred claims of copyright infringement of recordings and compositions against more than eight hundred artists. In preparing its lawsuits, Bridgeport had attempted to locate every sample from George Clinton's works and from other musical works in which it owned a copyright. Bridgeport claimed that *any* sampling of a sound recording it owned was copyright infringement. Many of the cases Bridgeport brought quickly settled. Others were dismissed because Bridgeport had named the wrong party or for other technical reasons. Bridgeport also lost a number of cases on the merits. However, Bridgeport's legal position that all sampling is illegal was endorsed in a 2005 decision by a panel of the U.S. Court of Appeals for the Sixth Circuit in *Bridgeport Music v. Dimension Films*.[4]

The defendants in that case had sampled from Funkadelic's 1975 recording of "Get Off Your Ass and Jam" in the rap song "100 Miles and Runnin'," which was included in the soundtrack to the defendants' 1998 movie *I Got the Hook Up*. Clinton's tune begins with a three-note combination solo guitar riff that lasts four seconds. "100 Miles" copied a two-second sample from that riff and lowered the pitch. The copied piece was looped and extended to sixteen beats. The sample appeared in five places in the background of "100 Miles," with each loop lasting about seven seconds. The lower court found that because the copying either was de minimis or lacked substantial similarity to the Funkadelic recording, it did not infringe Bridgeport's copyright. The lower court reasoned that the quantity taken was small and that listeners would not be able to identify the source of the sample. On appeal, the Sixth Circuit panel disagreed and held that the de minimis doctrine had no application to sound recordings. The court's bottom line: "Get a license or do not sample."[5] This ruling, based upon inferences the court drew from the text of the Copyright Act,[6] and raising the possibility that sampling even a single note would be infringement,[7] is of dubious merit.[8]

While the Sixth Circuit panel denied it, Bridgeport Music's shotgun litigation strategy probably influenced the court's decision to reject the de minimis doctrine. The problem with applying the de minimis rule to sound recordings, the court explained, was that it would require judges to perform "mental, musicological, and technological gymnastics" in order to determine whether the rule covered particular instances of sampling.[9] While praising the trial judge's efforts in the case, the court noted that "[w]hen one considers that he has hundreds of other cases all involving different samples from different songs, the value of a principled bright-line rule becomes apparent."[10] The obvious objection, though, is that a bright-line rule need not be the rejection of the de minimis doctrine in the case of sound recordings and a resulting ban on all sampling. The court could have held, for example, that four seconds or less is de minimis sampling and not infringement. That too would have allowed the district court to deal quickly with many of the other Bridgeport cases on its docket.[11]

The Sixth Circuit's analysis assumed also that those who sample without permission could have instead obtained a license. "We do not see this as stifling creativity in any significant way," the court said of its ruling, because "many artists and record companies have sought licenses as a matter of course."[12] The court predicted its decision would simply make licensing universal and more efficient: "[T]he record industry, including the recording artists, has the ability and know-how to work out guidelines, including a fixed schedule of license fees, if they so choose."[13] However, many copyright holders do not want their works sampled at any price. David Bowie, for example, has said, "I would not give permission if I felt the work to be morally or politically repugnant."[14] Copyright owners are also in a position to charge fees for samples that make the new recording prohibitively expensive. The Sixth Circuit thought that "the market will control the license price" so that the copyright owner could never "exact a license fee greater than what it would cost the person seeking the license to just duplicate the sample in the course of making the new recording."[15] There is, however, no market if the copyright owner flat out refuses to allow sampling. Moreover, the very reason for sampling may be that, even with sophisticated technology, a particular vocal or instrumental *cannot* be perfectly replicated in the studio.

After the panel's decision in the *Bridgeport* case, the defendants unsuccessfully petitioned the entire Sixth Circuit Court of Appeals for review. Remarkably, three of the four major record labels submitted an amicus brief in which they set out strong objections to the rule that sampling must always be licensed. Their brief stated that the "Record Companies—much of whose business depends on copyright protection— view the [p]anel's rule as a significant threat, both to creativity and to their businesses." The record companies argued that, far from protecting their interests, the *Bridgeport* decision would subject them to litigation because "many commercially successful records have been distributed that embody samples of sound recordings that were unlicensed because the artists or producers considered them too brief to require a license." In addition, the labels contended, the panel's decision "will deprive creators of sound recordings of the ability to do what creators in all other media may do—use de minimis (and therefore non-actionable) portions of prior works to build on and create new works." The labels disputed the panel's assumption that its rule would simply shift sampling from litigation to licensing. For one thing, the brief stated, there was in the industry a "recognition that de minimis sampling is not, and should not be, actionable." For another, the court's invitation to labels and artists to work out guidelines, including a fixed schedule of license fees, was impractical and, in the absence of congressional authorization, raised antitrust problems.[16] When major music labels say that a court has *over*-protected copyrights in sound recordings, we should listen.

An especially troubling consequence of the *Bridgeport* case is that its bright-line rule—"Get a license or do not sample"—comes without *any* analysis of fair use. Because the lower court applied the de minimis standard and found no infringement, it did not consider whether the fair use defense applied. On appeal, the Sixth Circuit panel declined to decide whether the sample at issue was protected by fair use because it wanted the lower court to consider that issue first upon remand of the case.[17] However, after the Sixth Circuit's decision, the dispute settled. There was, therefore, never a fair use ruling in the case. It is unfortunate that a seemingly decisive decision by a federal appellate court on the lawfulness of sampling comes without any consideration of whether fair use protects sampling.

Here, a difference between the doctrine of de minimis copying and fair use matters a great deal. The doctrine of de minimis copying is a judge-made rule. In the final analysis, it is the prerogative of courts to tailor the doctrine as they see fit. Fair use, however, is a statutory provision that binds judges. It limits, without exception, all the exclusive rights of copyright owners.[18] *Some* copying from copyrighted recordings is, necessarily, fair use. Because of the procedural history of *Bridgeport*, however, we never learn if fair use protects the defendants' use of the sample from Funkadelic's tune. The unsurprising result is that copyright owners (and samplers themselves) treat *Bridgeport* as standing for the proposition that all sampling is infringement. Even though the Copyright Act protects fair use of all species of copyrighted works, a legal decision on the question of de minimis copying enables copyright owners to assert that there is no fair use when it comes to sound recordings.

Subsequent case law has also not dealt squarely with the fair use issue. Although the Sixth Circuit has decided a slew of additional disputes involving litigation by Bridgeport Music, it has never decided whether sampling is protected by fair use. Another federal court could disagree with the Sixth Circuit and find that the de minimis doctrine applies to sampling. A different court could also find that sampling is protected by fair use. But *Bridgeport* has cast a wide shadow, and rather than go before a (different) court to test the legality of sampling, producers have instead opted to obtain sampling licenses. While courts have held that fair use applies to compositions, courts have provided no guidance on when sampling from an existing sound recording constitutes fair use. Says Philo T. Farnsworth, the owner of a label that releases sampled recordings, "We'd love to see a court case or legislation recognize transformative sampling as fair use. As of this moment it seems to exist in a very gray area."[19]

CREATIVITY STIFLED:

THE BURDENS OF LICENSING

In the *Bridgeport* case, the appellate court confidently asserted that requiring that all samples be cleared will not stifle creativity because it is easy enough to obtain a license. However, licensing samples can be costly and difficult. Record labels pass the costs of licensing on to the artist, and recording contracts require the artist to indemnify the record company and distributor in the case of any copyright infringement claim. For instance, rapper Buck 65 cites the "Pandora's box of legal and financial problems" that he encountered in using samples on his 2005 album *Situation*.[20] Recall that licensing a sample generally requires permission both from the owner of the copyright in the composition, typically a music publisher, and from the owner of the copyright in the recording, usually a record company. In licensing the composition, the music publisher typically receives an ownership interest of 15 percent to 50 percent in the new song. In exchange for the license to sample from the recording, the record company typically receives an advance that generally ranges from $2,000 to $15,000, with a royalty rate of two to seven cents per unit sold, and sometimes higher.[21] When a recording makes use of many samples, licensing fees can quickly run hundreds of thousands of dollars. For his song "I'll Be Missing You," Sean "Diddy" Combs (recording under the name Puff Daddy) reportedly paid 100 percent of his royalties to sample "Every Breath You Take" by the Police.[22] Sometimes the math is impossible: the percentages demanded by rights holders exceed 100 percent. Licensing negotiations occur *after* the recording is made so that the copyright owners can listen to the entire track or album. This means that the investment in creating the sound recording has already been made and the copyright owner can extract higher fees than it would be able to if negotiations preceded production. Copyright owners know they can hold up release of an album and demand additional payment on this basis.

Major artists signed to big labels are able to license samples. Their recordings generate sufficient revenue to make payment of licensing fees feasible. Their representatives can negotiate successfully with copyright holders, typically other major labels whose own artists will also be seeking to license samples. Small-time artists, however, are in a quite different position. They often cannot afford licenses, nor do they have the benefit in seeking licenses that comes from being signed to a major label. Further, while the Internet has created new distribution streams, smaller artists cannot usually sell through many mainstream channels such as iTunes or Best Buy unless their works have been cleared. Risk-averse gatekeepers who adhere to conservative interpretations of what copyright law allows thereby prevent sampling by artists prepared to invoke fair use.

Even though sampling technology is now more readily available, there is widespread agreement that many of the hip-hop songs and other works of the 1980s that were based heavily on samples would be prohibitively expensive to release today. It has been estimated that in 2004, fifteen years after the original release of the Beastie Boys' *Paul's Boutique*, it would have cost $3 million to clear the samples on the album, even assuming that the rights holders consented.[23] Likewise, Public Enemy's producer Hank Shocklee says that while it would be possible today to clear the samples for *It Takes a Nation of Millions*, it would be "very, very costly," because for an album that sells more than two million copies, "you're looking at one song costing you more than half of what you would make on your album."[24]

Artists who cannot afford licensing fees have few good choices. One is not to use samples. Singer-songwriter Beck explains why his 2005 album, *Guero*, relied less extensively on sampling than did his earlier recordings: "There's a lot of fun in sampling, and the sampling that we did do was a lot of fun and sparked a lot of creativity, but I think now it's a little bit prohibitive to sample. It's just so damn expensive, and it's such a hassle trying to clear things. As far as sampling goes, it's an interesting area these days, because it's definitely been dying out. It hasn't been arranged in a way where it's workable for musicians to do it."[25] For electronic music producer Morgan Page, sampling is off limits because of the threat of litigation: "I never sample anymore. It just creates needless complications and red tape down the line, especially when your music is licensed to film or television."[26]

A producer might mask samples so that they are hard to identify; some producers go to great lengths to conceal the sources for their samples. Yet there are listeners who take pride in uncovering sample sources and posting the information on websites—a practice the hip-hop community refers to as "dry snitching." (Asked about the reactions of producers to those who reveal sample sources, hip-hop producer Steve "Steinski" Stein says, "I've heard all kinds of stories—death threats and things."[27])

An artist might also replace samples with live instruments and new vocals, but this can be an imperfect choice. Hank Shocklee describes how Public Enemy's use of instrumentals in the 1990s produced a different sound from the sample-heavy music of *It Takes a Nation of Millions*:

We were forced to start using different organic instruments, but you can't really get the right kind of compression that way. A guitar sampled off a record is going to hit differently than a guitar sampled in the studio. The guitar that's sampled off a record is going to have all the compression that they put on the recording, the equalization. It's going to hit the tape harder. It's going to slap at you. Something that's organic is almost going to have a powder effect. It hits more like a pillow than a piece of wood. So those things change your mood, the feeling you can get off of a record. If you notice that by the early 1990s, the sound has gotten a lot softer.[28]

Gregg Gillis, who goes by the name Girl Talk, performs mash-ups, songs created from multiple samples layered on top of each other, live at clubs and has released recordings of his work through the label Illegal Art. Girl Talk's 2006 album *Night Ripper* comprises sixteen continuous dance tracks that sample from 167 artists. Many of Gillis's samples draw from recordings that contain samples themselves. On the track "Friday Night," the lyrics "Engine, engine, number nine / On the New York transit line" are sampled from rapper Fatman Scoop, who in turn sampled the lyrics from hip-hop artists Black Sheep, who sampled them from a song by country singer Roger Miller. Although the *New York Times* has called Gillis's music "a lawsuit waiting to happen," he contends that his work is protected by fair use: "I've always tried to make my own songs. They're blatantly sample based but I tried to make them so that you'd listen and think, 'Oh, that's that Girl Talk song,' as opposed to just a DJ mix. . . . My label, Illegal Art, and I . . . stand by the fair use law; that we do recontextualize the source material into a new whole. . . . I really don't feel like we're potentially hurting the sales of the artists sampled on the record."[29] Nonetheless, Gillis states that he doesn't know "if our [legal] argument would hold any water" and that he is therefore "just a little worried about potential repercussions," and "just waiting for a cease and desist letter to come in the mail."[30]

Copyright owners do not necessarily want the current ambiguity about sampling and fair use to be resolved. Girl Talk has never been sued for copyright infringement; the most likely reason is that the owners of the works from which Gillis samples recognize that there is a reasonable chance that a court would rule that what he produces is indeed fair use. Such a ruling would lead artists who currently seek licenses and pay fees to refuse to do so. It would also open mainstream distribution channels (which demand clearance) to smaller producers who cannot currently afford the licensing fees demanded and paid by major labels.

This reliance on the ambiguity of fair use by copyright owners may explain a curious aspect of a recent copyright infringement lawsuit against Sean "Diddy" Combs's label, Bad Boy Records, and Justin Combs Publishing, in connection with Notorious BIG's use of a five-second sample from "Singing in the Morning" by the Ohio Players. Combs's label did not assert a fair use defense in the case, and the jury awarded the plaintiffs $4 million (an amount that was later reduced on appeal).[31]

Anthony Falzone suggests that the defendants' decision not to assert fair use may have been strategic: "Combs and his label can afford to pay for samples. Many aspiring artists and their fledgling labels—the next generation of would-be moguls hungry to unseat Diddy—cannot."[32]

Regardless of industry norms, given the expense and difficulty of clearance, some artists do not bother. With the wide availability of sampling technology, copyright owners cannot keep track of all sampling. Underground DJs and producers can therefore try to fly beneath the radar. In addition, copyright owners may elect not to pursue remedies unless the work sampling their copyrighted recording has commercial success. Indeed, bringing attention to an unauthorized sample can make the problem worse from the perspective of the copyright owner. In late 2003, musician and producer Brian Burton, under the name Danger Mouse, created the *Grey Album*—a mash-up of vocals from rapper Jay-Z's *Black Album* and instrumentals from the Beatles' *White Album*. Burton released his album in limited quantities through select Internet sites. After the album gained popularity, EMI, which owns the sound recording rights to the *White Album,* and Sony/ATV Music Publishing, which owns the musical compositions on that album, threatened to sue Danger Mouse and retailers distributing the *Grey Album* for copyright infringement. Fans rebelled. On February 24, 2004, proclaimed "Grey Tuesday," hundreds of websites made the *Grey Album* available for free downloads to protest what they saw as corporate interference with fair use. EMI and Sony/ATV backed down.

The *Grey Album* incident highlights the ambiguous relationship major entertainment companies have to sampling. Even though they promote strong intellectual property rights in sound recordings and compositions, entertainment companies also benefit when new artists can draw from earlier works. These benefits go beyond the ability of a company's own artists to sample. As the *Grey Album* incident illustrates, Sony/ATV, a subsidiary of the Sony Corporation of America,[33] aggressively protects its music from uses it does not approve. Yet at the same time, Sony's Creative Software unit makes and sells the popular ACID sampling software in versions for home users ($64.95) and for professional producers ($299.95). Therefore, while one Sony subsidiary is concerned with unauthorized uses of copyrighted music, another Sony subsidiary makes and sells the device that permits the practice. (Indeed, Danger Mouse created the *Grey Album* using the professional version of Sony's ACID sampling software.[34]) Sony does not, of course, tell its software customers to make liberal use of the Sony music catalog. But like other entertainment companies, Sony does have interests both in limiting sampling and promoting sampling technology.

COMPULSORY LICENSING FOR SAMPLES

In Chapter 9 we will see how the law should be reformed to protect fair uses of copyrighted works. Restoring fair use to sampling of sound recordings, however, might merit a more targeted approach. One remedy is simply for Congress to write into the Copyright Act a provision setting out how much of a copyrighted sound recording may be sampled as a matter of fair use law. The benefit of this approach is that it would provide instantaneous clarity in sampling. The downside is that sampling that exceeds the statutory quantity would be curtailed even if there were a good argument that traditional fair use analysis permits it.

An alternative is compulsory licensing of samples. Compulsory licensing provisions allow a person to make use of a copyrighted work in a way that would otherwise constitute copyright infringement, upon payment of a fee to the copyright owner. Copyright owners cannot prohibit uses allowed for by the compulsory licensing system. The Copyright Act includes provisions for compulsory licensing in certain circumstances. For example, an artist may release a new recording of a copyrighted musical work, an act that ordinarily would constitute copyright infringement, upon payment of a fee that is determined in advance by the Copyright Royalty Board within the Library of Congress.

Compulsory licensing could usefully be extended to sampling.

Artists who wished to sample from prior sound recordings would be able to do so provided they pay the royalty fee. As is true of compulsory licenses for musical compositions, a compulsory license for a sound recording would specify how the recording may be used and what uses are prohibited. Uses beyond what the license permits would constitute copyright infringement.

This fix would not be perfect. Such an approach would not change the current industry norm that all samples must be licensed. It would not, therefore, encourage fair use of copyrighted sound recordings. Nonetheless, a system of compulsory licensing would have benefits over how things stand today. Compulsory licensing would allow artists to sample without having to negotiate with individual copyright owners. In some cases, a fee set by the Copyright Royalty Board would likely be lower than that charged by copyright owners for sampling. Copyright owners could not allow sampling to some artists but not others.

For the creator of a work, compulsory licensing represents a loss of control over the work, something that is often central to creative endeavors. For this reason, compulsory licensing is an exceptional feature of copyright law rather than the norm. In the sampling context, the interests of the artist in maintaining control of the work do not outweigh the benefits that will come from a properly functioning sampling regime. For one thing, the owner of a copyright in a sound recording is typically the record label, not the artist, who has already given up control over the uses that may be made of the recording. In addition, if fair use worked as it is supposed to, some sampling of sound recordings would be permissible and would already be occurring. The owner of a copyright who has convinced the world that fair use does not exist has only a weak claim to artistic integrity when compulsory licensing is proposed because fair use is not working.

WHAT SAMPLING TEACHES US ABOUT
INTELLECTUAL PROPERTY LAW

Whether or not Danger Mouse had a valid claim to fair use in making the *Grey Album*, EMI and Sony's acquiescence represented a rare instance of public pressure sufficient to persuade copyright owners to back down. Most sample and mash-up artists who draw attention to themselves run the risk of finding lawyers at their doorsteps. Fair use is not functioning properly when it is driven underground. Yet in the music industry, in which norms dictate that uses of copyrighted sound recordings be licensed and gatekeepers who control distribution channels enforce that requirement, this is exactly what has happened.

In sampling, there are three lessons for intellectual property law as a whole. The first lesson is that vagueness in the law of intellectual property allows the rights of intellectual property owners to expand. The short history of sampling is one in which owners' rights quickly triumphed over users' interests. This outcome occurred because the Copyright Act does not define with clarity how fair use applies to sound recordings. Copyright owners have been able to fill this void with their own vision of the law (in which fair use is prohibited) because the risk of litigation deters sampling and because music distributors prevent artists who have not obtained licenses from entering mainstream channels. Viewed as a case study, sampling shows that it is difficult to protect the interests of users (and, by extension, of the general public) without clear legal rules that define and protect lawful uses of copyrighted works.

A second lesson from sampling is that there are significant risks in relying upon courts to balance the interests of intellectual property owners with those of the public. From the district court's biblical admonition to Biz Markie to the circuit court's advice in the *Bridgeport* case to "get a license," the courts have done a poor job in applying fair use law to sound recordings. We should not leave to the judiciary the task of defining how fair use applies in an entire industry, because courts lack the information and the tools to do more than decide specific disputes. A single case, such as the *Bridgeport* case, is not a good vehicle for making general rules of intellectual property law. Cases typically involve the interests of private parties with a specific dispute and with nobody in the courtroom to represent the public as a whole. Determining how intellectual property law applies to sampling—and how it applies in other contexts—should not be the work of judges.

The third lesson from sampling is that technological advances that allow for increased creativity can also lead to stronger protections for intellectual property. Music sampling thrived as a low-tech practice on the streets of the South Bronx, where copyright owners saw no reason to claim infringement. Today, when sampling technology is widely and cheaply available, owners of sound recordings take the position—backed up with the threat of litigation—that unlicensed sampling is categorically illegal. Sampling continues to occur without the authorization of copyright owners: underground DJs sample without licenses, and Girl Talk performs on stage without being sued. But the strengthening of copyright claims that has accompanied the development of sampling technology means that the creative potential of that technology has not been met.

Advances in technology have done more than encourage copyright owners to assert stronger rights. The next chapter shows how technology has also allowed copyright owners to decide for themselves the proper scope of their rights and to dismantle wholesale the protections intellectual property law provides to users.

CHAPTER 4

TAKEDOWNS AND
LOCKUPS

I N TODAY'S DIGITAL WORLD we can all be creators
and publishers. Digital technology allows anybody
with a laptop or other electronic device to become an author, artist, or
composer. The Internet permits creators of digital works to share their
writings, art, and music on an unprecedented scale. These same tools
have also facilitated copyright infringement and threatened the publishing, music, movie, and other content industries. Providers of digital content have therefore sought to control tightly uses of works they
make available. As a result, the advent of digital technology and the
availability of the Internet have opened up a new forum for overreaching claims of intellectual property rights. While digital technology has
facilitated an outpouring of creativity, it has also permitted individuals
and corporations to interfere with creative expression in new ways and
to impose novel restrictions on how copyrighted works may be used.
And while the Internet is a place to distribute globally creative works,
it is also a Wild West in which copyright owners stake out and defend
aggressively new property claims.

Enacted to address copyright infringement in the digital environment, the 1998 Digital Millennium Copyright Act (DMCA) gives copyright owners new tools to protect their copyrights. However, these tools have been used not just to prevent and remedy copyright infringement but also to make false copyright claims and to interfere with lawful uses of copyrighted works. Using the DMCA, copyright owners have taken down from websites materials that do not infringe any copyright. Digital works, including public domain works, have been locked up behind technological protection measures so they cannot be accessed and used in ways the Copyright Act permits. With content increasingly produced in digital form, and with the Internet fast becoming the principal way in which we receive information, the costs of overreaching are growing and spreading.

THE DMCA AND DIGITAL TAKEDOWNS

As more and more material—both original and preexisting—has made it onto the web, disputes concerning online copyright infringement have arisen as well. In light of this reality, the DMCA sets out procedures for copyright owners and service providers to follow when one of the former believes an online service provider is hosting infringing material uploaded by its users.[1] The copyright owner must send a written notice conforming with the requirements of the statute (commonly referred to as a DMCA or takedown notice) to the service provider's designated agent.[2] The service provider can avoid liability for its customers' activities if it expeditiously removes or disables access to the material, does not receive any financial benefit directly attributable to the infringing activity, and was not previously aware of the presence of the infringing material or any facts or circumstances that would make the infringing material apparent,[3] in addition to satisfying certain other requirements necessary to take advantage of the DMCA safe harbor.[4] The service provider need not make a determination as to whether the material identified by the copyright owner in fact infringes a copyright. The service provider is also not required to notify the user before removing or disabling access to the material. Moreover, the statute provides that (subject to conditions discussed in the following pages) the service provider is not liable to the user for removing material or disabling access.[5] In sum, the service provider has no obligation to monitor its users' behavior in order to identify the presence of infringing behavior but, to avoid liability, must act when it receives notice of copyright infringement by its customers.

The obvious risk of these provisions is that DMCA notices might be used to remove material that is not in fact infringing. The statute anticipates this and provides some protection for users whose content is removed as a result of a takedown notice. For one thing, the statute imposes civil liability for knowingly misrepresenting in a DMCA notice that material is infringing.[6] In addition, the service provider must comply with some additional requirements in order to avoid liability to the subscriber for wrongful removal of material. The service provider must take reasonable steps to promptly notify the subscriber that it has removed or disabled access to the material. It must also restore the material, or access to it, upon receipt of a proper counter-notification from the subscriber to the service provider.[7] Once the service provider receives a valid counter-notification, it must promptly provide the person who filed the original takedown notice with a copy of the counter-notification and inform that person that the material, or access to it, will be restored in ten business days. It then must restore the material no less than ten and no more than fourteen business days following receipt of the counter-notice, unless the issuer of the DMCA notice notifies the service provider that it has begun a court action against the alleged infringer.[8] Complying with the counter-notice and restoring access to the allegedly infringing material does not subject the service provider to a copyright infringement claim, and doing so allows the service provider to avoid liability to the alleged infringer for removing content. Yet while users are able to restore material taken down as a result of a DMCA notice, the method is far from perfect—a delay of ten days can be an eternity in the fast-paced world of the Internet.

The DMCA's takedown procedure increases the power and ability of corporations and individuals to assert copyright claims where none exist and to interfere (if only temporarily) with web-based expression. The deck is stacked in favor of the issuer of the DMCA notice. The service provider has a strong incentive to remove material rather than risk liability to a copyright owner for failing to comply with the safe harbor terms. While the service provider might lose customers who find their online materials inaccessible, the risk of angering a deep-pocketed copyright owner (or supposed copyright owner) typically is a greater concern. Likewise, service providers have little reason to negotiate with the issuer of the DMCA notice or serve as an intermediary between the alleged copyright owner and the user who has posted the material in order to settle the dispute. The easiest, and safest, course of action is to remove the material upon request.

Overreaching by copyright owners combined with conservatism by service providers leaves little recourse for the Internet user whose postings are improperly taken down. While Internet users can cancel their accounts in protest, going without Internet access is not likely to be an option, and different service providers will have the same incentives to remove material at the request of a purported copyright owner. Liability for sending a false DMCA notice requires that the sender knowingly misrepresent that material is infringing. This is often hard to prove, and ordinary Internet users generally do not have the resources to go to court anyway. The Internet is a gateway to sharing information with the entire world. But the DMCA turns online service providers into gatekeepers, blocking publication of material that is deemed by a DMCA takedown notice to be infringing.

Takedown Notices and Overreaching:
From Pricing to Paranormalists

Despite protections against the targeting of non-infringing material, the DMCA enables copyright owners to overreach: copyright holders—

as well as individuals and corporations asserting they hold a copyright—abuse the system, deploying DMCA notices to interfere with Internet content that does not infringe any copyright. There have been many reports of the misuse of DMCA notices. For example, various retailers have used DMCA notices to prohibit comparison-shopping websites from posting advanced information about sales. In November 2002, Wal-Mart, Best Buy, Target, and Staples issued takedown notices to force the popular site FatWallet to remove user postings in its "Hot Deals" section that listed products that would go on sale on "Black Friday," the day after Thanksgiving, along with their sales prices.[9] FatWallet CEO Tim Storm stated at the time, "We don't think sales prices can be copyrighted, or that the DMCA was meant for this type of thing. But it would cost us a heck of a lot of money to be right."[10] Product prices are indeed facts that cannot be copyrighted, but the safer course was to remove the information.[11] Likewise, in 2007, Macy's legal department sent the operator of the website Black Friday Ads a notice that claimed that "sale dates and times, as well as sale merchandise selection and pricing, are the product of substantial time and effort on the part of Macy's, and constitute proprietary information," and that by displaying this information, the website was violating "copyright, trade secret, and other federal and state laws." Macy's demanded that the website remove the materials and disclose the source from which they were obtained.[12]

Some companies have automated the processes for issuing DMCA notices, generating mass notices based on keyword searches of websites, with the unsurprising result that notices are issued to remove content to which the company has no plausible copyright interest. (Inasmuch as the DMCA requires a good-faith belief that copyright infringement has occurred, it stands to reason that automated searches and issuance of notices violate the DMCA's requirements.) For example, in 2003, the search program of the Recording Industry Association of America reported that Penn State had unlawfully posted songs by the artist Usher, and a takedown notice was sent. The search engine had apparently flagged Penn

State because Peter Usher is listed as a faculty member in the Department of Astronomy and Astrophysics and the department's website contained a song performed by astronomers about the Swift gamma ray satellite.[13] In 2007, Viacom demanded that YouTube remove one hundred thousand user-posted videos that Viacom said contained clips from *The Daily Show* and other Viacom-owned content. Nikolaus Gebhardt, developer of the cross-platform game engine Irrlicht, found his videos caught up in the net. From Gebhardt's blog: "Viacom, the corporation behind MTV, DreamWorks and Paramount[,] is now claiming they own the copyright on a video of an Irrlicht tutorial. Which is completely ridiculous, of course: The whole thing has been written by me and the Irrlicht team, even textures and skins and logos have been created by me, and an Irrlicht Engine user . . . simply filmed and published it on YouTube.com."[14] There was speculation in the blogosphere that the error was attributable to Viacom's commercial interest in Klaus Schulze's album *Irrlicht*. In 2003, Universal Studios sent a takedown notice to the Internet Archive, which collects and makes available public domain films, after Universal's search engine mistakenly identified public domain films about home economics labeled "19571.mpg" and "20571a.mpg" as illegal copies of *U-571*, the 2000 movie about a German submarine.[15] One company, Righthaven, does not even bother with takedown notices at all. Righthaven is not a publisher; instead, it scours the Internet for newspaper and magazine articles and photographs that have been republished on blog sites. Righthaven then purchases the copyright in the material from the newspaper or magazine that produced the material, sues the owner of the blog that reposted it, and then offers the blog owner a quick settlement to end the litigation. There is never any legal determination of whether the blog posting actually infringes any copyright.[16]

Takedown notices are also often deployed to stifle competition rather than protect intellectual property interests per se. One study found that 55 percent of takedown notices sent to Google involved businesses targeting their competitors, and that a whopping 31 percent of the notices included no valid copyright claim.[17] Examples of this abound. In 2008, Apple demanded that OdioWorks, LLC, which runs the BluWiki website, remove a discussion among users about making Apple iPods and iPhones interoperate with software other than Apple's own iTunes. Apple's attorneys claimed that the discussion itself constituted copyright infringement and violated the DMCA's prohibition on circumventing copy protection measures. In April 2009, OdioWorks fought back. Represented by the Electronic Frontier Foundation, the company filed a lawsuit for a declaratory judgment that the discussions did not violate any of Apple's copyrights and did not violate the DMCA.[18] Apple withdrew the takedown notice.

Takedown notices can be a powerful weapon to silence critics, even if only temporarily. In 2001, a medical research firm with a history of bringing lawsuits against animal rights activists used a takedown notice to disable an animal rights organization's entire website; the notice did not identify any specific materials on the site that violated the research firm's copyright.[19] In a well-publicized incident in 2002, the Church of Scientology issued takedown notices to Google demanding the removal of links from its search engine that took users to a site critical of Scientology with postings of materials copyrighted by the church.[20] In 2007, spoon-bending psychic Uri Geller used a takedown notice to remove a YouTube video challenging Geller's techniques and sued the YouTube user who had posted the clip for copyright infringement. Geller's copyright interest in the fourteen-minute video extended to an eight-second clip. The YouTube user thereafter sued Geller for issuing a false takedown notice. The case settled, with Geller agreeing to make the eight-second clip available for anyone to use. These incidents illustrate the use of DMCA notices not for the purpose of protecting intellectual property interests but to gain an edge in a dispute.

When service providers remove content posted by users in response to a takedown notice, material in which the user owns a copyright is often removed as well. Blogger Kevin Lee operates a website called Shooting

Down Pictures. Since 2006, Lee has been watching what he calls "The 1000 Greatest Films of All Time" and posting on his website reviews of the films. As part of this project, Lee has uploaded to YouTube video essays containing clips from the films he watches along with his own commentary and criticism. In 2009, in response to the third DMCA notice YouTube received in connection with Lee's activities, YouTube disabled Lee's account and removed all his work—without regard to who owned the copyright in the video essays or whether the essays infringed any copyright.[21] Because online service providers have little incentive to implement mechanisms for sorting out infringing from non-infringing content, takedowns can easily reach material lawfully posted online.

Taking Down Fair Use

DMCA takedown notices are also deployed to remove material from websites that in all likelihood constitutes fair use of a copyrighted work. In many such instances, the point of the notice is not to protect a copyright but to stifle criticism, gain an advantage in a political debate, or otherwise interfere with freedom of speech. (Some courts have held that before sending a takedown notice, a copyright owner is required to consider whether the use of copyrighted material is fair use,[22] but few copyright owners abide by this practice.) One such case involved disparaging comments made by Michael Savage about Muslims during the October 29, 2007, broadcast of his nationally syndicated talk show, *The Michael Savage Show*. The Council for American-Islamic Relations thereafter posted criticism of Savage's comments on its website, including more than four minutes of copyrighted audio excerpts from the offending broadcast. In response, Savage sued the council for copyright infringement. The federal district court ruled that the council's use of the excerpts from Savage's show was fair use and therefore did not infringe Savage's copyright.[23] In 2008, Brave New Films posted a short video titled "Michael Savage Hates Muslims" on YouTube. The video, which criticized Savage, contained one minute of the same audio the

Council for American-Islamic Relations had used from the October 29, 2007, broadcast. Original Talk Radio Network, the syndicator and distributor of *The Michael Savage Show* (and other radio broadcasts), filed a takedown notice with YouTube demanding the removal of "Michael Savage Hates Muslims" plus 258 other videos that Original Talk Radio said violated its copyrights or those of copyright owners it represented. YouTube disabled access to the video and to Brave New Films' entire YouTube channel. YouTube also notified Brave New Films that the video had been taken down, whereupon Brave New Films submitted a DMCA counter-notice to YouTube. Brave New Films sued Original Talk Radio and Savage for a judgment that the video did not infringe copyright and for misrepresentation in violation of the DMCA.[24] Savage claimed he did not send the DMCA notice. Original Talk Radio claimed it did not own the copyright in the October 29, 2007, broadcast, and that it had included Brave New Films' video by mistake in its DMCA notice. It did not dispute the legality of the video, and the case later settled.[25]

In 2003, Diebold, Inc., a manufacturer of electronic voting machines, sent dozens of notices to online service providers hosting leaked internal e-mails that showed problems in Diebold's e-voting machines. At worst, posting Diebold materials "fell within a classic gray area between unlawful infringement and lawful fair use."[26] Nonetheless, Diebold stridently maintained that any use of its e-mails constituted copyright infringement. Under public pressure, Diebold later retreated from its blanket copyright violation claim. But one of the service providers targeted by the notices, along with two students at Swarthmore College who had posted the e-mails and as a result of a takedown notice had their postings removed, sued Diebold under section 512(f) of the DMCA for misusing the takedown process. The district court found that there was no commercial market for the e-mails and so no market harm to Diebold; the postings served a clear public interest, and Diebold "acknowledged that at least some of the emails . . . [were] subject to the fair use doctrine."[27] The court concluded that "[n]o reasonable copyright holder could have believed that the portions of the email archive discussing possible technical problems with Diebold's voting machines were protected by copyright."[28] Diebold had, therefore, knowingly used a takedown notice when it knew that infringement had not occurred and it was liable to the plaintiffs for damages.[29]

Parody, a classic form of fair use, has also been a victim of takedown notices. In 2008, Savitri Durkee, concerned with preserving the character of Union Square in New York City, created a website parodying the official website of the Union Square Partnership (USP), a group that supports redevelopment of the area. In response, USP sent Durkee's Internet service provider a takedown notice asserting that her site infringed USP's copyright. USP also filed a lawsuit against Durkee for copyright infringement in addition to a claim with the World Intellectual Property Organization pursuant to the Uniform Domain-Name Dispute-Resolution Policy seeking the transfer of Durkee's domain name to USP.

Fair use facilitates criticism but takedown notices thwart it. In the spring of 2009, during the Miss USA contest, Carrie Prejean, the contestant from California, stated that she was opposed to same-sex marriage. Prejean was runner-up in the contest and subsequently appeared in an ad for the National Organization for Marriage (NOM), an organization opposed to same-sex marriage. The ad, which was posted to YouTube, included a short excerpt from a video-blog depicting blogger (and Miss USA judge) Perez Hilton denigrating Prejean. Hilton used a DMCA notice to remove NOM's ad from YouTube. NOM itself is no stranger to using DMCA notices to stifle criticism: when leaked audition tapes for a TV ad purportedly featuring ordinary Americans opposed to gay marriage were posted to YouTube, NOM turned to DMCA notices to force their removal.

The Conversion of Senator John McCain

In the fall of 2008, the threat the DMCA poses to fair use garnered the attention of an unlikely critic. Presidential candidate John McCain, who as a senator voted in favor of the DMCA, and his running mate, Sarah Palin, found their campaign videos that included footage from television broadcasts subject to takedown notices from television networks and removed from YouTube. In a letter to YouTube complaining about the removal of the videos, Trevor Potter, general counsel for the McCain-Palin campaign, wrote that "overreaching copyright claims have resulted in the removal of non-infringing campaign videos from YouTube, thus silencing political speech."[30] The videos, Potter stated, were "clearly privileged under the fair use doctrine" in making use of "fewer than ten seconds of footage from news broadcasts . . . as a basis for commentary on the issues presented in the news reports, or on the reports themselves." The campaign took particular issue with YouTube's immediate removal of videos upon receipt of a takedown notice:

Despite the complete lack of merit in these copyright claims, YouTube has removed our videos immediately upon receipt of takedown notices. This is both unfortunate and unnecessary. It is unfortunate because it deprives the public of the ability to freely and easily view and discuss the most popular political videos of the day. And it is wholly unnecessary from a legal standpoint. We recognize that YouTube has said it adheres to the notice-and-takedown procedures established by the DMCA. But nothing in the DMCA requires a host like YouTube to comply automatonically [sic] with takedown notices, while blinding itself to their legal merit (or, as here, their lack thereof). The DMCA provides hosts with a safe harbor from liability for infringement—but there is no need for a safe harbor where, as here, there is no infringement in the first instance.

The campaign complained that the DMCA's counter-notice procedure was inadequate to protect online speech because reposting does not occur until ten days following the receipt of the counter-notice. Ten days, the campaign stated, "can be a lifetime in a political campaign, and there is no justification for depriving the American people of access to important and timely campaign videos during that period." However, it recognized that it would be too burdensome for YouTube to review the legitimacy of every takedown notice. Accordingly, the McCain-Palin campaign proposed that with respect to takedown notices directed at videos posted from accounts controlled by political candidates and campaigns, YouTube conduct "a careful legal review, including fair use analysis, to determine whether the infringement claim has substantial merit." Under this proposal, YouTube should refuse to act on takedown notices directed at campaign videos if it concludes that the use of copyrighted material is fair.

YouTube's response to the letter from the McCain-Palin campaign was also illuminating. YouTube rejected the idea that it could review videos with any degree of certainty before complying with a takedown notice: "Any such review would have to include a determination of whether a particular use is a 'fair use' under the law, which is a complex and fact-specific test that requires the subjective balancing of four factors. Lawyers and judges constantly disagree about what does and does not constitute fair use."[31] In addition, YouTube was not in a good position to attempt a review because it lacked information about the source and ownership of content that is uploaded. As for the McCain-Palin campaign's suggestion that YouTube conduct reviews only of videos posted by political candidates, here is what YouTube had to say in response:

[W]hile we agree with you that the U.S. Presidential election–related content is invaluable and worthy of the highest level of protection, there is a lot of other content on our global site that our users around the world find to be equally important, including, by way of example only, political campaigns from around the globe at all levels of government, human rights movements, and other important voices. We try to be careful not to favor one category of content on our site over others, and to treat all of our users fairly, regardless of whether they are an individual, a large corporation or a candidate for public office.

YouTube concluded its response by stating that now that the McCain-Palin campaign understood the problems the DMCA poses to those who upload content, "[w]e look forward to working with Senator (or President) McCain on ways to combat abuse of the

DMCA takedown process on YouTube, including, by way of example, strengthening the fair use doctrine so that intermediaries like us can rely on this important doctrine with a measure of business certainty." When a senator who voted to enact the DMCA reports from his own experience that copyright owners use DMCA notices to remove non-infringing materials, that the counter-notification process is inadequate, and that expression is curtailed as a result, we should pay attention.

DRM AND DIGITAL LOCKUPS

With the rise in digital media and the mass availability of copying technologies on personal computers as well as elsewhere, content providers naturally are concerned about protecting their copyrights. In the old days, most people did not have the tools required to make perfect reproductions of copyrighted works. For example, the original sound quality was not reproduced when a recording was copied to a blank audio cassette, since content in analog form loses its quality when it is copied. Today, however, digital media files can be easily duplicated an unlimited number of times with no degradation. In addition, technology readily allows for conversion of media originally in analog form (or in broadcast form) to digital form.

Digital rights management (DRM) is the response of copyright owners to the threat that digital technology presents to their interests. "Digital rights management" is a collective term for technologies that set *conditions* on how digital media or devices can be used. These technologies allow providers of digital content to lock up the content and make it available only under the conditions they specify. DRM terms are encoded into the media or device and determine how it behaves. DRM terms might limit the number of times digital content can be viewed; whether it can be copied, and if so, how many times; which devices it can play on or be transferred to; and whether the content can be converted to other formats. Technological protection measures such as encryption and access controls safeguard DRM terms.

In addition to restricting uses of content through digital lockups, technological measures may be deployed to keep track of a particular copy. Digital watermarks embedded within files can be used to identify the copyright owner, record the chain of distribution, and identify who uses the copy. For example, in the summer of 2009, the Associated Press (AP) announced that search engines and websites could not link to AP articles without a licensing agreement and that the AP would henceforth use digital "wrappers," software invisible to users that sends signals back to the AP, to keep track of uses of its articles across the web.[32]

There are numerous examples of DRM. The Content Scramble System (CSS) has been in place on commercially produced DVDs since 1996. It encrypts the data on a DVD so that only licensed DVD players are able to decode and play the file. To receive the license, device manufacturers must restrict features that would allow for digital copying of movies. Many DVDs also contain region codes that limit the playing of the DVD to designated areas of the world. Likewise, broadcast flags are used to set limits on the recording of digital television programs, including whether the program can be recorded at all, which devices the program can be recorded to, the quality of the recording, and whether commercials can be skipped. For example, pay-per-view movies on cable and satellite television are flagged so that recordings cannot remain for more than twenty-four hours on digital video recorders provided by the cable or satellite provider.

Software discs may contain a tethering restriction that prevents the software from being used on any computer other than the one on which it is first loaded. This means the consumer can only use the software on one computer and that consumers who purchase a new computer must purchase again the software. The software disc also cannot be sold on a secondary market unless the computer is sold with it. And even when the copyright expires on the software, nobody else can use it.

For a time, virtually all online music stores used DRM as well. Until early 2009, music tracks purchased from the iTunes Store were encoded with Apple's FairPlay technology. FairPlay prevented iTunes customers from playing the tracks on portable digital music players other than iPods, iPhones, and approved Motorola devices. After Apple announced it would no longer use DRM on iTunes, it told users they could "upgrade" their existing collections to DRM-free songs so long as they upgraded every track at once and paid an additional thirty cents per track.[33] Publishers of audio CDs have likewise experimented with DRM. In 2005, Sony BMG sold CDs with technology that installed stealth DRM software on the user's computer to prevent copying; among the titles affected was Neil Diamond's *12 Songs*, released by Columbia Records, a Sony subsidiary. However, the software installed on the CDs included a rootkit that exposed the user's computer to external security threats. This, combined with public protests against the technology, led Sony to end the distribution of CDs with DRM, to recall millions of CDs it had sold, and to settle lawsuits filed in connection with the security breach the software created.

E-books purchased from Amazon for use on the Kindle have restrictions on the number of devices to which they can be downloaded, and they cannot be shared or printed. Amazon's e-books are in a proprietary software format called Topaz: e-books in Topaz can only be read on devices for which Amazon has licensed use of Topaz. The Kindle itself is, likewise, designed to read only e-books and other digital content purchased from Amazon (although hackers have overcome this restriction). Some restrictions on e-books are simply absurd. For example, when first launched, Adobe Systems' Adobe Acrobat eBook Reader edition of *Alice's Adventures in Wonderland*, which is in the public domain, included a series of restrictions described in a notice accompanying the e-book:

Permissions on: Alice's Adventures in Wonderland

Copy

No text selections can be copied from this book to the clipboard.

Print

No printing is permitted on this book.

Lend

This book cannot be lent or given to someone else.

Give

This book cannot be given to someone else.

Read Aloud

This book cannot be read aloud.

Adobe quickly faced ridicule, in particular for purporting to restrict the right to read the book aloud. Ignoring the March Hare's advice to say what you mean, Adobe responded that reading aloud meant using the book in conjunction with an electronic reader's text-to-speech function. Furthermore, Adobe claimed that the restrictions on lending and giving the book to others also didn't mean what they sounded like but instead referred to *rights* in the book, not the actual book. Adobe removed these particular restrictions; however, it continues to use technology to impose other limits on the use of its e-books. An edition of *Alice's Adventures in Wonderland* that I purchased for $2.89 prohibits the printing, copying, and pasting of the text of this public domain book.

Not surprisingly, consumers have a litany of complaints about technological protection measures. Protection measures can prevent users from making backup copies of CDs and DVDs or storing them on computer hard drives. DVDs do not play on all DVD players. Digital music files purchased online play only on devices of the store from which the files were purchased. Computer printers print only if an approved cartridge is installed. Protection measures can also make computers vulnerable to outside security threats; some devices and content even come with technology that spies on consumers, tracking and reporting how they use the device or content. And in some instances, consumers are left without access to the protected content they have paid for when the provider goes out of business.

The DMCA, DRM, and Circumvention

Throughout its history, DRM has been a cat-and-mouse game, with hackers finding ways to disable or circumvent technological protection measures to gain access to works, and copyright owners developing ever-more sophisticated control systems. Consider the case of DVDs. In 1999, teenage Norwegian programmer Jon Lech Johansen and two collaborators reverse engineered the algorithm used by CSS and released on the Internet DeCSS, a program that decrypts content and allows a CSS-encrypted DVD to play on an ordinary computer using Linux. Once an unencrypted source video becomes available in digital form, it can be copied without any loss of quality. Johansen was prosecuted under Norwegian law but acquitted at trial. Within a short period of time following the release of DeCSS, scores of other programmers had produced software that performed the same function. In response, the movie industry deployed more sophisticated measures: newer systems, notably Content Protection for Recordable Media and Pre-recorded Media and Advanced Access Content System (used for HD DVD and Blu-ray discs), use different algorithms that offer more secure protection. And so the cycle continues.

In 1998, content providers gained an important edge in this game with the enactment of the DMCA. The DMCA prohibits the act of circumventing a technological protection measure that controls access to a copyrighted work.[34] The DMCA also prohibits making or trafficking in both devices that circumvent access controls and devices that circumvent copy control technologies.[35] The DMCA does not specifically prohibit the act of circumventing *copy* control technologies, most likely because Congress assumed that such an act would already probably involve copyright infringement. However, courts have understood the DMCA's prohibition on circumventing access controls to extend to circumvention of copy control measures, on the theory that such circumvention allows access to content. The DMCA provides for civil liability for violations of the anti-circumvention provisions.[36] In addition, the DMCA imposes criminal sanctions for willful violations and for commercial advantage or private financial gain from such violations.[37]

The enactment of these anti-circumvention provisions followed heated debate. While the entertainment and software industries strongly supported the provisions and saw them as essential to the protection of their digital content from piracy, librarians and educators warned that the provisions would stifle public access. In recognition of the concerns on both sides, Congress included in the DMCA two sets of exemptions from the ban on circumventing access controls. First, the DMCA excuses certain users from liability when they circumvent an access control on a work. These include nonprofit archives, libraries, and educational institutions that circumvent access controls for the purpose of making acquisition decisions; law enforcement and intelligence agencies; software developers who reverse engineer computer technology for the purpose of developing interoperable software products; and encryption and security researchers.[38] Second are exemptions that the DMCA directs the Librarian of Congress to issue for the circumvention of access controls to specific classes of works when it is shown that access control technology has had a substantial adverse effect on people's ability to make non-infringing uses of those copyrighted works.[39] Proposals for these administrative exemptions are submitted by the public to the Register of Copyrights, which conducts hearings, receives public comments, and then recommends a final rule to the Librarian of Congress. Once adopted, an administrative exemption expires after three years unless it is renewed.[40]

The DMCA, the Public Domain, and Fair Use

Despite these statutory and administrative exemptions, the DMCA enables content providers to control the public domain and to interfere with fair use. The DMCA does not prohibit circumventing technological measures on public domain works. However, if the public domain materials are compiled with copyrighted materials, circumvention is unlawful. If, for example, a database contains both public domain materials and copyrighted materials, the DMCA prohibits circumventing the database's access controls—even if the individual who circumvents the access control does so only to reach the public domain elements of the database. A provider of public domain materials can, therefore, prohibit circumvention of technological protection measures simply by including with those materials some copyrighted materials. Even the minimal addition of copyrighted material—for example, a short introduction to a public domain work—triggers the DMCA's ban on circumvention. Public domain materials can therefore be locked away in the same way as copyrighted works.

The DMCA also contains no exemption to the circumvention ban for obtaining access to a copyrighted work for fair use or other uses that do not constitute copyright infringement. The DMCA thus enables copyright owners, through technology, to prevent others from using their works in ways that copyright law itself deems permissible. In enacting the DMCA, Congress rejected calls to exempt circumvention for fair use of a copyrighted work. At the same time, Congress chose to include in the statute a statement that the DMCA's liability provisions were not intended to "affect rights, remedies, limitations, or defenses to copyright infringement, including fair use."[41] This simply meant, however, that the DMCA did not create any new grounds for claiming copyright infringement, which remained governed by the Copyright Act. Several bills have been introduced to render lawful circumvention to make fair use of copyrighted works (and to access public domain works); however, none of these bills have been enacted.[42]

Accordingly, in a series of early cases construing the DMCA, courts found that while fair use is a defense to a copyright infringement claim, it is not a defense to an anti-circumvention claim. In one case, movie studios sued website operators who posted, and thereby made available to the public, DeCSS, the software that circumvents CSS protection and allows CSS-protected DVDs to be copied and played on devices that lack the licensed decryption technology.[43] The court held that by posting DeCSS, the defendants had violated the provision of the DMCA prohibiting trafficking in technology that circumvents measures controlling access to copyrighted works. The defendants in the case argued that the DMCA should not be construed to reach their conduct because DeCSS permits those who want to make fair use of a work to access the work for lawful, non-infringing purposes. However, the court rejected this interpretation. It found that Congress had carefully considered the fair use issue and in the end elected to protect the ability of copyright holders to use technological measures that "prevent fair uses of copyrighted works as well as foul."[44] Similarly, the court rejected the defendants' argument that because DeCSS is capable of substantial non-infringing uses, and in accordance with the Supreme Court's decision in *Sony Corporation of America v. Universal City Studios*,[45] they were not liable. The court found that the *Sony* rule simply did not apply to a case under the DMCA.[46] Other courts have reached similar conclusions, refusing to excuse circumvention for non-infringing uses of copyrighted works. If Congress had wanted to allow circumvention for fair use, these courts reason, it would have done so.

Contrary to what the Copyright Act intends, therefore, the DMCA allows copyright owners themselves to determine whether fair use may be made of their works. The ban on circumvention means that copyright owners can prevent more than copyright infringement: it is impossible to overcome technological measures that prevent fair use and other forms of lawful copying, or that prevent lending and other activities that do not run afoul of copyright law, without violating the anti-circumvention ban. For educators, this is a serious problem. Teachers, for example, often wish to show their classes short clips from films. However, most DVDs are protected by technology that prevents users from cuing up a specific scene. The teacher can play the DVD from the beginning, but this route is both inefficient and, as opposed to screening a short clip, might not be protected by fair use. Alternatively, the teacher must circumvent the protection measures on the DVD, thus violating the DMCA.[47] The Motion Picture Association of America takes the position that teachers don't need to circumvent protection measures because they can simply play the DVD at home, use a camcorder to record the relevant clip from the television, and then play the home recording in class. Educators rightly complain that this approach is technologically difficult for many teachers, requires equipment (including a tripod) that is not always available, and results in unacceptable degradation of the clip.

The DMCA also inhibits the use of excerpts from DVDs for commentary, criticism, remixes, and other creative uses that, depending on the circumstances, may be fair as a matter of copyright law. "Vidding" is a form of filmmaking, practiced predominantly by women filmmakers, in which clips from movies and television shows are set to music for the purpose of criticism or social commentary. Some "vids" take and rework clips from a single production, while others bring together clips from hundreds of different productions and put them together to make a point. For example, in one vid, a filmmaker used clips of partnered male police officers and other pairs of male protagonists to argue in favor of the legalization of same-sex marriage.[48] Similarly, creators of videos in the fan fiction genre, in which a fan of a preexisting work uses characters and other elements from that work to create a new story, often seek to use clips from DVDs of the movies or television shows to which they pay homage.[49] The DMCA's anti-circumvention ban makes such forms of filmmaking problematic because even if use of a clip is fair use, circumventing an access control to obtain it violates the DMCA.

Although the DMCA does establish a rulemaking process for the Library of Congress to create exemptions to the anti-circumvention ban, use of this process has so far proved limited. The Library of Congress has been very cautious about adopting exemptions, and persuading it to do so is, by all accounts, laborious. In addition, the statute imposes significant limitations on what the Library of Congress can even accomplish. The rulemaking procedure only occurs every three years, and exemptions that are adopted last for just three years (unless they are renewed). The statute gives the Library of Congress authority to exempt particular classes of *works* rather than classes of *use*. Thus in the most recent rulemaking, in 2010, the Library of Congress included an exemption for circumvention of DVDs in some circumstances. The exemption must be allowed "solely in order to accomplish the incorporation of short portions of motion pictures into new works for the purpose of criticism or comment" and is permitted for only three types of uses, for which the person engaging in circumvention must reasonably believe circumvention to be "necessary": (1) an educational use of the clip by college or university professors or by college or university film and media studies students, (2) use of the clip in documentary filmmaking, or (3) use of the clip in a noncommercial video.[50] This three-year exemption was welcome news for filmmakers and media studies professors and their students; still, it remains unlikely that rule-making will produce a general exemption for fair use of movies or other copyrighted works.

Moreover, the Library of Congress is authorized to issue exemptions only to the prohibition on circumvention. It has no authority to exempt from liability manufacturers and distributors of devices that allow circumvention to occur. As a practical matter, then, even those who benefit from an exemption and are allowed to circumvent may lack the means to do so. Indeed, it is not just the DMCA that limits the availability of circumvention devices. In addition to criminal prosecution under the DMCA, the possibility of the manufacturers of such devices being held liable for secondary copyright infringement looms large following the Supreme Court's 2005 decision holding Grokster and StreamCast liable for inducing copyright infringement by making available software that allowed users to share music files.[51] As a result of that case, manufacturers and distributors of devices that enable circumvention, even in accordance with the exemptions issued by the Librarian of Congress, risk liability if the devices allow for unlawful forms of circumvention. The tools for taking advantage of an exemption, therefore, might not be readily available.

The U.S. Court of Appeals for the Federal Circuit has read the anti-circumvention provisions of the DMCA in light of certain limitations on the rights of a copyright owner under the Copyright Act. These cases are hard to square with the language and history of the statute, and they do not involve fair use specifically. But they do raise the possibility that a future court could read into the DMCA a fair use exemption. One such case decided by the Federal Circuit involved a manufacturer of garage doors that created a garage-door opener with computer software that opened the door when an acceptable sequence of code was sent by the transmitter.[52] The software contained a reset function, by which a different code sequence reset the accepted codes and opened the door even if the transmitter had already sent an invalid code sequence. A competitor manufactured and sold a universal opener that worked by sending a code sequence that either was accepted or commanded a reset, thus opening the door. The garage-door manufacturer, which wanted to be the sole vendor of openers for its own doors, sued the competitor on the ground that under the DMCA the rival transmitter was an unlawful circumvention device enabling access to the copyrighted software in the door mechanism. In agreeing with the district court that the defendant was not liable under the DMCA, the Court of Appeals for the Federal Circuit focused on the statutory definition of "circumvention" as involving access "without the authority of the copyright owner."[53] The court turned that provision on its head, reasoning that because the DMCA does not create any new intellectual property rights, a copyright owner *has* no authority under the DMCA to grant or prohibit access that is otherwise permissible under the Copyright Act. Accordingly, if there is no authority to deny access in the first place, access cannot be unauthorized. The DMCA, the court explained, "prohibits only forms of access that bear a reasonable relationship to the protections that the Copyright Act otherwise affords copyright owners."[54] On the facts of the case, copyright law prohibited unauthorized copying of the garage-door software, but it did not prevent consumers who owned the garage doors from accessing the software.[55] Therefore, trafficking in the universal opener did not violate the DMCA. Still, it is important to underscore the limitations of the decision. It does not deal specifically with the question of whether circumvention for fair use is permissible under the DMCA. The court observed that understanding the DMCA to apply to circumventing an access control that does not protect a right of a copyright owner "would . . . allow any copyright owner, through . . . technological measures, to repeal the fair use doctrine with respect to an individual copyrighted work."[56] However, the court specifically declined to address whether fair use is a defense to a DMCA claim.[57] While the possibility remains that a court in the future will extend the logic of this case to the fair use context, current law prohibits circumventing an access control even to make fair use of a copyrighted work.

FIXING THE DMCA: THE DMCA AND THE COPYRIGHT BALANCE

Adjustments to the DMCA takedown and counter-notification procedures can reduce the problem of lawful materials being removed from websites. Not all speech is lawful, but the law generally requires a full determination by a court that speech is unlawful before the speech may be curtailed. The DMCA is in tension with that principle. It permits a private party to interfere with speech without having to persuade anybody that there is a legal basis for doing so. The DMCA allows a copyright owner to get what amounts to an automatic restraining order good for ten days whether any infringement case is ever filed or not. Keeping in mind that the point of the DMCA notice procedure is to protect service providers from liability to the copyright owner for hosting infringing material (and to the user for removing content), Congress should amend the DMCA to better reflect free speech principles.

Before material is removed pursuant to a DMCA notice, the copyright owner should be required to provide a copy of the takedown notice to the user. Because it can be hard to identify and locate users, the online service provider should be required to forward the notice to the user at the copyright owner's request and upon payment of a fee. Currently, users can file a counter-notice and have their material restored after ten days. Congress should amend this provision to allow users to oppose removal of their materials before it occurs. Following their receipt of the takedown notice, users should have three days in which to file an opposition with the service provider. Should the user fail to do so, the service provider would be free to remove the material. If, however, the user files an opposition, the service provider should do nothing unless the copyright owner provides notification that it has initiated a lawsuit against the user. In cases when a three-day delay would result in irreparable harm to the copyright owner, it could go to court to seek an order requiring removal of the material. The copyright owner should also be required to file any takedown notice with the Copyright Office, which would maintain such notices in a publicly accessible database. Individuals and organizations concerned with misuse of takedown notices would then be able to bring the worst offenders to public attention. Finally, users should be entitled to seek statutory damages against any copyright owner who files a takedown notice for material that is not infringing.

Congress should also amend the anti-circumvention provision of the DMCA. That provision should not apply to circumvention for the purpose of accessing public domain works or making fair use of copyrighted works. The right to access the public domain and the ability to make fair use of copyrighted works are essential; we should not permit content providers to eliminate or impede such access with digital locks. The failed Digital Media Consumers Rights Act, which was introduced into Congress in 2003 and again in 2005, provided that it is not a violation of the DMCA to circumvent a technological protection measure in order to gain access to or use a work if the circumvention does not result in an infringement of the copyright in the work. Congress should again take up this provision and make it law. Relying upon the Library of Congress to issue piecemeal DMCA exemptions good for only three years is not an adequate substitute for congressional action to protect the public domain and safeguard fair use in the digital age.

The DMCA was designed to protect copyrights in digital content and to prevent dissemination of infringing works via the Internet. These two goals are reasonable and in harmony with the rights of copyright owners under the Copyright Act. The DMCA supports our system of copyright laws when copyright owners use DMCA takedown notices to remove from websites materials that infringe their rights. Likewise, use of the anti-circumvention provisions of the DMCA to protect technological measures that prevent infringement of copyrighted digital content comports with the rights that copyright law grants copyright owners.

In practice, however, corporations and individuals use these DMCA tools not just to remedy and prevent infringement but also to interfere with activities that copyright law allows. The DMCA is regularly used to take down from websites content that does not infringe any copyright. The DMCA is also often deployed to lock up digital content so that it cannot be accessed and used in ways that copyright law permits. By enabling content providers to control public domain materials and to interfere with fair uses of copyrighted works, the DMCA is at odds with the Copyright Act's limitations on what can be protected by a copyright and how far copyright protections extend. Reforming the DMCA is essential to restoring the balance the Copyright Act sets between private rights and public interests.

The DMCA is not the only law that undermines the balance the Copyright Act sets. The next chapter takes up the problem of content providers using contract law to obtain rights beyond those copyright law gives them.

CHAPTER 5

FROM COPYRIGHT
TO CONTRACT

A T THE BEGINNING of his 1884 book *The Adventures of Huckleberry Finn*, Mark Twain included this notice: "Persons attempting to find a motive in this narrative will be prosecuted; persons attempting to find a moral in it will be banished; persons attempting to find a plot in it will be shot."[1] While the particular conditions Twain imposed remain absurd, terms of use attached to creative works are now commonplace. Federal copyright law gives strong protections to copyright owners while also protecting the interests of the public in copyrighted works. But many content providers are not satisfied with this balance. They have taken to using state contract law to impose terms of use upon consumers that exceed the protections that copyright law confers, and to assert rights to works to which they do not hold copyright. As a result, state contract law, which enables overreaching, is increasingly supplanting federal copyright law as the basis for protecting creative works.

Contracts allow content providers to limit access to works to those who agree to abide by their conditions. Whereas a copyright is limited in duration, contracts are used to give content providers perpetual rights. While copyright law permits fair use of copyrighted works, contracts prohibit it. While federal copyright law applies uniformly around the country, contract law can vary among states—and so the terms of use accompanying copyrighted works vary from one work to the next. Furthermore, as we shall see in this chapter, digital delivery greatly facilitates the ability of content providers to impose through contract what they cannot obtain under copyright law, with terms of use accompanying virtually every kind of digital content, from music files to software, from online news reports to social networking sites. In the digital age, private ordering is supplanting public law.

CONTRACTING AROUND COPYRIGHT LAW

Here is a scenario that is familiar to many researchers. An archive owns a physical copy of a letter of historical significance. To view the letter, the researcher must sign an agreement with the archive that provides, among other things, that the researcher will never publish the letter or any excerpts from it without the permission of the archive. While a contract cannot create a copyright where none exists, the conditions apply even if the letter is in the public domain and even with respect to copying that would be permissible fair use.

It is common practice for museums, libraries, and other archival collections to restrict access to their holdings to people who agree to forgo the sort of copying that the Copyright Act permits. In my office is an impressive stack of reproduction request forms and licensing contracts collected from the permissions departments of such institutions around the country. These contracts are often developed in house without the assistance of legal counsel and contain all manner of terms and conditions.[2] A museum's contract for the use of a reproduction of a work of art in a forthcoming publication, for example, may state the permissible and prohibited uses, place limitations on transmitting the image to others, prohibit cropping or manipulation of the image, restrict the number of images from the collection that a single author can use, specify the exact phrasing that must be used in credit lines, require that the museum be provided with a copy of the periodical or book in which the image is used, and so on.

The Schlesinger Library at Harvard University bills itself as "the largest and most significant repository of documents covering women's lives and activities in the United States."[3] Researchers must register, show a picture ID, and complete an application form just to visit the library. Among the rules researchers must adhere to: "Permission to examine library materials is not authorization to publish or to reproduce the examined material in whole, or in part. A separate 'Permission to Publish' application must be submitted to the library."[4] Columbia University says of its collection of the papers of John Jay: "[M]uch of the material may be in the public domain," but "[t]he University does not authorize any use or reproduction whatsoever for commercial purposes."[5] The Historical Society of Pennsylvania requires that users obtain the "[p]ermission of [t]he . . . Society . . . , as owners of the material, to cite or quote from the collections," even though "the Society does not claim to control literary rights" and "[t]he publishing party assumes all responsibility for clearing copyright."[6] For authorization to cite or quote from materials in the collection of the Massachusetts Historical Society, researchers must seek permission by giving the Society a "full description of publication plans."[7]

Some of the conditions archives impose on users result from restrictions applied to the archives themselves by the donors of the materials. In certain cases, an archive might be happy to allow researchers to publish material in its possession—but the donor has set limitations, with the threat that the gift will be taken back if the archive does not enforce them. Such conditions might limit who can access the materials, when they may be opened to researchers, and the circumstances in or purposes for which they may be copied or quoted. In some instances, materials are entirely off limits for a period of time. Donor restrictions can hamper the mission of an archive to provide researchers with access allowing them to make use of collection materials. The Society of American Archivists and the American Library Association have adopted a joint statement which says that while "private donors have the right to impose reasonable restrictions upon their papers to protect privacy or confidentiality for a reasonable period of time," archivists should "discourage . . . unreasonable restrictions" and "work toward the removal of restrictions when they are no longer required."[8] In reality, though, it is hard for archives to do more than gently encourage donors to relinquish some of their control over materials, because typically there are other archives willing to embrace the gift on the donor's preferred terms.

An archive that learns that a researcher has violated the conditions upon which access was provided can bring a claim for breach of contract; although litigation between archives and disobedient researchers might seem unlikely, it is not unheard of. In 2005, author Richard Schwartz filed a preemptive lawsuit against the Berkeley Historical Society in connection with his use of public domain photographs from the Society's collection.[9] The Society had given Schwartz access to its photographs and, in a "one-time use agreement," permission to use some of the photographs in his book *Berkeley 1900*.[10] Subsequently, in promoting the book, Schwartz displayed enlarged versions of seven of the book's photographs—two of which Schwartz had licensed from the Society—in the window of a hardware store where the book was sold.[11] The Society asserted that the store window reproductions violated the agreement Schwartz had signed and the Society's access policies, and it demanded they be taken down.[12] In Chapter 1, we saw how archives engage in copyfraud by falsely claiming they own a copyright in public domain materials in their collection. The Berkeley Historical Society's position was different. It did not assert a copyright in the photos but rather argued that it was entitled to damages because Schwartz had broken his promise. Nonetheless, in asking the court to rule that his use was lawful, Schwartz argued that the contract itself was unenforceable because the photos were in the public domain.[13] The parties ultimately settled the case without a court decision on whether a breach of contract had occurred.[14]

Even if an archive itself does not seek legal redress against a researcher who violates the terms of an access agreement, the researcher might be sued by the author of the materials or by the author's estate. In *Salinger v. Random House*, biographer Ian Hamilton accessed letters of J. D. Salinger, donated by the letters' original recipients, in the archives of Harvard University, Princeton University, and the University of Texas at Austin.[15] To consult the letters, Hamilton had to sign access agreements that limited what he could do with the letters. At Princeton, for example, the "Library Request for Access to Manuscripts" stated in part, "I understand that Princeton University holds manuscripts for purposes of research and scholarship. I agree not to copy, reproduce, circulate or publish them without the permission of Princeton University Library and of the owner of the literary property rights, if any. I assume all responsibility for any infringement by me of the literary property rights held by others in the material requested."[16] Despite agreeing to these terms, Hamilton decided to include in the biography excerpts from the letters. Salinger obtained a pre-publication version of the biography and sued Hamilton and his publisher for copyright infringement and breach of contract. Salinger claimed that as the author of the letters, he had the right to enforce the access agreements even if the archives themselves did not plan to sue Hamilton.[17]

Some contracts go so far as to require the licensee not to contest the licensor's asserted ownership of a copyright in a work. At least one federal circuit court has upheld a contract prohibiting the licensee from asserting that a copyright is invalid.[18] The case concerned a licensing dispute between the *Saturday Evening Post* and Rumbleseat Press. A contract between the parties gave Rumbleseat the exclusive right to manufacture and sell porcelain dolls designed after Norman Rockwell illustrations published in the *Saturday Evening Post Magazine*. The agreement contained a warranty that the *Post* had a valid copyright in the illustrations, and a provision under which Rumbleseat agreed not to "dispute or contest . . . the validity of any of the copyrights." After the licensing period had passed, Rumbleseat continued to produce the dolls, and the *Post* sued for copyright infringement. When Rumbleseat argued in its defense that the *Post* did not in fact own copyrights in the illustrations, the *Post* asserted that the contract barred Rumbleseat from making that claim. Judge Posner for the Court of Appeals for the Seventh Circuit agreed with the *Post*.[19]

The practice of contracting around copyright law is not limited to dusty archives and old works of art. A sports match is not a copyrighted work because it is not fixed in a tangible form. Nonetheless, sports organizations treat matches as their intellectual property and use contract law to limit what reporters may say about them. Minor League Baseball (MiLB) requires reporters seeking press credentials to sign an agreement that imposes strict limitations on the reporters' activities. The contract prohibits unauthorized uses of photographs and videos as well as of "any account, description . . . or other information concerning an Event . . . other than for news coverage of, or magazines, books or stories about, the Events, or for First Amendment–protected purposes."[20] During a game, the bearer of the press credential is prohibited from "transmit[ting] . . . any Event Information on a play-by-play or pitch-by-pitch basis more frequently than once every half-inning of play."[21] Other provisions limit the length of video and audio feed allowed, restrict online posting of video from inside the ballpark, and require photographers to sell prints to MiLB under the best terms made available to any other party.[22] MiLB has obvious business interests in limiting who can report on games. MiLB sells broadcasters rights to carry the game live. In addition, the league and the individual teams have their own websites with game footage, photographs, and reports that generate substantial revenues. However, copyright law allows activities that do not necessarily serve the business interests of a sports league.

CONTRACTS AND COPYRIGHT
IN THE DIGITAL ERA

We saw in Chapter 1 that a person or organization's ability to limit access to public domain materials provides an opportunity for that person or organization to claim rights in those materials equivalent or similar to copyright. In a similar fashion, the possibility of limiting access to copyrighted works to individuals who sign a contract presents an opportunity for content providers to prevent uses of works that are permissible under the Copyright Act. The ever-increasing electronic delivery of books, music, and other works facilitates such overreaching by allowing vendors to require consumers to agree to their terms as a condition of receiving these digital works. For example, software is often accompanied by *shrinkwrap* contracts, which provide that in tearing open the shrinkwrap packaging, the user assents to its terms (which often are displayed to the user when the software is run). Terms may also take the form of *clickwrap* (or click-through) contracts, which require the user to assent to terms by clicking electronically on an acceptance box; *browsewrap* contracts, which specify that the user agrees to terms simply by visiting the website; or *webwrap* contracts, in which, by downloading software, the user consents to its accompanying terms.

Although the specific terms of these agreements vary by provider, they typically begin with an identification of the parties to the agreement and an assertion that use of the product or service constitutes consent to the terms. At the website of the Associated Press, a browsewrap agreement provides, "Use of this Web site is conditioned on the acceptance, without modification, of all terms and conditions of this agreement. By using this Web site you represent that you have read and understand the terms and conditions and that you agree to be bound by these terms and conditions as set forth below."[23] Many agreements governing digital content prohibit activities that do not constitute copyright infringement. Agreements generally state that the licensor grants the user a non-exclusive, nontransferable license to use the product or service in accordance with the terms of the agreement. In addition, acceptable use is frequently limited to personal, noncommercial use, and restrictions are imposed on the user's right to copy content as well as distribute it or provide anybody else with access to it. Consider, for example, this provision in the terms and conditions accompanying *U.S. News & World Report's* online ranking of colleges: "The materials contained on the Web site are provided by U.S. News as a service to you for your noncommercial, personal use . . . and may be used by you for information purposes only. . . . All materials published on the Web site are protected by copyright laws, and may not be reproduced, republished, distributed, transmitted, resold, displayed, broadcast, or otherwise exploited in any manner without the express written permission of . . . U.S. News."[24] The fair use provision of the Copyright Act does not limit uses of copyrighted materials to noncommercial, personal, and informational uses. Fair use also allows some reproduction and dissemination without the permission of the copyright owner. By accepting the terms and conditions imposed by *U.S. News & World Report*, however, the individual who accesses the college rankings purportedly pledges to forgo activities that the Copyright Act permits.

There are many other examples of overreaching contracts. If you visit CBS.com, you agree to the following: "You may not . . . copy, reproduce, distribute, publish, [or] display . . . the . . . Content without our permission."[25] The terms and conditions of FirstSearch, which provides access to multiple subject-specific databases, such as business periodicals and medical articles, allow the user to "view screen displays of data accessed via the FirstSearch service, and . . . make one (1) copy per screen display of any portions of such data for that person's internal or personal, noncataloging and noncommercial purposes."[26] Visiting YouTube triggers a browsewrap agreement that provides, among other thing,: "You may access Content for your information and personal use solely as intended through the provided functionality of the Service and as permitted under these Terms of Service. You shall not download any Content unless you see a 'download' or similar link displayed by YouTube on the Service for that Content. You shall not copy, reproduce, distribute, transmit, broadcast, display, sell, license, or otherwise exploit any Content for any other purposes without the prior written consent of YouTube or the respective licensors of the Content."[27]

Digital contracts also contain a range of other provisions tilted to the interests of the content provider. Agreements typically carry a limited liability provision restricting the damages available for a breach of the agreement by the licensor. Also, agreements often include a territorial restriction limiting the use of the underlying product to the United States. Many agreements attempt to waive warranties that consumers might otherwise have when they purchase products.[28] Indemnification is another common provision whereby the user agrees to reimburse the licensor for claims by third parties related to the user's breach of the agreement. Agreements that govern Facebook and other interactive sites often provide that the user grants the site administrators a license to use any content that he or she uploads.[29] In addition, licensors often retain the right to change the terms of the agreement at any time.

Content providers may use contracts to limit criticism and to curtail speech they deem offensive. In making available trailers for display on websites, Disney's contract provides,

The Website in which the Trailers are used may not be derogatory to or critical of the entertainment industry or of [Disney] (and its officers, directors, agents, employees, affiliates, divisions and subsidiaries) or of any motion picture produced or distributed by [Disney] . . . [or] of the materials from which the Trailers were taken or of any person involved with the production of the Underlying Works. Any breach of this paragraph will render this license null and void and Licensee will be liable to all parties concerned for defamation and copyright infringement, as well as breach of contract.[30]

Similarly, Microsoft's software license terms prohibit in a webwrap agreement the "use [of] the service in any way that . . . harms Microsoft or its affiliates, resellers, distributors and/or vendors (collectively, the 'Microsoft parties'), or any customer of a Microsoft party."[31] Some contracts require the licensee's acquiescence to the possibility that the content provider may check up on him or her. A Symantec clickwrap software license provides, "An auditor, selected by Symantec and reasonably acceptable to You, may, upon reasonable notice and during normal business hours, but not more often than once each year, inspect Your records and deployment in order to confirm Your use of the Licensed Software complies with this License Agreement."[32]

Terms of use may also be used to interfere with software development. Some software manufacturers seek to develop new programs that are interoperable with other programs already on the market, which often requires reverse engineering of the original product to identify its components and determine how it operates. Under the Copyright Act, it is fair use to reverse engineer software to develop an interoperable program if the elements necessary to achieve interoperability are not otherwise available to the software engineer.[33] The Digital Millennium Copyright Act (DMCA) also permits circumvention of access controls in order to reverse engineer software under these circumstances.[34] Nonetheless, software owners use contract law to restrict all forms of reverse engineering. This permits software providers to maintain control over the development of interoperable products; if reverse engineering is not permitted, developers of interoperable products need to enter into licensing agreements with the software provider to obtain the information needed for interoperability. Use of Apple's digital download service is governed by the iTunes Store clickwrap terms of service. Those terms state that the user agrees "not to violate, circumvent, reverse-engineer, decompile, disassemble, or otherwise tamper with any of the security technology . . . or to attempt or assist another person to do so," thus prohibiting any circumvention that is permitted under the DMCA.[35] Users of Amazon's Kindle must agree before they can read a book in digital form to a series of conditions, including that they will not "bypass, modify, defeat or circumvent security features that protect the Digital Content."[36]

Software manufacturers also use contractual provisions to restrict licensees from publishing the results of any benchmark testing they conduct to test the software's performance capabilities. The licensing agreement that governs the use of Novell's Suse Linux Enterprise Server requires, for example, that users obtain Novell's permission before they publish or disclose to anyone else the results of any benchmark testing.[37] This is significant because in addition to allowing software vendors to compare the performance of their software against competing products, benchmark testing is used by magazines and websites to give consumers comparative information about different products. Software manufacturers contend that because the design of a benchmark test can affect how well the software appears to perform, they need to control the dissemination of the results of benchmark testing to ensure fair and accurate reporting of the software's capabilities. However, as consumer groups and trade publications understandably complain, when vendors unduly restrict the use of these results, consumers lack the information necessary to make informed purchasing decisions, and software improvements to which the publication of results would probably lead are stalled.

STATE LAWS VERSUS FEDERAL LAW IN THE ERA OF DIGITAL CONTRACTS

While federal law governs copyrights, contracts are governed by state law. When parties enter into a contract, the interpretation of the contractual terms and the enforceability of the agreement depend upon the laws of the applicable state as construed by that state's highest court. State law, rather than federal copyright law, therefore increasingly determines the scope of rights held by owners of creative works and sets the limits on uses of those works.

Under the Constitution's Supremacy Clause, federal law is supreme to state law if there is a conflict between the two.[38] When there is no conflict, state law may nonetheless have to yield to federal law if the federal law displaces or preempts state regulation. Preemption can be either express or implied. Express preemption exists when a federal statute specifically provides that it is displacing state law on a matter. Implied preemption exists when a statute does not expressly preempt state law but it is clear that Congress nonetheless intended to do so. Section 301 of the Copyright Act contains an express preemption provision: "[A]ll legal or equitable rights that are equivalent to any of the exclusive rights within the general scope of copyright . . . in works of authorship that are fixed in a tangible medium of expression and come within the subject matter of copyright . . . are governed exclusively by this title. Thereafter, no person is entitled to any such right or equivalent right in any such work under the common law or statutes of any State."[39] The federal Copyright Act therefore displaces copyright laws at the state level. At the same time, though, the section also states that federal preemption does not apply to state law rights with respect to "subject matter that does not come within the subject matter of copyright."[40]

When courts first confronted contractual restrictions on digital content, they were reluctant to allow state law to alter the copyright balance that Congress had struck. In a well-known 1988 case, for example, the U.S. Court of Appeals for the Fifth Circuit held that the Copyright Act preempted a provision of the Louisiana Software License Enforcement Act that permitted software manufacturers to prohibit all decompilation or disassembly of their programs.[41] However, this approach was adopted by the minority of courts. In construing the express preemption provision of the Copyright Act, most courts have since upheld contracts that enhance the interests of content providers.

Courts have conducted a two-step preemption analysis, asking first whether the work at issue comes within the subject matter of copyright, and, if that condition is satisfied, whether the rights granted under state law are equivalent to any of the exclusive rights within the general scope of copyright. In the second step, some courts have approached preemption through a factual analysis that looks carefully at the particular contractual term alleged to have been broken and asks whether the right at issue is one that is protected by the Copyright Act. For example, in *Altera v. Clear Logic*, the Ninth Circuit considered a software licensing agreement that restricted use of the software to users with the "sole purpose of programming logic devices manufactured by Altera."[42] When Clear Logic began manufacturing semiconductor chips that were based on bitstreams produced by Altera's software, Altera sued Clear Logic for intentionally inducing Altera's customers to violate their software license agreements and for intentional interference with contractual relations. The court held that the Copyright Act did not preempt enforcement of the "sole purpose" provision of the licensing agreements because it involved the use of the software's end product, which is not protected under the Copyright Act.[43]

A more common approach to preemption has been to treat contractual rights in general as different from those the Copyright Act protects. Under this approach, courts reason that even though the materials may fall within the general subject matter of copyright, the rights enforced through contract law are new rights, not equivalent to the rights under the Copyright Act. On this theory, the contract, in which the parties have exchanged something of value and agreed to be bound by the arrangement, is the very thing that makes the right at issue qualitatively different from those the Copyright Act protects.

Exemplifying the approach in *ProCD v. Zeidenberg*, an influential 1996 case, the U.S. Court of Appeals for the Seventh Circuit upheld a shrinkwrap license agreement for a CD-ROM of telephone listings.[44] ProCD, the plaintiff in the case, marketed the CD-ROM, which contained a database of information compiled from over three thousand telephone directories, to consumers for personal use and to businesses. The cost of the CD-ROM for businesses was higher than the cost for personal use even though the two groups received the same product. To

prevent consumers from selling their cheaper CD-ROMs to businesses
at a price lower than ProCD's own business price, the license that came
with the consumer version limited use of the application software
and the listings to noncommercial purposes. The terms of the license
appeared on the computer screen every time the software was run. The
defendant in the case had bought a consumer version of the CD-ROM
and resold the information in the database via a website at a price lower
than what ProCD charged its business customers. ProCD sued for
breach of contract, in addition to pursuing other causes of action. The
defendant argued that the shrinkwrap license was unenforceable as a
matter of contract law because the terms of the license did not appear
on the outside of the box and could not be assented to at the time
of purchase. In addition, the defendant argued that even if the license
were contractually valid, the Copyright Act preempted its enforcement
because it restricted use of un-copyrightable public domain information.
In support of this argument, the defendant cited the Supreme Court's
1991 decision in *Feist Publications v. Rural Telephone Service Company*
that, because telephone numbers are in the public domain, a telephone
directory could not be copyrighted: even though great effort may
have been involved in compiling the numbers, the directory was not a
sufficiently original work to merit copyright protection.[45]

In his opinion for the Seventh Circuit in *ProCD v. Zeidenberg*,
Judge Easterbrook upheld the shrinkwrap license. He concluded that
the license was valid as a matter of contract law: the contract was formed
when the defendant opened the package containing the license and used
the product rather than returning it. On the issue of preemption, Judge
Easterbrook agreed with the district court's conclusion in the case that
even though ProCD's data were in the public domain, they were "within
the subject matter of copyright" for the purposes of section 301 of the
Copyright Act. Judge Easterbrook explained that "[o]ne function of §
301(a) is to prevent states from giving special protection to works of
authorship that Congress has decided should be in the public domain,

which it can accomplish only if 'subject matter of copyright' includes all works of a *type* covered by . . . [the Copyright Act] even if federal law does not afford protection to them."[46] However, Judge Easterbrook disagreed with the district court's conclusion that the contract rights at issue in the case were "equivalent" to the rights granted by the Copyright Act. He reasoned, "Rights 'equivalent to any of the exclusive rights within the general scope of copyright' are rights established *by law*—rights that restrict the options of persons who are strangers to the author. Copyright law forbids duplication, public performance, and so on, unless the person wishing to copy or perform the work gets permission; silence means a ban on copying. A copyright is a right against the world. Contracts, by contrast, generally affect only their parties; strangers may do as they please, so contracts do not create 'exclusive rights.' "[47] In other words, contractual rights are different from copyrights because of the very existence of the contractual agreement. In addition, Judge Easterbrook noted, a two-party contract does not "withdraw any information from the public domain" because "[e]veryone remains free to copy and disseminate all 3,000 telephone books that have been incorporated into ProCD's database."[48] Accordingly, a "simple two-party contract" that did not lock away information from the public domain did not protect rights equivalent to any exclusive right within the general scope of copyright and was therefore valid under section 301.[49] *ProCD v. Zeidenberg* has been enormously influential. A series of cases since the decision have followed Judge Easterbrook's logic and upheld agreements giving additional rights to providers of digital content.[50]

At some point the issue of preemption of contracts is likely to make it to the United States Supreme Court. How the Supreme Court will rule is uncertain. The Court's prior cases involving preemption and intellectual property provide little guidance. In 1964, the Court stated that state laws cannot operate to prevent copying of something that is not protected by federal intellectual property law. "[W]hen an article is unprotected by a patent or a copyright," the Court explained, "state law may not forbid others to copy that article. To forbid copying would interfere with the federal policy, found in . . . the Constitution and in the implementing federal statutes, of allowing free access to copy whatever the federal patent and copyright laws leave in the public domain."[51] In accordance with this view, in 1989 in *Bonito Boats v. Thunder Craft Boats,* the Supreme Court held that federal law preempted a state law that prohibited reverse engineering of a public domain work.[52] However, the Court has never ruled on whether contracts in which contracting parties give up a right they may enjoy to copy or use a work are enforceable. Nor has the Court given any indication as to whether state contract law can give copyrighted works stronger protections than the Copyright Act confers.

BALANCING INTERESTS IN
AN ERA OF PRIVATE ORDERING

Commentators are divided on the issue of whether people should be permitted to use contracts to impose restrictions unavailable under copyright law. Raymond Nimmer argues that contract and intellectual property law have always coexisted peaceably and will continue to do so in the future.[53] One benefit Nimmer sees is that licensing agreements facilitate the transfer of information by allowing parties to offer different kinds of licenses for different markets; in contrast, denying parties the ability to set their own terms is likely to result in higher prices, restricted supply, or the copyright owner choosing not to release the work at all.[54] Other commentators see state contract law as improperly eroding the public domain and undermining federal copyright policy. These commentators argue against "unbargained . . . license provisions that reduce or eliminate the rights granted to licensees by the federal intellectual property laws," contend that "information law [should] be a . . . federal preserve," and assert that "attempts to rework, alter, or eviscerate aspects of copyright through the vehicle of state contract law are illegitimate."[55]

Even though a contract is an agreement between individual parties, contracts that govern the use of content, particularly digital content, can have broad public effects. First, the limitations that copyright law sets on the rights of the copyright owner protect the interests of individual users, but in doing so they also serve the public's interest in expression. An individual user who agrees to give up protections available under copyright law does not therefore bear all the costs of that decision: the public also loses out. For example, the public benefits when a filmmaker relies upon fair use and uses excerpts from copyrighted movies for the purpose of commentary or criticism. A filmmaker who gives up fair use suffers a private loss, but the public is also worse off because the film may be less powerful or might not be made at all. Contracts also have broad public effects when they affect large numbers of people. When everybody who receives information must accept the terms that the content provider imposes, particularly when that information is not otherwise readily available, it no longer makes sense to think of digital licenses as simple two-party contracts. Instead, such licenses give the content provider rights that are, in effect, held against the world. When, for example, millions of people get their music from iTunes, contractual terms displace copyright law as the basis for protecting musical works.

More generally, contracts undermine Congress's desire for a uniform law of copyright in two respects. First, content providers tailor specific terms to their own interests. Some content may be saved to a hard drive, while some must be accessed only online. Some content may be stored in one device, while other content may be stored on five. Sometimes printing and copying are permitted, sometimes not. Whereas copyright law is designed to impose a set of common rules that bind content providers and content users alike, contract law permits each content owner to decide which uses are permissible.[56]

The second source of variation comes from the fact that contracts are governed by state law. State laws of contract vary. Although the dissemination of digital content does not abide by state geographic boundaries, the enforceability of contractual terms accompanying that material depends upon the law of a particular state. The absence of uniformity presents problems not just for consumers but also for content providers. Content providers solve the problem (from their perspective) and impose uniformity by including a choice-of-law provision in their licenses specifying that the laws of a designated state govern any dispute, regardless of where the content is obtained or used.[57] This is also not ideal from the perspective of the general public. The content provider naturally elects a state whose laws are most favorable to it. This means, then, that a single state can dictate for the nation which kinds of digital contracts are valid. In place of federal law governing copyrighted works, and balancing the interests of copyright owners and the public, contracts can nationalize the unbalanced law of a single state.

Shrinkwrap, clickwrap, webwrap, and browsewrap licenses that bind everyone who accesses content should be viewed in terms of their implications for the balance that Congress has reached under the Copyright Act between the rights of creators and the interests of the general public to access and use works. This need not mean that we should condemn contracts simply because they are not subject to negotiation. In some sectors, it is feasible for licensors and licensees to negotiate the terms for use of content. For example, a library that is considering purchasing an expensive database may be in a position to negotiate with the database provider about the terms of the arrangement. In many other instances, however, it is simply impractical to expect digital content providers to negotiate with their customers about the terms of use. Amazon cannot feasibly negotiate with its millions of Kindle users. If there is to be contracting in the digital age, it will be, for the most part, of the standard-form variety. As an attorney for Microsoft has put it in explaining standard contracts accompanying software, "publisher[s] . . . can offer products at such low prices only if each transaction has very low transaction costs. The uniform terms

. . . facilitate high-volume distribution without the cost of individually negotiating individual licenses."[58]

Likewise, there is little reason to condemn digital licensing terms simply because they are not always visible to the user (to view a browsewrap agreement, for example, the user typically must scroll to the bottom of the website and click on a link).[59] From the perspective of users, there is no practical difference between terms of use that pop up on a screen or are printed on a box and those that are viewed only when one clicks on a link at the bottom of a website. There is also no practical difference between the user who tears open a wrapper or clicks on a box and assents to the license and the user whose assent is presumed from his or her visit to a site or installation of a program. Many consumers do not read through terms closely regardless of whether they are made visible or hidden from view, whether they require assent or presume it has been given. In a world in which consumers quickly click on "I agree" boxes in order to get immediately to content, the traditional contractual requirement that parties have notice and assent is largely meaningless. Moreover, it is unrealistic to expect that the consumer who is unhappy with the terms of the license will, rather than clicking to indicate his or her assent, stop using or return a product. A consumer who purchases software, begins to install it, and then sees a box with unfavorable terms of use is unlikely to return the software to the store or contact the provider for a refund.

The focus should remain on how contracts affect the public's interest in copyright law. Christina Bohannan persuasively argues that contractual waivers should be enforceable only if they involve a waiver of "rights under the Copyright Act that protect individual rather than public interests."[60] Under this approach, individual users should not be able to give up through contract a right that benefits the public because "[t]he right is not theirs to give away, and, if enforced, the waiver could interfere with the purpose of the federal statute."[61] According to Bohannan, this means that in general, "a contractual promise not to use public domain material or to make fair use of copyrighted material" should not be enforceable because the promise "affects copyright policy intended for protection of the public."[62] However, Bohannan argues that rather than create blanket rules to that effect, courts should decide on a case-by-case basis whether a specific contractual provision undermines public protections.[63] Bohannan thinks, for example, that the result in *ProCD v. Zeidenberg* was actually correct under her approach, because even though the user of ProCD's telephone number database waived a right to distribute public domain information, the contract did not interfere with copyright policy. She observes that (as the court reasoned) enforcement of the contract allowed ProCD to sell a cheaper personal CD-ROM along with the business version, thereby giving more people access to the database; in addition, the contract did not withdraw information from the public domain, as the telephone numbers in the database remained available to the general public in telephone books.[64] Similarly, under Bohannan's approach, not all waivers of fair use would be unenforceable, because a court would decide in specific instances whether the waiver had a public impact.[65]

THE EUROPEAN SOLUTION

While distinguishing between individual and public interests is useful, relying upon courts to decide in particular cases whether a contract is enforceable has a chilling effect. Content providers require users to give up most or all of the protections available to them under copyright law. If nobody knows whether a waiver of protections is enforceable until a court hears the case, users cannot be confident they will not be held liable if they ignore the contract and use the content in a way that the Copyright Act allows. Statutory limitations on contracts are a better approach because they provide clarity at the outset. Congress should therefore follow the lead of the European Union and amend the Copyright Act to prohibit contractual terms waiving protected uses that serve public interests.[66] At a minimum, Congress should prohibit outright waiver of the two categories of uses that Bohannan identifies: use of public domain materials and fair use of copyrighted materials.[67] This proposed statutory change would invalidate many of the contractual provisions discussed in this chapter. For example, archives could no longer use access agreements to prohibit researchers from publishing public domain materials within their collections or from making fair use of copyrighted materials without permission. *U.S. News & World Report* could not prohibit wholesale all copying from its college rankings, because some copying would be protected fair use under the Copyright Act. Because reverse engineering is a fair use of software, a software manufacturer could not use a contract to prevent users from reverse engineering its products.

Although Congress should prohibit contracts that limit the use of public domain materials, some other kind of legal protection for providers of databases of public domain work is desirable. Consider, for example, a database operator who digitizes and makes available for a fee public domain archival records that would-be users previously could access only by visiting the archive. Without some guarantee that somebody else will not immediately copy and disseminate the database, the database provider has little incentive to digitize and make available the materials in the first place. Copyright law will not provide that guarantee because the materials are in the public domain, and under the proposal I have offered, the database provider will not be able to use contract law to limit copying and distribution of the materials. Unless somebody takes on the task of digitizing the materials without an expectation of control and compensation (a not entirely unlikely scenario), the public will have less access to public domain materials than it otherwise could.

A sensible remedy to this specific problem is for Congress to create a right separate from copyright for creators of databases of public domain materials.[68] The sui generis right in databases that exists in the European Union provides a useful model.[69] The European database right is separate from any copyright protection that might apply, and it therefore extends to databases of public domain materials.[70] The database right, which is designed to promote the development of new databases, lasts just fifteen years.[71] To merit protection, the database maker must have made a quantitatively or qualitatively substantial investment in compiling the database.[72] The right protects the database creator from users extracting or reutilizing all or a substantial part of the contents of the database.[73] However, users are permitted to extract or utilize insubstantial parts of the database for any purpose.[74]

Asking Congress to create a federal statutory right in databases of public domain materials is preferable to allowing the creators of those databases to assign themselves rights through contracts. A statutory right in databases can be limited to the initial years after the database is created—when the database is most valuable and when wholesale poaching is most detrimental. The database right would be restricted to the database itself—it would create no rights in the individual public domain materials in the database—and even then some copying from the database would be permissible.[75] A statutory database right therefore allows database creators to recoup their investment without permitting them to lock up in perpetuity public domain works.

THE BROAD HARM OF CONTRACTS

Contracts governing content are now common. Accessing information today often requires agreement to a set of conditions imposed by the supplier. Contracts determine how archival materials, including public domain materials, may be used. Contracts dictate what we can do with computer software, whether we can share information from online news reports, and who controls what we post on social networking sites. Even baseball, America's national pastime, is governed by contracts specifying what can be shown of or said about a game.

As we have seen in this chapter, private ordering of intellectual property rights through contracts undermines the system of intellectual property law Congress has created. Contracts favor the interests of content suppliers over those of users and the general public. Contracts therefore upset the balance the Copyright Act sets between private and public rights.

Contracts also undermine our system of intellectual property law in more fundamental ways. Contracts reinforce the culture of licensing we have encountered in prior chapters, in which permission is the precondition to using content. Contracts also foster misunderstanding about the scope and nature of intellectual property law. Making use of the public domain and making fair use of copyrighted materials require ordinary people to know and to understand the ways in which copyrights are limited. This is increasingly difficult when content is routinely delivered with contractual terms that restrict public domain materials and that threaten lawsuits for unauthorized uses of copyrighted works. When contracts displace copyright law, consumers become used to having few or no rights; even when no contract actually applies, ordinary people may well assume that the content they would like to access and use is restricted. These effects are likely to be especially strong when consumers do not actually own the content they pay for. The next chapter takes up that problem.

CHAPTER 6

THE OWNERLESS
SOCIETY

THE INFORMATION SOCIETY is increasingly an
ownerless society. Digital delivery allows content
providers to give the consumer only *access* to a work, as opposed to
the consumer's own copy of the work itself. Thus, under the terms by
which it is made available, digital content is usually licensed, not sold.
Digital consumers are not owners of the content they receive, but mere
licensees with a right to read, view, or listen to the work. Ownership
remains with the content provider. The consumer's ability to maintain
the access for which he or she has paid depends upon his or her compliance with the provider's terms. If, for example, the consumer does not
keep up with subscription payments or violates some other condition
for access, he or she loses access to the content.

Even compliance with the provider's terms, however, does not
guarantee that the consumer will always have access to digital content
or that the terms of access will not change. The provider might, for
example, modify the functionality of the service. Digital materials that
once could be copied or shared might become locked. Content can
also simply disappear because the provider changes its mind about the

arrangement. In the summer of 2009, for instance, owners of the Kindle e-book reader who had downloaded George Orwell's *1984* or *Animal Farm* found the books removed from their devices. Those who lost a book received a refund, and Amazon later apologized and eventually arranged to have the books restored.[1] However, in such cases there is no certainty that concessions will be made. If a record label goes out of business, the records it sold can still be played, but if a digital music store goes out of business, the consumer can easily end up with nothing.

Because licensees of digital works do not own anything, they have nothing to sell, lend, or give to anyone else. Whereas the books on my bookshelf are mine to keep or to sell as I wish, the e-books on my Kindle belong to Amazon. As Nicholson Baker observes, I have bought not the books themselves, but "the right to display a grouping of words in front of [my] eyes for [my] private use with the aid of an electronic display device approved by Amazon."[2] I can read the e-books I have purchased so long as I adhere to the terms of use Amazon imposes. However, I cannot sell them to anybody, donate them to a library, or leave them to a friend in my will.

This is a radical development in the way in which we receive information. As long as books have been around, the owner of a book has been free to read it and then sell it, lend it, or give it away. So, too, if I buy a music CD, I am free to sell or give the CD to somebody else. Indeed, copyright law protects these activities. Today, however, publishers of e-books, record labels that offer digital music, and other providers of content in digital form assert that these rules do not apply to them.

THE FIRST-SALE DOCTRINE

The law traditionally has protected the ability of the owner of a lawful copy of a copyrighted work to transfer that copy to somebody else through the first-sale doctrine. The Supreme Court recognized the first-sale doctrine as a limitation on the rights of copyright owners in 1908 in *Bobbs-Merrill Company v. Straus*.[3] The Bobbs-Merrill Company had sold a copyrighted novel with this notice printed below the copyright notice: "The price of this book at retail is $1 net. No dealer is licensed to sell it at a less price, and a sale at a less price will be treated as an infringement of the copyright."[4] The defendant, a book retailer, purchased copies of the book at wholesale and sold them at eighty-nine cents a copy.[5] The publisher argued that the provision of the Copyright Act of 1891 (then in force) that gave a copyright owner the "sole liberty . . . of vending" a copyrighted book meant that the copyright owner could also "part with . . . [the right] to another to the extent that he sees fit, and may withhold to himself, by proper reservations, so much of the right as he pleases."[6] On this theory, the right to sell included the right to sell under specified terms. According to the publisher, failure to adhere to its price condition constituted copyright infringement. The Supreme Court rejected the publisher's argument, reasoning that "[t]o add to the right of exclusive sale the authority to control all future retail sales, by a notice that such sales must be made at a fixed sum, would give a right not included in the terms of the [copyright] statute, and, in our view, extend its operation, by construction, beyond its [intended] meaning."[7]

A series of subsequent cases firmly adhered to this first-sale rule, holding that a copyright owner cannot restrict the ability of the owner of a lawfully acquired copy to transfer that copy to somebody else. For example, in a 1961 case before the United States Court of Appeals for the Third Circuit, *Independent News Company v. Williams*, the distributor of a comic book sought to prevent sales of coverless versions of the comic book by secondhand dealers.[8] As was customary in the industry, the wholesaler could return the covers of unsold comic books to the distributor for reimbursement. A contract between the distributor and the wholesaler set out how the wholesaler could then dispose of the coverless books. To further effectuate this arrangement, the publisher printed the following notice in each comic book: "This periodical may not be sold except by authorized dealers and is sold subject to the conditions that it shall not be sold or distributed with any part of its cover or markings removed, nor in a mutilated condition, nor affixed to, nor as part of any advertising, literary or pictorial matter whatsoever."[9] In the *Independent News* case, the wholesaler sold the coverless comic books to a wastepaper dealer that, rather than dispose of them, sold them to a secondhand dealer, which then marketed the comics to the public. The distributor and publisher sued the secondhand dealer for copyright infringement. The Third Circuit held that the notice attached to the comic books was unenforceable.[10] Since there was no contract between the wastepaper dealer and the wholesaler (or distributor), the wastepaper dealer took full title to the comics. Accordingly, the plaintiffs could not, under copyright law, control how the comics were subsequently sold: "[O]nce there is lawful ownership transferred to a first purchaser, the copyright holder's power of control in the sale of the copy ceases."[11]

The first-sale doctrine was codified in section 109(a) of the 1976 Copyright Act. That section provides that notwithstanding the copyright owner's exclusive distribution right,[12] "the owner of a particular copy or phonorecord lawfully made under this title, or any person authorized by such owner, is entitled, without the authority of the copyright owner, to sell or otherwise dispose of the possession of that copy or phonorecord."[13] In other words, once the title in the physical embodiment of a copyrighted work is lawfully transferred to somebody else, that person can sell or give away the copy—or rent, lease, or lend it out—without infringing any interests of the copyright owner.

The idea behind the first-sale doctrine is that when a copyright holder chooses to sell a copy of the copyrighted work, he or she relinquishes the exclusive statutory right to control further distribution of the copy. A first sale does not, however, cause the copyright owner to relinquish other rights, such as the right to make additional copies of a work. Thus the doctrine allows a consumer who purchases a copyrighted novel to sell that copy to somebody else (the consumer is still not allowed, however, to make a photocopy of the novel).

One exception to the first-sale rule bears mentioning. The Record Rental Amendment of 1984 amended section 109 of the Copyright Act to prohibit commercial renting, leasing, or lending of phonorecords without the copyright owner's permission.[14] This exception came about because the recording industry persuaded Congress that record rentals, which once were common, were not genuine rentals, but designed to give people temporary access to a copyrighted record in order to make a copy of it. Particular evidence of this was the fact that record rental stores offered blank audio cassettes for sale to their customers along with the records they were renting. Congress prohibited rentals of records not, therefore, to limit the first-sale privilege (though the amendment had this effect) but to prevent unlawful copying. After Congress enacted the amendment, the former record rental companies adopted a new approach. They sold records to consumers and allowed them to return the records a few days later for a small restocking fee. Courts ruled that even though the practice involved a transfer of title, these transactions were not truly sales but rentals, and therefore also prohibited by the 1984 amendment.

This, then, brings us to an aspect of the first-sale right that merits emphasis: transfer of *ownership* is an essential element of the first-sale doctrine. Only owners of a copy of a work can invoke the first-sale privilege. The doctrine does not "extend to any person who has acquired possession of the copy or phonorecord from the copyright owner, by rental, lease, loan, or otherwise, without acquiring ownership of it."[15]

SOFTWARE LICENSING AND
THE END OF FIRST SALE

Providers of digital content seek to put an end to the first-sale doctrine. The first-sale doctrine is particularly vulnerable when it comes to computer software. Congress has set some limits on the first-sale doctrine with respect to software. The Computer Software Rental Amendments Act of 1990 amended section 109 of the Copyright Act to prohibit (as the statute does with records) unauthorized commercial renting, leasing, or lending of computer programs.[16] There is no prohibition on *selling* computer software, which remains permissible under the first-sale rule. Nevertheless, software publishers claim that the first-sale doctrine does not apply to software *at all* because software is not sold, but only licensed to the user. Under this theory, "owner[ship] of a particular copy," the condition for invoking first sale under section 109, remains with the software company itself, not the consumer—who never takes title to the product. The consumer is bound by an end user license agreement, which restricts what he or she can do with the software and includes a prohibition on transferring the software to anyone else. In sum, although the Copyright Act authorizes resale of software, the software license does not.

Software developers introduced licensing prior to the 1990 amendments in order to prevent consumers from renting software and copying it. The first-sale doctrine was at that time a barrier to suing companies that were renting the software to consumers. By licensing the software rather than selling it, software manufacturers sought to avoid the first-sale doctrine entirely and create a cause of action against the software rental companies in contract law. After Congress amended the first-sale doctrine in 1990 with respect to computer programs, software companies continued to use licensing to retain title in the software and impose restrictions on licensees, including restrictions on transferring the software in any manner. Typical of these restrictions is the user agreement accompanying Intuit's TurboTax, the popular tax preparation software, which states that "The Software is licensed[,] not sold, and Intuit reserves all rights not expressly granted to you in this Agreement. The Software is protected by copyright, trade secret and other intellectual property laws. Intuit and its licensors own the title, copyright, and other worldwide intellectual property rights in the Software and all copies of the Software."[17] Among the restrictions on the licensee: "You are not licensed or permitted under this Agreement to . . . rent, loan, resell or distribute the original CD or a copy of the Software to any other person or entity."[18]

Two legal questions arise in this context. One is whether, as a matter of statutory law, the consumer—who goes to, say, Best Buy, pays for his or her purchase, and returns home with software on a CD-ROM—is in fact the *owner* of the copy of the software, so that the first-sale privileges of section 109 are triggered. The second question is whether, if section 109 applies, the consumer's *surrender* in the licensing agreement of the right of transfer otherwise supplied by section 109 is valid. The latter question is the preemption question that we have already encountered in Chapter 5: does federal law trump contracts in which consumers give up things (here, the right of first sale) that the Copyright Act otherwise protects? The distinction between these two issues is not merely conceptually significant; it also has implications for the size and nature of the remedy a copyright owner can collect. If the consumer is not the owner of the copy of the software, then any subsequent transfer is copyright infringement. If the consumer is the owner, the only legal cause of action available to the copyright holder (assuming the transfer does not involve commercial rental, leasing, or lending) is breach of contract. Breach-of-contract damages are generally limited to the actual loss caused by the breach. Copyright damages allow the copyright owner to collect actual damages and any additional profits incurred by the infringer, or statutory damages—currently as much as $150,000 per infringed work. In addition, in cases of copyright infringement, a court may impose injunctive relief, order the seizure of infringing articles, and award the plaintiff costs and attorneys' fees.

Courts have reached different conclusions in cases involving software and first sale. In a 2001 case in the central district of California, software publisher Adobe brought a copyright infringement claim against a software reseller, SoftMan, which unbundled Adobe software collections and sold the pieces individually on a website.[19] Adobe distributed its products through signed licensing agreements with its own distributors. Among other things, these license agreements required that the software be distributed in its original form and packaging, and that distributors acknowledge that the software could only be licensed to end users in accordance with the original licensing terms. Each piece of Adobe software was accompanied by an end user licensing agreement that set out the terms between Adobe and the individual software user. The same agreement also appeared on the screen when users attempted to install the software; the user was required to agree to the terms before the software would install. Adobe's user agreement permitted the user to transfer all interests in the entire collection of software to someone else but prohibited transfer of individual components of the software package. Adobe claimed that by distributing unbundled collections, SoftMan violated the user agreement and infringed Adobe's exclusive distribution right under the Copyright Act. Adobe argued that the first-sale doctrine did not apply because Adobe does not sell or authorize *any* sale of its software. Instead, according to Adobe, in every transaction, from distributor through end user, each party receives only a license from Adobe to use the software. "Since no party can transfer more rights than it acquired," Adobe contended, "there was no 'first sale' in the transfer to SoftMan," which, too, was merely a licensee.[20]

The court rejected Adobe's argument. Looking to the economic realities of the transaction, rather than how Adobe chose to label it, the court found that SoftMan had in fact purchased, not licensed, Adobe's software. According to the court, Adobe sold its software to distributors: Adobe transferred large amounts of merchandise to the distributors, they paid full value for it, and they accepted the risk that the software might be damaged or lost or might not be sold. These transactions were, therefore, sales. In addition, the court reasoned, consumers took title to the software from the software distributors because each consumer obtained a single copy of the software, at a single price, paid at the time of the transaction, and Adobe's "license" ran for an indefinite term. Whatever Adobe called the transaction, the court viewed it as a sale. SoftMan therefore owned the software and could sell it as it wished.[21]

However, in another case from the northern district of California, a court agreed with Adobe that it licensed rather than sold its software.[22] In that case, the defendant, One Stop Micro, distributed educational versions of Adobe software to customers seeking to use it for noneducational purposes. Adobe made available the educational versions of its software, which lacked the full functionality of and were cheaper than retail versions, to authorized educational distributors, which then transferred the software to authorized educational resellers on college campuses. The educational reseller's relationship with Adobe was governed by a campus reseller agreement providing that the educational reseller would "make the Educational Software Products available to certain of Reseller's customers who are Educational End Users."[23] One Stop acquired educational versions of the software, removed packaging information identifying the software as such, and sold it to retail customers below the regular retail price. Adobe claimed that One Stop, by distributing educational software in violation of the campus agreement, infringed Adobe's copyright. One Stop invoked the first-sale doctrine as a defense. It argued that the campus agreement was actually a sales agreement: having obtained ownership of the software copies, One Stop could distribute them as it chose. The court agreed with Adobe that the first-sale doctrine was inapplicable because the campus agreement was in fact a licensing (not sales) agreement and therefore One Stop did not obtain title to the copies of the software. Accordingly, One Stop's distribution of educational versions of Adobe software to noneducational end users, which was outside the scope of Adobe's license, infringed Adobe's distribution right under the Copyright Act. Therefore, the court held, One Stop had committed copyright infringement.[24]

The question of ownership of software arises as well under section 117(a) of the Copyright Act. It provides that "it is not an infringement for the owner of a copy of a computer program to make . . . another copy or adaptation of that computer program" if the copy is an "essential step" in using the software or the copy is for archival purposes.[25] The meaning of "owner" is, presumably, the same under section 117(a) as it is under section 109. However, courts have not shown consistency in interpreting these provisions. In one case under section 117(a), the plaintiff was a programmer who wrote custom computer programs for the defendant and stored the programs on the defendant's computer network.[26] When the relationship between the plaintiff and the defendant ended, the plaintiff allowed the defendant to continue to use the executable code but prohibited any modification to the source code. To enforce this limitation, the plaintiff put a lock on the executable code to prevent its conversion back into source code. Inability to modify the source code rendered the program largely useless to the defendant, because it meant the defendant could not, among other things, add new customers, modify customer addresses, or fix bugs. The defendant therefore circumvented the lock and modified the source code. The plaintiff sued for copyright infringement based on the defendant's copying of his programs. The district court granted summary judgment to the defendant on the ground that its use and modification of the programs were protected by section 117(a). The Second Circuit Court of Appeals affirmed. In his opinion for that court, Judge Pierre Leval concluded that formal title in a program copy is not "an absolute prerequisite" to the benefits of section 117(a). He thought that courts should ask whether "the possessor of the copy enjoys sufficiently broad rights over it to be sensibly considered its owner."[27] Applying this approach, Judge Leval concluded that the defendant owned copies of the programs within the meaning of section 117(a) because the defendant paid the plaintiff a substantial amount to develop the programs for its sole benefit, the plaintiff customized the software to serve the defendant's operations, the copies were stored on the defendant's server, and the plaintiff had not reserved a right to repossess the copies when the relationship was terminated.[28]

Sections 109 and 117(a) came together in the 2008 case of *Vernor v. Autodesk*.[29] In that case, Timothy Vernor sought to sell copies of Autodesk's copyrighted AutoCAD design software on eBay. Autodesk claimed the sales constituted copyright infringement. Vernor initially bought one used copy of the software at a garage sale and posted it for sale. Autodesk responded by sending a takedown notice under the Digital Millennium Copyright Act (DMCA) to eBay claiming that the sale would infringe its copyright, whereupon eBay suspended the auction. Vernor responded with a DMCA counter-notice stating that his sale was lawful. Autodesk never responded. eBay therefore reinstated the auction and Vernor sold the disputed AutoCAD package. Subsequently, Vernor bought four used AutoCAD packages from an office sale at Cardwell/Thomas Associates, a Seattle architecture firm. Vernor sold three of those packages on eBay. Each sale provoked DMCA notices from Autodesk, suspension of the auction by eBay, a counter-notice from Vernor, and eventually reinstatement of the auction. When Vernor attempted to sell the fourth AutoCAD package and Autodesk filed a DMCA notice, eBay responded by suspending Vernor's eBay account for one month for repeated infringement. Vernor then filed a lawsuit seeking a ruling that his sale of AutoCAD did not constitute copyright infringement.

At the time of his lawsuit, Vernor had two AutoCAD packages that he wished to sell. By tracing the serial numbers on the packages, Autodesk determined that Cardwell/Thomas had acquired both copies from Autodesk as part of the settlement of an unrelated dispute. Under the terms of the settlement, Cardwell/Thomas agreed to adhere to the provisions of the AutoCAD software license agreement. That agreement stated that Autodesk granted the user a "nonexclusive, nontransferable license to use the enclosed program . . . according to the terms and conditions herein."[30] The license restricted the number of computers on which the software could be installed and the number of users by whom it could be used, and it prohibited any copying of the software, as well as the "rent, lease, or transfer [of] all or part of the Software, Documentation, or any rights granted hereunder to any other person without Autodesk's prior written consent."[31] Autodesk contended that the first-sale doctrine did not apply because under the terms of the license, the transfer of AutoCAD packages to Cardwell/Thomas did not constitute a sale. Thus, for purposes of section 109(a), Cardwell/Thomas was not an "owner" of the copies of the software it received. Since Cardwell/Thomas was not an owner, it could not pass title to Vernor, who, therefore, also was not an owner. If Autodesk was right, Vernor's transfer of the software infringed Autodesk's exclusive right under the Copyright Act to distribute the software. If, on the other hand, a sale had occurred, there could be no copyright infringement claim.[32]

Overturning the lower court's decision in favor of Vernor, the U.S. Court of Appeals for the Ninth Circuit held that Autodesk's software was merely licensed. The court held that "a software user is a licensee rather than an owner of a copy where the copyright owner (1) specifies that the user is granted a license; (2) significantly restricts the user's ability to transfer the software; and (3) imposes notable use restrictions."[33] Applying this test, the court ruled that customers who obtain copies of software from Autodesk are licensees of those copies rather than owners. Because Autodesk's customers are not themselves owners, they cannot give ownership of the software to somebody else. Accordingly, since Cardwell/Thomas never owned the software, Vernor was not an owner either, and he could not invoke the first-sale doctrine.[34]

Software manufacturers that *permit* the transfer of software impose terms of use that are designed in such a way that the conditions for using the software always remain with it and apply to *anybody* who comes into possession of the software. For example, the end user license agreement for Adobe Shockwave Player states,

You may not rent, lease, sublicense, assign, or transfer your rights in the Software, or authorize all or any portion of the Software to be copied onto another user's Computer except as may be expressly permitted by this agreement. You may, however, transfer all your rights to Use the Software to another person or legal entity provided that: (a) you also transfer (i) this agreement, and (ii) the Software and all other software or hardware bundled or pre-installed with the Software, including all copies, Updates, and prior versions, to such person or entity, (b) you retain no copies, including backups

and copies stored on a Computer, and (c) the receiving party accepts the terms
and conditions of this agreement and any other terms and conditions upon
which you obtained a valid license to the Software.[35]

Part c of these terms is critical. It sets the arrangement apart from
those we have seen thus far. Adobe binds downstream transferees by
requiring them to assent to a contract to which Adobe is a third-party
beneficiary. If the transferee subsequently violates the terms, Adobe can
claim a breach of the contract; if a court accepts that the software is only
licensed and not sold, Adobe can also assert copyright infringement in
the event of unauthorized distribution.

Turning software buyers from owners into licensees gives software
manufacturers powerful tools for controlling the use of their products.
In 2004, Blizzard Entertainment and Vivendi Games released the
multiplayer online role-playing game World of Warcraft (WoW),
a virtual universe in which player-controlled characters explore the
landscape, interact with each other, fight monsters, complete quests, and
build skills. Along the way, each character gains experience points, which
allow him or her to advance in the game, encountering new challenges
and opportunities. The game proved enormously popular—it was the
best-selling PC game of 2005 and 2006, and by 2008 there were more
than ten million players worldwide. Blizzard owns the copyright in the
WoW software, which consists of the game client software and the game
server software. A user obtains the game client software by purchasing
a copy at a retail store or downloading it from the WoW website. He
or she can then play by loading the game client software on a personal
computer and accessing the game server software through an online
subscription account. Use of WoW is governed by two agreements: an
end user license agreement and a terms-of-use agreement.

In June 2005, MDY Industries began marketing a bot called the WoW
Glider, created by MDY's founder, Michael Donnelly. Glider plays WoW
for its owner while he or she is away from the computer. By continuing to
play during a player's absence, Glider allows the player to advance faster in

the game. In October 2006, representatives of Blizzard and Vivendi went to Donnelly's home and told him that the sale and use of Glider violated Blizzard's rights in WoW, and they threatened legal action. In response, MDY filed a lawsuit in federal court, seeking a ruling that Glider did not infringe any rights owned by Blizzard. Blizzard also sued, asserting a series of claims against MDY, including claims for contributory and vicarious copyright infringement. Under the case law, contributory copyright infringement occurs when someone intentionally induces or encourages direct infringement. A person commits vicarious infringement by profiting from direct infringement while declining to exercise a right to stop or limit it. There was no dispute between the parties that by selling and profiting from Glider, MDY would be liable for contributory and vicarious infringement if, by using Glider, players were indeed infringing Blizzard's copyright. The relevant issue, then, was whether Glider users infringed Blizzard's copyright in the WoW software.

In a welcome decision, the U.S. Court of Appeals for the Ninth Circuit held that use of Glider did not violate Blizzard's copyright.[36] The court explained that because of the extent of control Blizzard retained over the software copies, WoW users were licensees not owners of the game client software under section 117(a) of the Copyright Act.[37] Nonetheless, the court also held that Blizzard could not claim copyright infringement from the use of Glider. The terms-of-use agreement prohibited WoW users from using any bots or "third-party software designed to modify the [WoW] experience."[38] However, the court explained, the use of the Glider bot did not infringe any of Blizzard's exclusive rights under copyright law because "the use does not alter or copy WoW software."[39] Blizzard might have a contractual claim against WoW users for violating the conditions to which they agreed when they obtained and installed the software, but Blizzard could not transform the license provision into a right enforceable through copyright. Instead, "for a licensee's violation of a contract to constitute copyright infringement, there must be a nexus between the [license] condition and the licensor's exclusive rights of copyright."[40] The court explained the far-reaching implications of accepting Blizzard's copyright infringement claim: "Blizzard—or any software copyright holder—could designate any disfavored conduct during software use as copyright infringement, by purporting to condition the license on the player's abstention from the disfavored conduct. . . . This would allow software copyright owners far greater rights than Congress has generally conferred on copyright owners."[41] The court's decision represents a rare rebuke to efforts by software providers to augment through contract their rights over what copyright law provides.

FROM SOFTWARE TO DVDS AND BEYOND

Providers of other kinds of digital content also seek to curtail the first-sale doctrine. Despite industry pressures, Congress has made no exception to the first-sale rule for video cassettes, DVDs, or Blu-ray discs; these products may be rented and leased commercially. Nonetheless, manufacturers attach notices to these products that suggest that their rental is prohibited. For example, this warning appears on DVDs of HBO's television series *The Wire*: "The motion picture contained in this videodisc is protected under the copyright laws of the United States and other countries. This disc is sold for home use only and all other rights are expressly reserved by the copyright owner of such motion pictures." That is not the law. The owner of a DVD may rent it out commercially.

Consider also the exclusive distribution agreement between the Weinstein Company and Blockbuster Video. In a deal reached at the end of 2006, the Weinstein Company agreed to provide its movies for DVD rental exclusively at Blockbuster stores and on Blockbuster's online rental site. Blockbuster, for its part, agreed to promote Weinstein movies to its customers and to pay a minimum guarantee for each title to the Weinstein Company. Through its distributor, Genius Products, the Weinstein Company would continue to sell DVD copies of the movies to retailers. Thus, rental companies other than Blockbuster would still be able to purchase copies. However, DVDs made available to retailers would carry a notice stating that the Weinstein Company authorized only the sale of the DVD; consumers would be encouraged to call an 800 number if the DVD was rented to them in violation of this policy.

Shortly after the Blockbuster deal was announced, the National Entertainment Buying Group, a three-hundred-member-strong organization, along with two independent video stores filed suit in Massachusetts state court against the Weinstein Company and Genius to block the "intended for sale only" labeling. The plaintiffs' legal argument was that by marking DVDs with such a notice and asking consumers to report rentals through an 800 number, the defendants were wrongly suggesting that it was unlawful to rent the DVDs, and this constituted unfair competition in violation of state law.[42] The defendants removed the suit to federal district court, where the plaintiffs conceded that the "intended for sale only" notice did not by itself violate state law and the record showed that the defendants had not yet included in the DVDs an 800 number and might not ever do so. The district judge therefore dismissed the case as unripe for adjudication.[43]

The same issues come into play in the case of journals that are published in electronic rather than print form. The library purchasing a subscription does not own the journal but rather has a right of access so long as the subscription is paid up. Libraries cannot lend these journals, and readers cannot typically make fair use of them. College textbooks are also increasingly available in digital form. The student purchases a subscription, which allows for access to the book during a specified period. Rather than keep a copy of the text after the course ends, the student, a mere licensee, has nothing when the subscription expires.[44]

Developments in the recording industry are especially notable. With encryption and digital rights management leading to consumer backlash,[45] the recording industry has turned to a novel means of distribution—the streaming of music to subscribers, who are bound by licensing agreements. Whereas consumers once purchased physical records and CDs, consumers accessing streamed music receive no physical or digital file. Essentially, streaming is paid radio on demand. The consumer purchases nothing other than the right to stream the music. An obvious benefit to the record labels is that streaming helps prevent copyright infringement because there is nothing for an infringer to copy and transfer to others (there is also no recording from which to sample).

To receive streamed music, the subscriber must agree to terms that specify that no title is acquired and restrict use of the music. According to the terms of use at Rhapsody, a popular service providing streamed audio, "[Rhapsody] and its licensors retain exclusive ownership of the Application, the Content, the Services, and all intellectual property rights associated therewith."[46] Subscribers must agree that Rhapsody is "for . . . personal, non-commercial use only" and that they will not "reproduce, record, retransmit, redistribute, disseminate, sell, rent, lend, broadcast, publicly perform, adapt, sub-license or circulate the Application or any Content received through the Application or any Service (including music content) to any third party."[47] Rhapsody "reserves the right, at any time, to change its subscription fees,"[48] and while it promises to "make reasonable efforts to keep your account and the Service(s) operational," Rhapsody also "reserves the right at any time and from time to time to modify or discontinue, temporarily or permanently, functions and features of the Application and Service(s) with or without notice" and "to change or remove the Content at any time."[49] Indeed, under the agreement, Rhapsody can simply stop providing music altogether: "[Rhapsody] may also in its sole discretion and at any time . . . discontinue providing the Application and/or any Service. . . . [Y]ou agree that . . . [Rhapsody] shall not be liable to you or any third-party for any interference with or termination of your access to the Application and/or any Service."[50]

The shift from ownership to access in the digital realm has also spilled over to traditional media. Even some *physical* copies of works are deemed no longer owned. With the rise of Internet sites reselling all manner of goods, anybody can now buy a used copy of a book (or CD)—for which the publisher receives no revenue—rather than purchase the item new. The first-sale doctrine combines with a well-functioning secondary market to cut into publisher profits. In response, publishers have sought ways around the first-sale doctrine so that they can continue to make new sales. For example, exam preparatory courses provide printed study materials under contractual terms that prohibit resale, deny fair use, and otherwise impose restrictions beyond those available as a matter of copyright law. Kaplan PMBR, a bar review course for law school graduates, requires enrollees to agree to these terms: "All course materials that you receive during your enrollment are protected by Federal Copyright law and are meant for your personal use only. By signing this agreement, you agree not to reproduce, redistribute, share, sell, auction, or give away any such materials either during or after your enrollment. Violation of this agreement is harmful to Kaplan PMBR and may subject you to civil penalties and/or criminal prosecution."[51]

PROTECTING DIGITAL TRANSFER RIGHTS

Congress should update section 109 of the Copyright Act to protect first-sale rights in digital works. A sensible approach would be to eliminate the ownership requirement of section 109 and protect, as a statutory matter, the right of anybody who lawfully obtains a copy of or access to a digital work to transfer that copy or the access to somebody else. To balance the interests of consumers with those of content providers, the transfer right should be limited to the first end user of the content. Thus content could be transferred a single time as of right, but it could not subsequently be transferred by the new recipient without the permission of the original content provider.

This right of transfer would be protected only if the person making the transfer gives up his or her entire interest in the digital content. Therefore, the transferor would not be permitted to retain a copy of the digital work or retain any right of access to it. The recipient would receive the copy or the right of access on the same terms as the person who made the transfer. The transfer would therefore not result in the transferee gaining any additional rights or protections beyond what the transferor held. If the original purchaser has already exhausted his or her interest in the work, there would be nothing left to transfer.

By protecting a right of transfer as a statutory matter, the Copyright Act would override any provision in a licensing agreement eliminating or restricting the transfer right (including a restriction on using the content on a single device). Thus, for example, an individual who purchases a copy of computer software on a CD-ROM and installs it on a computer would be entitled, regardless of any restriction in the terms of use accompanying the software, to sell or give that software CD-ROM to anyone else. The transfer would be lawful under the Copyright Act so long as the original purchaser of the CD-ROM deleted the installed software from his or her computer and did not otherwise retain a copy of it. The transferee could not later sell the CD-ROM to anyone else.

For a digital file that is downloaded from the provider's website and so not stored on a CD-ROM or other device (besides the computer or device to which the file is initially downloaded), the right of transfer would include a right to copy the file so that it may be sold or given away. The right to make a copy under these circumstances would override the DMCA's prohibition on circumventing technological protection measures that limit access to or copying of the digital file. Again, the person making the transfer would be required to give up all his or her interests in the file, which would mean deleting the file from his or her own computer once the copy for transfer has been made, and the transferee would receive only the interests that the transferor possessed. If, for instance, I pay for and download to my computer tax preparation software, I would be entitled to copy the software to a CD-

ROM and sell it to somebody else provided I deleted the software from my own computer. If the software allows me to prepare and file two federal and two state tax returns and I use it to file a federal return and a state return, all I would be able to transfer is the right to file one more of each. Transfer of a right of access would operate in a similar way. A database subscriber could then transfer the subscription so long as the subscriber gave up his or her right to access the database; the recipient would have access to the database until the subscription the original subscriber purchased ran out.

As a practical matter, technological innovations might well be needed to ensure that transfers can be made. Congress should therefore exempt such technology from the DMCA's prohibitions on manufacturing and distributing devices that circumvent access controls. With respect to content that is tethered to the content provider's own device, for which there might not already be an easy way to execute a transfer, Congress could simply require the content provider to provide, along with the device and content, practical means of transferring the content. For example, Amazon would be required to incorporate within the Kindle's design the means to transfer e-books from one Kindle to another—or else provide another means for potential transferees to obtain e-book files, for example, by downloading the files from Amazon's website. It is likely that if Congress protects a digital transfer right, content providers will quickly develop technological measures to prevent transferors from retaining rights following a transfer. (For example, we should expect to see technology that automatically deletes or prevents access to a digital file once it has been copied to a CD-ROM.)

If Congress protects a digital transfer right, some content providers will respond by imposing, through contracts and technology, new limitations on how their content can be used. In particular, by restricting the rights of the initial purchaser to a single or other very limited use of the content, content providers could render the transfer right of little practical value. The provider of an e-book might prevent a user from turning each page more than one time, thereby limiting use of the e-book to a single reading; providers of digital music might allow each song to be played just one time; a database subscription might expire after one hour. However, market forces will deter many such restrictions. Consumers will not readily accept e-books that can only be read once or music that can be heard just one time; they will not pay for content with severe use restrictions unless the price reflects the content's limited utility. The most likely scenario is that in response to the digital transfer right, content providers will make available at different prices content in single-use and multiple-use versions, the latter of which will have transfer value after the initial use. A statutory transfer right would thus restore to digital content a right that consumers have always held in copyrighted works while adequately safeguarding the interests of content providers, in addition to offering consumers more options.

OWNERSHIP AND THE COPYRIGHT BALANCE

For as long as there have been books, book owners have had the right to sell, lend, or give their books to others. From piano rolls to LPs to CDs, music collections have always been owned, and collectors have been entitled to bequeath their collections to heirs, donate them to museums, or sell them at garage sales. Today, content providers assert that they retain title to the products consumer pay for. In their view, consumers do not own the books they read, the music they listen to, or the software running on their laptops. The information society is fast becoming a society of renters and, as with renting a home, once the payments stop or the landlord decides to end the arrangement, the renter is left with nothing.

Turning owners into renters is the last in a series of steps taken by content providers who do not favor the balance that copyright law sets between the rights of copyright owners and the interests of the public. As we have seen in the preceding chapters, to undermine this balance, content providers have claimed copyrights in public domain works. They have sought enhanced control over copyrighted works by interfering with fair use. Content providers have misused DMCA takedown notices to remove non-infringing works from web sites, and they have installed digital locks that prevent permissible uses of digital content. Using contract law, content providers have imposed their own rules on how content may be accessed and utilized, tilting the copyright balance further and further in their favor with each of these mechanisms.

The forced transformation of owners into renters negates the transfer rights that the Copyright Act gives owners of lawfully obtained copies of a copyrighted work, and it further undermines the copyright balance. By selling only a subscription to view or listen to digital content, providers gain increased control over the ways in which the content is available to be accessed and used. When content is merely streamed via the Internet or is visible only on the provider's own device, authorized uses can be determined by the provider at the outset; if there are any violations of the terms, the content can be made immediately to disappear.

Eliminating ownership buttresses the forms of overreaching considered in the previous chapters and has its own impact on the copyright balance. At the end of the day, in order to be effective, copyfraud requires persuading somebody that ignoring a copyright notice will result in a lawsuit. Interfering with fair use depends upon the presence of risk-averse users or gatekeepers with a fear of being sued. Taking down content from websites requires sending a DMCA notice and a cooperative online service provider. Locking up digital content means identifying people who circumvent the lock and making a credible threat of litigation. Enforcing contractual terms requires, ultimately, willingness to bring a lawsuit for breach of contract and a favorable court ruling. Content providers have been very successful in using each of these mechanisms to control public domain and copyrighted works, but each mechanism requires monitoring, policing, and, in the final calculation, willingness to carry through on a threat. Eliminating ownership is easier and it has a bigger payoff. It gives control to providers of digital content without obliging them to do the same work or meet the same conditions that other forms of overreaching entail. For these reasons, restoring transfer rights in digital content is of special urgency.

With the account of overreaching in copyright law now complete, the next chapter turns to trademarks.

CHAPTER 7

TRADEMARKS UNBOUND

I N 2006, the Hell's Angels Motorcycle Corporation sued Disney, Buena Vista Motion Pictures, and a movie production company in connection with *Wild Hogs*, a then-upcoming movie about a group of middle-aged suburban men turned bikers—played by Tim Allen, William H. Macy, Martin Lawrence, and John Travolta—who encounter on the road and are involved in various confrontations with a chapter of the Hell's Angels. The lawsuit contended that by showing bikers identifying themselves as Hell's Angels and wearing jackets with the Hell's Angels insignia, and having the characters refer to the Hell's Angels by name, the movie violated the corporation's rights in its registered Hell's Angels trademark. The Hell's Angels Corporation asserted that the use of the mark implied that it had sponsored *Wild Hogs*. In addition, the corporation claimed that the movie tarnished the Hell's Angels trademark.[1] We are a long way from the bounds of trademark law when there may be no movies with Hell's Angels bikers unless the Hell's Angels Motorcycle Corporation approves. Nonetheless, Disney and its partners caved. When *Wild Hogs* was released in 2007, all references to the group had been removed. Instead of happening upon members of the Hell's Angels, the movie's protagonists encounter a biker gang called Del Fuego. Filing a lawsuit was enough for the Hell's Angels Motorcycle Corporation to prevail.

Overreaching by trademark owners is common. They prevent lawful uses by others of their trademarks, and they interfere with uses of other marks that are not infringing. At times, trademark owners falsely claim rights they do not possess. In other cases, trademark owners overreach by threatening to sue when, in all probability, no violation of their rights has occurred. Trademark overreaching produces economic costs that hurt businesses and consumers. More significantly, trademark overreaching curtails many kinds of expression that the law permits and encourages.

SOME TRADEMARK LAW BASICS

A trademark is a distinctive name, symbol, slogan, or design that a business uses to identify its products or services to consumers and to distinguish its products or services from those of other businesses. For example, the word *Nike* and the Nike "swoosh" (both trademarked) identify shoes made by Nike, Inc., and distinguish them from shoes made by other companies. The law gives the owner of a trademark the right to prevent others from using the mark or any similar mark if the use is likely to confuse consumers about the origin of a product or service or otherwise undermines the commercial value of the trademark.

Whereas copyrights and patents protect original creations, trademarks serve a quite different purpose. A trademark designates *source*. It allows consumers to identify where a good comes from, thereby facilitating purchasing decisions: a consumer who believes that Nike makes high-quality shoes can easily identify Nike shoes when he or she wishes to purchase them. Trademark law ensures that consumers don't have to worry that a pair of shoes with a Nike label and swoosh was made by somebody else. Creativity is not required in order for a mark to receive protection. As the Supreme Court has stated, trademark protection does not "depend upon novelty, invention, discovery, or any work of the brain. It requires no fancy or imagination, no genius, no laborious thought. It is simply founded on priority of appropriation."[2]

Congress protects trademarks through its constitutional power to regulate interstate commerce, not, as with respect to copyrights and patents, its power "[t]o promote the progress of science and useful arts."[3] This has some important implications. Trademarks are intended to lubricate commercial transactions rather than promote scientific or artistic progress. In addition, while Congress may authorize copyrights and patents only for "limited times,"[4] no such limitation applies to trademarks. Assuming the trademark owner continues to use the mark, it can last forever. Also in contrast to copyright and patent, trademark law is not exclusively the province of Congress. Trademarks are governed simultaneously by state and federal law. State common law provided the earliest protections for trademarks. In 1946, Congress enacted the Lanham Act, the principal federal trademark law in force today. That act codified the protections the common law gave to trademark owners and provided for protection of trademarks around the country. Even so, state law continues to provide supplemental trademark protections.

The Lanham Act of 1946 defines a trademark as "any word, name, symbol, or device, or any combination thereof" that a person uses "to identify and distinguish his or her goods . . . from those manufactured or sold by others and to indicate the source of the goods."[5] On the basis of this definition, the United States Patent and Trademark Office (USPTO) and the courts have recognized all of the following as potentially protectable as trademarks under the Lanham Act: words, phrases, symbols, numbers, pictures, characters, graphic designs, colors, and even sounds and smells. The Lanham Act's protections extend also to eligible product and packaging designs, usually referred to as "trade dress."[6] For example, Apple holds a trademark in "the design of a portable and handheld digital electronic media device comprised of a rectangular casing displaying circular and rectangular shapes therein arranged in an aesthetically pleasing manner"—in other words, in the design of the iPod.[7] The design of a building, exterior or interior, that serves to identify the goods of a particular merchant can likewise qualify for protection from confusingly similar usages as a trademark.[8] For example, there are federally registered trademarks for the facade of the New York Stock Exchange building and the spire of the Chrysler Building.

Not all marks can be protected as trademarks. A basic requirement for trademark protection is that the mark be distinctive. For example, calling a brand of breakfast food "Cereal" is not distinctive, and such a mark could not be protected as a trademark. To determine whether a mark is distinctive, courts evaluate the mark by reference to five categories that may describe it in terms of its relationship to the underlying product: (1) fanciful, (2) arbitrary, (3) suggestive, (4) descriptive, and (5) generic.[9] A fanciful mark is a made-up word or symbol created for the purpose of a trademark. *Xerox* and *Kodak* are examples of fanciful marks. These words have no preexisting meaning in any language. A mark is arbitrary if it has a meaning but the meaning bears no logical relationship to the underlying product. *Ivory*, for soap, is an arbitrary mark, as is *Apple* for computers. There is nothing apple-related in an Apple computer. Fanciful and arbitrary marks are inherently distinctive and therefore receive strong protection as trademarks.

A suggestive mark is a mark that evokes or suggests the good or service but does not describe it. The consumer who sees the mark does not instantly think of the good or service; some imagination is needed to draw the connection. For example, *Coppertone* is a suggestive mark (while "suntan lotion" is not). Suggestive marks are inherently distinctive and are also given a high degree of protection.

A descriptive mark is a mark that simply describes the qualities of the underlying product. For example, "100% cotton" and "No animal by-products" are descriptive marks. Descriptive marks are not inherently distinctive, and ordinarily they are not protectable. This makes sense when one recalls that the purpose of a trademark is to identify the unique source of a product. Competing manufacturers often use similar descriptive terms to describe the qualities of their products, and so a description does not readily identify a unique source. A descriptive mark can be protected as a trademark, however, if it has acquired "secondary meaning."[10] This occurs when consumers have come to identify the descriptive term with a *particular* good or service so that the term signifies two things: first, it describes the features of a product, and second, it identifies a particular source. For example, "holiday inn" is a mark that is descriptive (a place to stay on vacation), but it has acquired secondary meaning because consumers understand that it designates a particular hotel chain, Holiday Inn. The mark therefore serves to identify a specific company's product, not merely a product in general. In considering whether a descriptive mark has acquired secondary meaning and can be protected as a trademark, courts look to such things as consumer surveys, the duration of the use of the mark, success in the markets, and amounts spent on advertising.

Finally, a generic mark is the noun that is used in ordinary language to name a good or service, for example, "computer" or "sweater" or "fence." Generic terms are not eligible for trademark protection even if they acquire secondary meaning, as granting rights in generic marks would remove common terms from ordinary language. (As we shall see, however, this does not stop overreaching trademark owners from attempting to do so.)

If a mark qualifies for protection, the user of the mark obtains trademark rights by being the first to use the mark in commerce or by being the first to register the mark with the USPTO with the intention to use the mark in commerce.[11] Registration with the USPTO is not required for a trademark to be protected, but it offers a number of benefits. Registration constitutes constructive notice of ownership, confers the right to use the mark nationwide, and facilitates bringing trademark infringement suits in federal court for monetary damages.[12]

The symbol ® indicates that the mark is registered with the USPTO, while the ™ symbol is used to designate rights that are claimed in a trademark that is not registered with the USPTO.[13]

INFRINGEMENT, FAIR USE, AND THE FIRST AMENDMENT

Infringement of a trademark occurs when someone other than the trademark owner uses a mark in a way that is likely to confuse consumers about the origin (or sponsorship or approval) of his or her goods or services.[14] An owner of a trademark who establishes infringement can obtain an injunction to halt the unauthorized use of the mark as well as monetary relief in the form of the damages sustained and the defendant's profits, and in some instances costs and attorneys' fees; if the defendant acted in bad faith, the plaintiff can obtain treble damages.

Likelihood of confusion is the central element of a trademark infringement claim. To prevail, the trademark owner must demonstrate the likelihood that consumers will be confused or deceived about the origin or source of a product (or about sponsorship or approval of the product). For example, if Continental Grain wants to stop an airline from calling itself Continental, it would need to show that consumers are likely to be confused into thinking that the grain company had branched out into the airline business.

In evaluating a likelihood-of-confusion claim, courts consider a variety of factors, including the distinctiveness of the plaintiff's mark, the degree of similarity between the marks, the proximity of the parties' products or services in the marketplace, the likelihood that the plaintiff will enter the defendant's market, evidence of actual confusion, whether the defendant acted in good faith, and the sophistication of the buyers. To take a simple example, if Nike's competitor attaches the Nike swoosh to its shoes, it has probably infringed Nike's trademark: the mark is arbitrary (Nike is the Greek goddess of victory) and therefore highly distinctive, and consumers are likely to believe Nike is the manufacturer of the competitor's products, which are in the very same market in which Nike sells. Not every use of the same or a similar mark is infringement, however. If goods designated by the mark are sufficiently different from the trademark owner's own goods that there is no likelihood of consumer confusion, there is no infringement of the trademark. If I market Snapple Dog Shampoo, consumers will probably not imagine that the tea company has begun selling canine grooming products, and I have probably not infringed the trademark in Snapple Tea. (There are, however, courses other than infringement that the owner of the trademark might take to prevent others from using the same or a similar mark, as this chapter will show.)

In the same way that copyright law deems fair uses of copyrighted works non-infringing, trademark law also acknowledges the fair use of trademarks. There are two types of trademark fair use. The first, descriptive fair use (sometimes called classic fair use), exists when a descriptive term is used not in a trademark sense, that is, not to designate source, but to describe the goods or services of the user.[15] An example helps demonstrate this point. As we have seen, a mark that is merely descriptive of a product does not ordinarily qualify for trademark protection because it is not distinctive. Thus, if I decide to manufacture umbrellas strong enough to withstand high winds, I cannot ordinarily claim a trademark in the phrase "Strong Umbrella" because those words simply describe my product. For a descriptive mark to be protected as a trademark, it must acquire secondary meaning. That is, consumers must primarily associate the mark with a particular producer, rather than with the underlying product it describes. "Strong Umbrella" acquires secondary meaning when consumers hearing the phrase think of *my* product, not a generic umbrella that happens to be strong.

Under the doctrine of descriptive fair use, when a descriptive mark acquires secondary status and so can be protected as a trademark, the trademark owner cannot prevent others from using the mark in its original descriptive sense. The trademark owner's rights are limited to

the secondary meaning, that is to say, to the significance of the mark
in identifying the trademark owner's goods or services. Thus, even
when my Strong Umbrella mark acquires secondary meaning, I cannot
prevent another umbrella vendor from saying, "Our umbrellas are strong
enough for Chicago winds" in describing its own products. In one case,
for example, a court accepted this defense when the manufacturer of
SweeTARTS candy sued Ocean Spray for running ads describing its
cranberry juice as sweet-tart. Holding that Ocean Spray's use of "sweet-
tart" was protected as descriptive fair use, the Seventh Circuit explained,
"That SweeTARTS is an incontestable mark for sugar candy does not
make [the plaintiff] the gatekeeper of these words for the whole food
industry."[16]

The second type of trademark fair use is nominative fair use.[17]
Unlike descriptive fair use, nominative fair use involves using another's
trademark to identify the *trademark owner's* goods or services. Such use
is not an infringement provided there is no likelihood of confusion.[18]
Nominative fair use has its origins in a 1992 decision of the Court of
Appeals for the Ninth Circuit in *New Kids on the Block v. News America
Publishing*.[19] In that case, *USA Today* ran a survey asking its readers to
vote for their favorite member of the pop group New Kids on the Block.
To vote, readers called a 900 number and paid a fee. New Kids sued *USA
Today* for making commercial use of their trademarked name. The Court
of Appeals for the Ninth Circuit held that the use of the New Kids mark
in the survey was a non-infringing fair use. The court explained that
"*nominative* use of a mark—where the only word reasonably available
to describe a particular thing is pressed into service—lies outside the
strictures of trademark law . . . because it does not imply sponsorship
or endorsement by the trademark holder."[20] The fact that New Kids
on the Block has a trademark does not prevent the world at large from
referring to their existence. The doctrine has intuitive appeal, in that
nominative use facilitates ordinary communication. Without it, instead
of mentioning New Kids on the Block by name, *USA Today* would have

had to ask its readers to "vote for your favorite member of the all-male pop group from Boston that consists of five members, two of whom are brothers." Nominative fair use is also important for comparative advertising. The doctrine permits a vendor to make use of its competitor's trademark in order to say something about the competitor's products. For example, nominative fair use allows Progresso to advertise that its soups taste better than Campbell soups, and Mac Guy to tell PC Guy why Apple's operating system is superior to Windows.

Trademarks are often an important component of expression. Many trademarks enter popular speech. For example, the common phrase "Where's the beef?" began as an advertising slogan for Wendy's restaurants. "Xeroxing" has become a synonym for "photocopying." The trademark "TASER," which is an acronym for "Thomas A. Swift Electric Rifle," has become a verb. Artists routinely incorporate trademarks into their works. Andy Warhol's uses of Campbell soup cans and Coca-Cola bottles are prominent examples. Book titles such as Tom Wolfe's *The Electric Kool-Aid Acid Test* (1966) and Robyn Okrant's *Living Oprah: My One-Year Experiment to Walk the Walk of the Queen of Talk* (2010) include trademarks ("Kool-Aid" and "Oprah," respectively). Commentators often invoke trademarks to make a point, and cartoonists use them to lampoon corporations. Movies frequently depict trademarks on screen.

Recognizing the significance of trademarks to expression, courts have held that there is also a First Amendment defense to trademark infringement.[21] For this we can partially credit Ginger Rogers. She brought a case against the producers and distributors of *Ginger and Fred* (1986), a film directed by Federico Fellini that tells the story of two fictional Italian cabaret performers who imitate Ginger Rogers and Fred Astaire. Ginger Rogers claimed that the film title violated her trademark in the name "Ginger." In deciding the case, the Court of Appeals for the Second Circuit adopted a balancing approach that many other courts have since followed. The test weighs the free speech values at issue against the value in avoiding consumer confusion by protecting the trademark. Under the test, a mark used in an expressive work is prohibited infringement only if it has "no artistic relevance to the underlying work" or, if there is artistic relevance, if the title of the work "explicitly misleads as to the source or the content of the work."[22] Applying that standard, the Second Circuit held that the use of Ginger Rogers's name in the film title was permissible.

Under the *Rogers* test, once First Amendment interests are found, "the finding of likelihood of confusion must be particularly compelling" to overcome them and support a finding of infringement.[23] The *Rogers* test applies to "expressive" works such as books, commentary, and movies; it does not apply to advertising and other forms of purely commercial speech, which receive less protection under the First Amendment. This does not, however, mean that expression must *entirely* lack commercial value in order to qualify for a First Amendment defense in a trademark infringement action. Rather, courts have found no infringement where commercial products *also* entail a degree of protectable expression. For example, parodies of trademarks, even in the case of retail products, are often entitled to protection.[24] In one case, the Court of Appeals for the Fourth Circuit held that the manufacturer of Chewy Vuiton dog toys did not infringe the Louis Vuitton trademark because the plush toys, designed to resemble the expensive Louis Vuitton handbags, were a parody and therefore there was no likelihood of confusion as to the source of the toys.[25] In another case, a court held that a porcine character called Spa'am in a Muppets movie did not infringe the Hormel Foods Corporation's Spam trademark.[26]

Even so, not all parodies preclude a finding of infringement. If a trademark owner produces evidence (for instance, in the form of survey results) demonstrating that a parodic use of its trademark results in consumer confusion, the owner may well prevail in an infringement action. For example, one court held that a poster with "Enjoy Cocaine" written in white flowing script on a red background violated Coca-Cola's trademark in "Enjoy Coca-Cola."[27] Although this was obviously parody, Coca-Cola produced evidence that "some persons of apparently average intelligence did attribute *sponsorship* to plaintiff and discontinued their use of Coca-Cola as an expression of resentment."[28] Accepting Coca-Cola's evidence, the court barred distribution of the poster.

DILUTION: BLURRING AND TARNISHMENT

Trademark law also protects against dilution of a famous trademark. Dilution is what it sounds like: a lessening of the capacity of a mark to identify and distinguish goods and services.[29] Dilution occurs when the use of a mark resembling a famous trademark results in blurring or tarnishment of the latter.[30] According to the Lanham Act, blurring takes place when an "association aris[es] from the similarity between a mark . . . and a famous mark that impairs the distinctiveness of the famous mark."[31] Marks that courts have found to blur include "Tiffany's Restaurant and Lounge" (blurring of the Tiffany & Co. mark) and "HERBOZAC," an herbal antidepressant (blurring of the PROZAC mark).[32] Tarnishment results from an "association arising from the similarity between a mark . . . and a famous mark that harms the reputation of the famous mark."[33] For example, courts have found tarnishment from the use of "Papal Visit" and "Pastoral Visit" on an adult website (tarnishment of the St. Louis Archdiocese) and from the use of Candyland.com, also an adult website (tarnishment of the children's board game).[34]

The availability of dilution as a cause of action protects interests different from those safeguarded by prohibitions against infringement. Traditional trademark infringement law protects consumers from confusion, but the law of dilution protects the integrity of the mark itself. Thus while trademark infringement, which is concerned with consumer confusion, depends upon competition between the parties' goods, dilution has no such requirement. Nike could therefore use the law of dilution to prevent a wide range of uses of its trademarked swoosh that might not rise to the level of trademark infringement; for example, it might claim dilution by blurring if somebody attached the Nike swoosh to roof shingles—even though Nike would have a hard time proving in an infringement action that consumers are likely to be confused into believing that Nike manufactured the shingles. Likewise, Nike could claim dilution by tarnishment if somebody used the Nike swoosh as an icon on a pornographic or racial supremacist website; even though it is unlikely visitors to those sites would believe Nike sponsored them, the use of the Nike swoosh in this manner would whittle away its value.

Only "famous marks" qualify for protection from dilution. The Lanham Act defines a famous mark as one that is "widely recognized by the general consuming public of the United States as a designation of source of the goods or services of the mark's owner," and it provides a list of factors (such as the extent of advertising and the amount of sales) for courts to consider in determining whether a mark qualifies.[35] Meeting the standard is difficult; to do so, a trademark must normally be a household name, like Big Gulp or Pepsi.[36] Because most trademarks do not qualify as famous, dilution was designed to be an exceptional cause of action.

The Lanham Act contains specific exemptions for uses that, though potentially dilutive, are permitted. The statute permits "[a]ny fair use, including a nominative or descriptive fair use . . . of a famous mark by another person other than as a designation of source for the person's own goods or services."[37] Such uses may include those for purposes of comparative advertising or "identifying and parodying, criticizing, or commenting upon the famous mark owner or the goods or services of the famous mark owner."[38] The statute therefore specifically recognizes in dilution actions the two types of fair use—descriptive and nominative— we have seen in the infringement context, along with a quite broad expressive use defense. Further, the statute exempts from dilution claims news reporting and commentary and noncommercial uses of a famous mark.[39]

In one case, for example, Ralph Nader's 2000 presidential campaign ran a television ad that borrowed from MasterCard's well-known "priceless" ad campaign. The MasterCard ads show a series of goods that can be purchased with a credit or debit card and their prices, and then some intangible good followed by the words "Priceless. There are some things money can't buy. For everything else there's MasterCard." Nader's ads showed a series of items, with the price of each, including "promises to special interest groups: over $100 billion," followed by the phrase "Finding out the truth: priceless. There are some things that money can't buy." MasterCard claimed trademark dilution and infringement. The court dismissed the dilution claim because Nader's use was not commercial and was therefore exempt under the statute. Recognizing the expressive interests at stake in a political campaign, the court also dismissed the infringement claim on the ground that there was no likelihood that the public would be confused into thinking that MasterCard had sponsored Nader's campaign.[40]

OVERREACHING TRADEMARKS

Trademark owners overreach. They seek to expand the scope of their trademark rights by preventing others from using on their own products marks that are not infringing. This undermines the purpose of trademark law—to facilitate commerce—and it imposes economic costs. Trademark law protects fair uses of trademarks, but, like overzealous copyright owners, trademark owners take the position that no use without their authorization is permitted. Interference with trademark fair use chills expression.

Trademark owners often assert baseless infringement and dilution claims to silence their critics and prevent commentary they find objectionable. In 2003, Fox News sought to block publication of Al Franken's book *Lies (and the Lying Liars Who Tell Them): A Fair and Balanced Look at the Right* (2003), on the ground that the title infringed and diluted a trademark Fox had registered in the phrase "fair and balanced."[41] Fox plainly brought its lawsuit to interfere with Franken's speech rather than to defend any legitimate trademark interest. In its complaint, Fox described Franken as "shrill and unstable" and stated that Franken's "views lack any serious depth or insight."[42] Denying Fox's motion for a preliminary injunction that would prevent distribution of Franken's book, U.S. District Judge Denny Chin stated, "There are hard cases and there are easy cases. This is an easy case . . . because it is wholly without merit, both factually and legally." On the merits, Judge Chin said, "Parody is a form of artistic expression protected by the First Amendment. The keystone to parody is imitation. In using the mark, Mr. Franken is clearly mocking Fox." Further, the judge, who suggested that Fox's trademark in "fair and balanced" is probably invalid because it is "plucked out of the marketplace of ideas and slogans," chided the news service for bringing the lawsuit in the first place. "[I]t is ironic," he noted, "that a media company that should be fighting for the First Amendment is trying to undermine it by claiming a monopoly on the phrase 'fair and balanced.' "[43]

Trademark infringement claims require that the defendant make *commercial* use of the plaintiff's mark.[44] However, trademark owners regularly disregard this element of the law and threaten or bring lawsuits even when there is no plausible claim that the defendant is using a mark commercially. In one case, Bosley Medical Institute brought a trademark infringement claim (along with other claims) against a former patient, Michael Kremer, who, dissatisfied with the hair restoration services he had received from Bosley, created a website, BosleyMedical.com, where he criticized the institute. Affirming the district court's decision in favor of Kremer on the trademark infringement claim, the Court of Appeals for the Ninth Circuit explained that "trademark infringement law prevents only unauthorized uses of a trademark in connection with a *commercial transaction* in which the trademark is being used to confuse potential consumers." The Lanham Act was simply not available to Bosley "as a shield from Kremer's criticism, or as a sword to shut Kremer up."[45]

Mattel Corporation, the producer of Barbie, is also guilty of invoking trademark law to interfere with protected expression. Mattel wrongly pursues noncommercial uses of *Barbie* that it considers "libelous or objectionable."[46] Mattel also takes the false position that *any* commercial use of the term *Barbie* violates its Barbie trademark. Among many other overreaching claims it has made, Mattel has sued the creator of a satirical "Exorcist Barbie," a collector who referred in his catalog to the Elizabethan Queen Barbie as "ugly," and a doll magazine that portrayed Barbie with cigarettes and champagne.[47] Although there was little legal basis to Mattel's claims, these defendants all settled with an agreement to refrain from referring to Barbie in ways Mattel found objectionable.

When Mattel has been forced to defend in court its claims of trademark violations, it has lost. Asserting trademark infringement and dilution, Mattel sought an injunction against the distributors of Aqua's 1997 song "Barbie Girl." Mattel objected to the song's lyrics, which include "Life in plastic, it's fantastic. You can brush my hair, undress me everywhere," and "I'm a blond bimbo girl, in a fantasy world / Dress me up, make it tight, I'm your dolly." Affirming the district court's decision, the U.S. Court of Appeals for the Ninth Circuit rejected Mattel's claims in their entirety. The court correctly explained that there was no trademark infringement because while the song title used Mattel's mark, it did so to indicate what the song was about, not the source of the song. In other words, members of the public would not think that the use of the Barbie mark in the title meant that Mattel had produced or approved of the song. With respect to Mattel's dilution claim, the defendant agreed that the use of the mark was potentially dilutive, in that consumers would think of both the doll and the song and therefore the distinctiveness of the Mattel mark was blurred. However, as the court rightly held, even though the song was offered for sale, because it lampooned Barbie's image, it was not purely commercial and, as parody, therefore fell within the noncommercial use exemption of trademark dilution law.[48] Mattel likewise lost its trademark infringement and dilution action to enjoin a

series of photographs titled "Food Chain Barbie," which showed a naked
Barbie under attack by household appliances. The court in that case held
that the parodic use of Barbie in the photographs was protected by the
First Amendment and fell within the statutory dilution exemptions.[49]
These losses have not, however, stopped Mattel from pursuing others
who scoff at Barbie.

Barney the purple dinosaur has also been deemed off limits by his
corporate creators. In 1998, Stuart Frankel created a personal website on
which he portrayed Barney as leading a double life: a friendly television
character who turns evil when the cameras are not rolling. Frankel's
webpage had two images of Barney: one in his familiar form, and a
second captioned, "What Barney Looks Like After the Show!!" with
scribbled-on horns, sharp teeth, and a pentagram and the number 666
on his chest. Beginning in early 2002, the Lyons Partnership, which
owns the Barney brand, sent Frankel a series of letters alleging that the
website violated Lyons's trademarks and copyrights and threatening legal
action if Frankel did not remove the material from his site. Lyons has a
long history of successfully threatening litigation to shut down websites
that parody or criticize Barney. Represented by the Electronic Frontier
Foundation, Frankel sued Lyons for a declaratory judgment that the site
constituted fair use and did not infringe any copyright or trademark.[50]
The case settled, with Lyons agreeing not to threaten or pursue any
further legal action against Frankel and paying him $5,000.[51]

MOVIES AND PRODUCT DISPLACEMENT

Movies often feature trademarked products because such products
are a part of everyday life. Although trademark law provides little basis on
which to object to a product's appearance on screen, trademark owners
regularly invoke trademark law and interfere with "unauthorized"
product placement. In a well-known case, a district court rejected
Caterpillar's trademark infringement and dilution-by-tarnishment
claims against Disney, the producer of the movie *George of the Jungle 2*,

in which Caterpillar bulldozers appear. On the infringement claim the court found that there was no likelihood that moviegoers would think Caterpillar had sponsored the movie, and that trademark law did not prevent the mere unauthorized appearance in a movie of trademarks or products.[52] Nor did Caterpillar have a viable dilution claim, because the presence of the bulldozers in the movie did not, as Caterpillar claimed, tarnish the Caterpillar brand. The court wrote that it was "incredible . . . to imagine a consumer's decision to purchase Caterpillar's primary product line of heavy machinery and equipment, costing substantial sums of money, being affected after watching this film."[53]

This decision, clearly correct, has not stopped trademark owners from claiming violations of their rights when their products appear in movies. In 2006, the manufacturer of a garbage disposal device sued NBC for trademark infringement and dilution when the pilot of NBC's television show *Heroes* showed a high school cheerleader's hand mangled by the device, the brand name of which was visible to viewers. In its complaint, the manufacturer alleged that the episode "implies an incorrect and dangerous design for a food waste disposer" and depicted the garbage disposal unit "in an unsavory light, irreparably tarnishing the product."[54] While NBC thought the lawsuit lacked merit, this did not stop it from editing the episode for rebroadcasting. The case thereafter settled. NBC similarly declined to exercise its right to make fair use of product names when it sought Yankees owner George Steinbrenner's permission to post a Yankees pennant on the wall of Jerry's apartment in the television series *Seinfeld*.[55] There is no plausible argument that the appearance of an item of Yankees memorabilia in a television character's home constitutes trademark infringement.

If NBC does not defend itself from overreaching claims, it should come as no surprise that independent filmmakers are unable to do so. We saw in Chapters 1 and 2 the problems that documentary filmmakers confront in using public domain footage in their works and in invoking fair use as a basis for using copyrighted materials, as well as the aggressive role that gatekeepers play in preventing them from doing so. A similar phenomenon exists with films in which trademarks appear. Insurers and distributors require filmmakers to clear any depiction of a trademark.[56] As a result, many documentary films and reality shows blur out products so that their trademarks are not recognizable to viewers.[57]

Photographing a trademarked building or capturing the building in a movie scene does not ordinarily infringe the trademark. This is because there is no likelihood that the public seeing the photograph or viewing the movie will be confused into thinking that the owner of the trademark in the building somehow sponsored the photograph or movie.[58] Nonetheless, owners of trademarks in buildings interfere with photographs and movies that depict the buildings. Lawyers have told photographers that photos taken in Times Square violate the trademark in the design of a background building and therefore cannot be sold or posted on the Internet. Managers at Starbucks stores have informed customers they may not take photographs inside the store because the interior is trademarked. In 2002, Sony released *Spider-Man*, a scene of which shows buildings in Times Square bearing advertising signs. Sony digitally substituted new ads for those that appeared on the buildings at the time the scene was shot; among other changes it made, Sony replaced a Samsung ad with an ad for *USA Today*. The owners of three of the buildings whose signs had been altered sued Sony under the Lanham Act for trademark infringement (and on other grounds). The building owners claimed, implausibly, that Sony had caused confusion in the minds of moviegoers as to their buildings' association with the substituted advertisements.[59]

We saw in Chapter 1 that copyright claims over public domain materials are a common occurrence, in part because copyright law provides no specific penalty against those who falsely assert a copyright. In the same way, there also is no specific penalty under the Lanham Act for falsely asserting a trademark or for using the symbol ® to indicate a registered trademark where none exists.[60] While there are fewer instances than in the copyright context of individuals or corporations claiming to own a trademark when they do not, false claims do occur. In one case, a plaintiff claimed that it owned a trademark in the Three Stooges' 1936 film *Disorder in the Court* (the copyright of which had already expired) and sued for trademark infringement the producer of *The Long Kiss Goodnight* (1996), which contained a scene in which a thirty-second clip from the Stooges' film played on a background television set. The U.S. Court of Appeals for the Ninth Circuit dismissed the claim to trademark in film footage as "fanciful."[61]

HIJACKED DOMAIN NAMES

Trademark overreaching also occurs with respect to Internet domain names. Beginning in the late 1990s, as it was preparing recommendations for the resolution of domain name and trademark disputes, the World Intellectual Property Organization collected evidence of "reverse domain name hijacking," in which trademark holders "improperly threatened to sue" owners of lawfully registered domain names.[62] In one such incident, the Prima Toy Company, owners of the Gumby and Pokey trademarks, threatened a twelve-year-old boy whose personal website, which had nothing to do with toys, was at www.pokey.org. The boy's father had registered the site because "Pokey" was his son's nickname. So too, Archie Comics sued the parents of a two-year-old girl, Veronica Sams, after they registered the domain name www.veronica.org. Negative publicity ultimately led to these lawsuits being dropped.

The 1999 Anticybersquatting Consumer Protection Act amended the Lanham Act to create a cause of action against those who register, traffic in, or use a domain name identical or confusingly similar to a trademark or personal name or dilutive of a famous mark.[63] As a remedy, a court may order the transfer of the domain name to the owner of the mark. This law was designed to deal with the problem of "cybersquatters," who register an Internet domain name containing a trademark and, rather than create a website, aim to sell the domain name to the trademark owner or a third party. The statute therefore requires that the plaintiff demonstrate that the defendant acted with "a bad faith intent to profit from" the use of the mark.[64] Disregarding this requirement, trademark owners have sought to shut down, as squatters, lawful sites. In particular, corporations have sued or threatened to sue "gripe" sites that criticize their products and sites that are protected parodies.[65] Likewise, famous individuals have sought to use the cybersquatting law to shut down websites critical of them. In one case, the Reverend Jerry Falwell (who held a trademark in his own name) claimed that the operator of www.fallwell.com, a website that contained criticisms of Falwell's stated opinions about homosexuality and other issues, was violating the cybersquatting law. Rejecting Falwell's claim, the Fourth Circuit Court of Appeals rightly explained that the website operator did not have the requisite bad-faith intent to profit from the use of the domain name because he "clearly employed www.fallwell. com simply to criticize Reverend Falwell's views" and "use of a domain name for purposes of comment . . . and criticism . . . constitutes a bona fide . . . fair use under the statute."[66]

HOW TRADEMARK LAW
ITSELF ENABLES OVERREACHING

Trademark claims are expensive to prosecute and to defend. In particular, to establish a likelihood of confusion in an infringement action, the plaintiff generally must submit evidence, typically in the form of commissioned surveys, to demonstrate that the defendant's use of a mark confuses consumers. To defend itself, the defendant must then submit its own survey evidence demonstrating that the likelihood of confusion is not serious. Preparing surveys and bringing in experts to testify about them are expensive undertakings. A trademark infringement claim usually entails significantly greater costs than a copyright infringement claim. Most trademark disputes do not therefore make it to trial, and those that do tend to involve litigation between large corporations with the resources to support their respective positions. The high cost of trademark litigation means that if they are sued for violating a major corporation's trademark rights, smaller entities and individuals rarely have the financial capacity to defend themselves before a judge and jury. Our legal system thereby enables wealthy trademark owners to overreach by threatening legal action or by filing a legal complaint. The prospect of litigation deters most people from using a trademark over a trademark owner's objection even if the law permits the use.

Trademark law not only enables trademark owners to overreach: it also creates an incentive for doing so. If a trademark owner fails to police its trademark, a court may determine that the trademark owner has acquiesced in the use of the mark by somebody else or deem the mark abandoned because it has lost its distinctiveness.[67] As with copyright, there is little downside to over-enforcement, but trademark law itself imposes a penalty for under-enforcing rights. This built-in punishment for lax trademark owners results in some owners taking a scorched-earth approach to enforcement. For instance, McDonald's polices all uses of the "Mc" prefix, claiming that any such use infringes what its lawyers call the "McFamily of brands." Among McDonald's targets: Lauren McClusky, a teenager who tried to use the name "McFest" for concerts she organizes to raise money for the Special Olympics and other charities.[68]

When applied to trademarks that involve ordinary words, this approach means that trademark owners claim a monopoly on language. Lawyers for Richard Branson, founder of the Virgin Group, have claimed that *any* use of the word *virgin* in a company or product name is trademark infringement.[69] Among other things, Virgin has targeted Virgin Cigars and Virgin Mortgage, when there is little likelihood of consumer confusion.[70] Monster Cable Products, a manufacturer of audio cables, has similarly sought to monopolize the use of the word *monster*. According to the *Wall Street Journal*:

Over the years, [Monster Cable] has gone after purveyors of monster-branded auto transmissions, slot machines, glue, carpet-cleaning machines and an energy drink, as well as a woman who sells "Junk Food Monster" kids' T-shirts that promote good eating habits. It sued Monster.com over the job-hunting Web site's name and Walt Disney Co. over products tied to the film "Monsters Inc." It opposed the Boston Red Sox trademark applications for seats and hot dogs named for the Green Monster, the legendary left-field wall in Fenway Park. All in all, Monster Cable says it has fought about 190 monster battles at the U.S. Patent and Trademark Office and filed around 30 monster lawsuits in federal courts.[71]

In 2006, the company sued the operators of Monster Mini Golf (golf courses featuring glow-in-the-dark ghouls). Following public pressure, the lawsuit was dropped.[72] This is a rare outcome. Virtually every other lawsuit Monster Cable has brought has quietly settled, without the company needing to defend its extravagant claims in a court of law or public opinion.

Other examples of monopolizing words abound. When the Australian Institute of Management listed a twenty-year-old course on its website titled "Effective Negotiation Skills," it received a notice from Karrass, a U.S. training group that claimed the course description infringed its trademark rights in the phrases "effective negotiating," "advanced effective negotiating," and "effective sales negotiating."[73] Eric Menhart, a technology lawyer, sought a trademark in the word *cyberlaw* in connection with the practice of law and sent threatening letters to other lawyers who used the term to describe their work.[74] (The USPTO rightly refused to register the mark on the ground that it is merely descriptive.[75]) *Playboy* sued "Playmate" Terri Welles for referring to herself on her own website as a former Playmate of the Year.[76] The NFL has claimed that trademark law precludes advertisers from referring to the "Super Bowl" or the "Big Game"—as in "Get your new plasma TV in time for the Big Game!"[77]

Most trademark disputes settle, usually with the target of the trademark owner's grievance backing down. This is true even when the trademark owner's claims are meritless. Leo Stoller, operating a company called Stealth Industries, has filed dozens of lawsuits and sent out scores of cease-and-desist letters to prevent any use of the word *stealth*. Among the targets: a fishing tackle company, Pure Fishing, for producing and selling the Spiderwire Stealth fishing line, and Brett Brothers Sports International, which makes the Stealth baseball bat.[78] None of Stoller's trademark infringement suits have succeeded. Indeed, one court has described Stoller as "running an industry that produces often spurious, vexatious, and harassing federal litigation" and issued an order prohibiting Stoller from bringing further litigation without the court's prior approval.[79] Nonetheless, a large number of small businesses and individuals have ceased using the word *stealth* to describe their products as a result of Stoller's threats.[80] Acquiescence is less of a hassle than going to court.

PROTECTING TRADEMARK FAIR USE

Altering the economic incentives that trademark owners face can help remedy trademark overreaching. Right now, the cost to trademark owners of overreaching is low because the Lanham Act gives victims of overreaching no remedy. Not only is the benefit to trademark owners of overreaching high, because increased control over marks confers economic value, but the cost of not overreaching is also potentially high, because the trademark owner who does not protect his or her rights can lose the benefits of trademark protection.

Trademark overreaching should be made more expensive. The Lanham Act should be amended to permit those injured by trademark overreaching to bring a civil action to collect damages. A good place to begin is with overreaching that deters fair uses of trademarks because it has the greatest impact upon freedom of speech.

A helpful model for imposing civil liability against overreaching trademark owners is found in the law of the United Kingdom. Section 21 of the United Kingdom's Trade Marks Act of 1994 creates civil liability against those who make "groundless threats" to bring proceedings for infringement of a registered trademark.[81] The law allows anybody who is injured by such a threat to file an action for monetary damages (along with other remedies) against the person making the threat.[82] According to one High Court jurist, this law, which "covers any intimation that would convey to a reasonable man that some person has trade mark rights and intends to enforce them against another," was designed to curtail the activities of those trademark owners "who were (in Pope's words about Addison) 'willing to wound but afraid to strike.'"[83]

A section 21 claim can be brought against the owner of the trademark or against anybody acting on a trademark owner's behalf. The individual who brings a claim for damages has to show only that a threat was made and that as a result of the threat, his or her commercial interests have been affected. To avoid liability under section 21, the person who threatened the trademark infringement proceeding has to prove in defense that his or her threat was justified because the threat was directed at activities that actually did constitute trademark infringement.[84] The person making the threat is on the hot seat.

Section 21 claims are not available in all circumstances. Notably, there is no cause of action for threats directed at the application of a mark to goods or their packaging or to the supply of services under a mark.[85] A trademark owner can therefore threaten with litigation manufacturers who attach a mark to a product as well as providers of services under a mark without risking liability under section 21. This limitation makes considerable sense. It allows trademark owners to zealously protect the core benefit that a trademark is designed to confer, identification of the source of goods or services, while punishing the trademark owner who issues threats against uses of trademarks in comparative advertising, in commentary, or for other lawful purposes.[86]

Congress should adopt a measure similar to section 21 to protect fair uses of trademarks. As we have seen, trademark law in the United States protects fair uses of trademarks from claims of infringement as well as dilution. Because fair use serves First Amendment interests, threats by trademark owners that deter fair use merit special attention.

Adding to the Lanham Act a provision analogous to section 21 that allows individuals who encounter unsustainable threats when they seek to make fair use of a trademark to bring a claim for damages could go a long way in curing this form of overreaching by altering the economic incentive structure facing trademark owners. Unless the trademark owner (or those acting on his or her behalf) could prove that the use against which the threat was made was not a fair use, monetary damages would issue.[87] Most claims could be decided expeditiously. Because fair use, a legal question, would be the basis for a claim, there would be no need for a trial on the issue of consumer confusion, the most expensive part of trademark litigation.

Under this proposed change to the Lanham Act, building owners would face civil liability when they threaten trademark litigation against photographers. Owners of websites that criticize products or services could obtain damages when corporations demand the sites be disabled. A documentary filmmaker would have a claim against the trademark owner who insists that products caught on film be excised. Prima Toy Company would be held accountable when it threatens the twelve-year-old operator of www.pokey.org. Imposing liability for these and other threats against fair use would protect uses of trademarks that closely serve freedom of speech without burdening the ability of trademark owners to enforce the actual rights that trademark law gives them.

FROM SOURCE TO CENSORSHIP

Like giant oil slicks, trademarks resist containment. Designed to help the public identify where products come from, trademarks have become tools to silence critics, prevent parody, control the use of words, and squash small businesses. If you poke fun at Barbie, you face Mattel's wrath. If you say you hate Barney, his handlers will find you. If your name begins with "Mc," McDonalds has your number. If you use the word *monster* in your business name, you can expect to find lawyers at your doorstep.

While trademark rights are meant to be limited in scope, and fair use applies to trademarks, trademark law itself enables overreaching to occur. There is no provision in the Lanham Act allowing a victim of overreaching to obtain compensation for the losses he or she has suffered. There is therefore little reason for trademark owners to act cautiously in asserting violations of their rights. Further, the law gives trademark owners an incentive to act aggressively because it penalizes owners who do not adequately protect their interests. Overreaching by trademark owners succeeds because it is too costly for most individuals, businesses, or other entities to go to court and defend themselves against a trademark infringement or dilution claim: individuals confronted with lawyers' demands that they cease using a mark refrain from activities that trademark law permits. Conservative uses lead trademark owners to continue to act aggressively. The cycle repeats, and overreaching flourishes.

While trademark overreaching has some of the same causes and effects as copyright overreaching, there is an important difference between the two when it comes to their impact on freedom of speech. As we have seen, when it comes to copyright there is a strong licensing culture in which permission must be sought, and a fee paid, in order to make use of works even when the Copyright Act deems the use lawful. This makes speech more expensive than it should be (and it inhibits some expression altogether), but speech can occur when a license is obtained. The expressive effects of trademark overreaching are more severe. Copyright owners have reason to license their works because, in addition to generating royalties, dissemination brings renown to the author. A trademark owner, however, does not have the same incentive for its marks to be used by others because the whole value of the mark lies in its being identified with the company that owns it and the products that company creates. Trademark licensing is therefore much more limited.[88] Licensing uses of a mark for expressive purposes offers the trademark owner virtually no benefit. (There is, for example, no trademark equivalent of the Copyright Clearance Center for ordinary users to license marks.) In the absence of licensing and as a result of the prohibitive costs of defending a lawsuit, lawful uses of marks are not made. Copyright overreaching makes some speech more costly. Trademark overreaching prevents expression altogether. Protecting trademark fair use by imposing liability for unfounded threats can safeguard freedom of speech.

The next three chapters show how to stop copyfraud, protect copyright fair use, and restore the public domain.

CHAPTER 8

COPYFRAUD LIABILITY

I T IS TIME to restore the balance between private intellectual property rights and the interests of the public in accessing and using intellectual creations. As we have seen, overreaching by content providers takes different forms. There is, therefore, no single way to remedy it. Rather, multiple tools are needed to reduce the causes of overreaching and to minimize its effects. This chapter and the next two present a series of mechanisms that governmental and private actors can use to confront copyfraud, interference with fair use, and the other forms of overreaching discussed in this book and thereby restore the public-private balance. We begin with a proposal to reform the law in order to punish directly those who commit copyfraud.

TREATING COPYFRAUD AS FRAUD

Copyfraud is the most egregious form of overreaching because it involves a claim of intellectual property rights where none exist. False claims require strong medicine. The law should impose liability on those who falsely claim copyrights in public domain works. In the law, liability can take the form of a criminal penalty, in a criminal case initiated by a government prosecutor, or a civil penalty, in a civil case brought by a private litigant or by a governmental agency. Section 506(c) of the Copyright Act criminalizes fraudulent use of copyright notices, but the fact that this provision is rarely enforced shows that the government has little interest in prosecuting copyfraud in criminal court. It therefore makes sense to turn to a system of civil liability for copyfraud so that private parties and the courts can deter and remedy copyright claims in public domain works.

Congress should amend the Copyright Act to require publishers and other content providers to specify clearly which portions of a book, article, play, film, musical composition, database, or other work are protected by copyright, and which are not. This requirement is not especially onerous. Many reprints, compilations, and digitized versions of public domain works are not copyrightable because nothing original has been added to them: they should therefore carry no copyright notice. Works that combine public domain and copyrighted materials would require only a simple explanatory statement setting out what is protected and what may be freely reproduced. In most instances, the designation is easily made: publishers and other content providers are already accustomed to using notices to designate licensed reproductions of copyrighted materials, and indicating that part of a work is in the public domain would be an equally straightforward task. In this regard, the practices of Signet, a Penguin imprint, are notable. The copyright notice in Signet's 1985 collection of Mark Twain's short stories (all in the public domain) properly states that "the texts in this book are reproduced from *The Writings of Mark Twain* . . . from an original edition in the collection of The New York University Libraries," but that the new introduction by Justin Kaplan is copyrighted.[1] Similarly, Signet's reprint of Frederick Douglass's autobiography carries a copyright notice limited to a new introduction.[2] In some instances, original copyrighted materials might be so intermingled with a public domain work that there is no easy way to specify in a brief statement what is protected and what is not. In such circumstances, some other kind of statement—perhaps one explaining that the work is based on a specific public domain work itself not copyrighted—would be appropriate. The point is that copyright notices should, as a general rule, make clear what is copyrighted and what is not.

To ensure that content providers use copyright notices accurately, the Copyright Act should be amended to impose liability against anyone who claims a copyright in a public domain work and to allow individuals injured by false copyright claims to collect damages. The clearest cases in which copyfraud liability should arise are those falling under a straight-up fraud theory. The law defines fraud as a false representation made with the intention of causing somebody to act upon the falsehood to his or her detriment and resulting in injury. The injured party can bring a civil lawsuit to collect damages for the resulting monetary loss.[3] If, therefore, a content provider intentionally attaches a copyright notice to a public domain work in order to cause deception and then extracts licensing payments from individuals who rely on that false notice, the content provider should be liable to the licensees for damages incurred. The Copyright Act should be changed to allow a lawsuit to go forward. Some statutorily specified bonus amount might also be appropriate in these circumstances so as to deter content providers from engaging in copyfraud and to make bringing the lawsuit worth its cost. Class action litigation should also be permitted, because it can prove a useful remedy to copyfraud when there are large numbers of individuals who have suffered the same injury.

Also on a simple fraud approach, somebody who intentionally claims copyright ownership in a public domain work should be held liable to individuals who refrain, to their own detriment, from using the work as a result of that false claim. Exactly what would be required to prove detrimental reliance here would depend on the individual circumstances of the case, but the clearest kind of proof would be evidence that a plaintiff, believing that a copyright notice was valid, purchased the work instead of making a duplicate of a copy to which he or she already had access. In many such instances, the precise amount of actual damages will be readily calculable. Members of a choral society who purchase additional sets of public domain sheet music marked as copyrighted rather than making copies suffer a determinable loss, as do college students directed to pay for works because their professors believe the material cannot be posted on a website or otherwise made freely available. Likewise, the person who forgoes using freely an image of a public domain painting from a website or database and instead purchases a license to use the image from a museum suffers a loss that can be readily calculated. Additional deterrence-based damages might also be appropriate in such circumstances. In other cases, the actual loss may be more nebulous: a teacher forgoes using a particular work in class and chooses something different to use instead, a film society shows its second-choice movie or decides against showing anything at all, a website owner posts one set of materials instead of another, a screenwriter decides against adapting a novel. In such instances when there is detrimental reliance on a defendant's false copyright notice, an appropriate penalty would be some specific statutory award.

MODIFYING THE ELEMENTS OF FRAUD:
LESSONS FROM THE PATENT ACT

Requiring that the traditional elements of fraud be met before somebody can be held liable for copyfraud has the advantage of deterring frivolous litigation and limiting compensation to situations in which someone has suffered an actual, demonstrable loss as a result of a content provider's deliberately false copyright claim. However, a strong case exists for relaxing the elements of fraud and drawing a wider circle of liability in order to deal with copyfraud. Because false copyrights have a constitutional dimension—interfering with creativity and free expression—they deserve a more vigorous enforcement approach than do other kinds of fraud. Falsely marking a public domain work as copyrighted undermines expression even if the false marking was not made with the intent to trick anyone into making payment. Thus copyfraud has broad effects beyond the injury to individual victims who can demonstrate detrimental reliance: when public domain works are marked as copyrighted, the public as a whole, in addition to any particular individual who suffers a loss, is the victim.

For this reason, it makes sense to impose liability for copyfraud without requiring plaintiffs to establish all the elements of the traditional tort of fraud. A regime of strict liability—in which any false use of a copyright notice, intentional or not, triggers liability—would probably be too burdensome on publishers and other content providers, so intent should still be required; however, plaintiffs should be permitted to establish intent by inference. For instance, because it is impossible to believe that a play by Shakespeare is copyrightable, a publisher who attaches a copyright notice to the play would easily be found to have acted with deceptive intent. Likewise, the database provider who attaches copyright notices to the pages of public domain newspapers would have the requisite intent. (On the other hand, liability would not attach when a publisher or other content provider has acted in good faith—for example, when a book author represents that he or she owns the copyright in an image and the author's publisher, relying on that representation, marks the image as copyrighted.) Deceptive intent could also be found when a defendant received notice of a false copyright and continued to attach the copyright notice to the work. Allowing deceptive intent to be inferred would lead most content providers to be careful about their use of copyright notices and produce far less copyrighting of the public domain than we see today. As explored in greater detail in the following pages, two other elements of a traditional fraud claim should also be relaxed in a copyfraud case. First, a copyfraud plaintiff should not be required to prove detrimental reliance. Second, the cause of action should not be limited to individuals who have suffered an actual injury; instead, any member of the public should be empowered to bring a copyfraud claim.

Here the Patent Act is instructive. The Patent Act prohibits falsely marking a good as patented by use of the word *patent* or other words or numbers, or falsely marking the good as covered by a pending patent.[4] The false-marking provision, which imposes a monetary fine,[5] requires a showing that the defendant intended to deceive the public.[6] However, the statute does not require proof that anybody actually was deceived or detrimentally relied upon the deception. In addition, the statute permits any person, whether personally harmed or not, to bring a lawsuit and retain half of the recovered penalty.[7] Further, in construing this provision of the Patent Act, courts have found that the intent to deceive can be inferred on the basis of the defendant's conduct in knowingly mismarking the product as patented.[8]

While copyright law and patent law both protect intellectual property, the differences between copyrights and patents are pronounced enough that we should not automatically assume that rules that work well for one will also work well for the other. In particular, patent litigation is circumscribed in a way that copyright litigation is not. Patent holders are inventors; patent infringers are other inventors and manufacturers. By contrast, anyone can acquire a copyright simply by creating an original work. An ordinary person can also easily infringe a copyright—and can easily become the victim of copyfraud. In drawing upon patent law to design rules for copyright and copyfraud, it is therefore important to keep in mind that the universe to which those rules will apply is potentially extremely large. Nonetheless, the patent law standards described here can usefully be extended to the context of copyright. If Congress couples the relaxed liability scheme with careful specification of the damages and other penalties to be assessed when liability is established, copyfraud can be deterred without unduly burdening publishers and other content providers.

STANDING AND ENFORCEMENT

Standing is the legal term for the right somebody has to bring a lawsuit in court. In creating a civil liability scheme to deal with copyfraud, Congress should grant standing to a broad set of actors. Clearly, private parties who have suffered injuries as a result of copyfraud should have standing to seek relief. But limiting standing to parties who can demonstrate personal injury is likely to lead to an insufficient response to the broad problem of copyfraud. Furthermore, individuals who suffer a specific copyfraud injury—for instance, unnecessarily purchasing a copy of a work rather than photocopying it—might not readily recognize they have been wronged and might lack sufficient incentive or resources to bring a legal claim. Copyfraud often entails a series of small individual injuries over a period of time rather than a large wrong against a single party on one occasion. Accordingly, and in light of the important public interest at stake in protecting the public domain, it makes sense to assign standing to a broad set of plaintiffs to bring copyfraud claims. Besides individual victims, two sets of actors should be authorized to bring copyfraud lawsuits: government agencies acting on behalf of citizens, and individuals who, though they have not suffered an injury themselves, are willing to act as private attorneys general and go to court to enforce the law.

Governmental Enforcement

Both federal and state agencies can be granted standing to seek civil relief and could prove useful in combating copyfraud. The experience with section 506(c), the rarely enforced provision of the Copyright Act criminalizing fraudulent use of copyright notices, suggests that as a practical matter federal agencies are reluctant to pursue copyfraud. However, this history of non-enforcement in the criminal context does not necessarily mean that federal agencies will not vigorously pursue civil penalties once Congress makes them available. Bringing a civil case is typically easier than bringing a criminal prosecution (among other things, there is a higher standard of proof required of the government in a criminal trial), and government agents might see civil liability as a more appropriate response. Accordingly, it makes sense for Congress to authorize the U.S. attorney general to seek civil penalties for copyfraud.

When federal enforcement efforts fail to achieve a statute's goals, enforcement by state governmental agencies can be effective. Congress has provided authority to state attorneys general to seek relief for violations of certain federal laws, including antitrust laws. On the assumption that federal agencies might not zealously or fully enforce a civil copyfraud scheme, Congress should grant standing under federal law to state agencies to bring civil claims on their citizens' behalf. Congress should also ensure that the available penalties for copyfraud violations are sufficient such that the state will devote its resources to bringing these kinds of claims. State agents would therefore be both empowered and encouraged to take up some of the enforcement slack.[9]

Private Attorney General Enforcement

Congress should also give standing to private attorneys general to enforce the law. A private attorney general is "a plaintiff who sues to vindicate public interests not directly connected to any special stake of her own."[10] Giving private attorneys general standing in copyfraud cases would likely be more effective and less expensive than relying on government agents to bring lawsuits, and it would promote enforcement of the law when government is unable or unwilling to devote public resources to enforcement. Moreover, lawsuits by private attorneys general would create stronger enforcement than would waiting for a victim of copyfraud to bring an action.

Congress authorizes private attorney general litigation in several other contexts. For example, since the 1970s, many federal environmental laws have authorized any individual to bring a lawsuit to enforce the law's provisions. Similarly, many states permit individuals to bring lawsuits to enforce state environmental, consumer protection, and other laws—even though the person bringing the suit may not have personally suffered an injury. Indeed, Congress has already recognized in the patent context the benefits of private attorney general enforcement. As we have seen, in addition to providing for government prosecution for misuse of patent marks,[11] the Patent Act creates a broad private cause of action.[12] Congress should create a similar mechanism for actions against those who falsely mark public domain works as copyrighted. Private attorneys general would be entitled to act as plaintiffs and to bring claims for copyfraud even if the claims do not correspond to any specific injury they themselves have suffered. In essence, private attorneys general would function as copyfraud bounty hunters: they would monitor published books, websites, movies, databases, and other works for false claims to copyright, and they would be entitled to collect a bounty for each instance of copyfraud uncovered.

Beyond pursuing claims on behalf of the general public, private attorneys general could also bring actions to remedy injuries to the government itself. It is not difficult to see that the perpetrators of copyfraud, by misusing the copyright notice designated by Congress to identify rights protected under copyright law, cause injury to the government, and federal statutes have long authorized otherwise disinterested private individuals to bring claims on the government's behalf.[13] For example, the federal False Claims Act, the law that imposes civil liability on those who defraud the federal government, allows private individuals to sue on behalf of the government—representing the United States in the litigation and redressing the government's injury.[14] To encourage private enforcement of this nature, the act allows private individuals who bring a successful claim to share in the assessed penalties and damages.[15]

Private attorney general litigation is not, however, without its problems. Commentators have argued that private attorney general litigation can result in profit-seeking lawyers filing frivolous lawsuits and settling claims quickly and cheaply, resulting in poor enforcement of the laws and burdens on businesses. Constructing a private attorney general scheme to deal with copyfraud therefore requires attention to potential problems. For instance, the bounty should probably be payable only to the first private attorney general locating and collecting on a particular false copyright. Private attorneys general could be required to take a course of instruction—which might be web-based—on principles of copyright and mechanisms of enforcement. To discourage private attorneys general from making spurious reports, some penalty—for example, suspension of bounty-hunting privileges for a specified period, or a reduced payment for the next successful "capture"—could be imposed if an allegation of copyfraud turns out to be wrong. Settlement might require court approval, and the U.S. attorney general could have standing to intervene in especially important cases to fully protect the public's interest. With a little imagination, the benefits of private enforcement can be coupled with mechanisms to prevent abuses and undesirable results.

There is one important limitation on Congress's ability to allow private attorney general litigation in federal courts. The Supreme Court has held that because the federal judicial power is limited to "Cases" and "Controversies" under Article III of the Constitution, to bring a lawsuit in federal court, a plaintiff must allege an "injury in fact" caused by the defendant's conduct and redressable by a favorable court decision.[16] The Court has explained that to qualify as an injury in fact, the injury "must be concrete in both a qualitative and temporal sense. The complainant must allege an injury to himself that is distinct and palpable, as opposed to merely abstract, and the alleged harm must be actual or imminent, not conjectural or hypothetical."[17] Applying this rule in *Lujan v. Defenders of Wildlife*, the Court held that an environmental organization did not have Article III standing to bring a lawsuit in federal court to challenge a regulation issued under the Endangered Species Act if the organization could not show that the regulation caused it or its members any injury in fact.[18] Although *Lujan* has generated criticism, and the full reach of the decision is not clear, the case does indicate limitations on Congress's ability to assign standing in federal court to otherwise disinterested parties. Nonetheless, Congress can give plaintiffs standing to bring lawsuits in state court, where the requirements of Article III do not apply.[19] In addition, the Supreme Court has held that the federal government is entitled to "assign" to a private individual an injury that the government has suffered. Assignment of an injury allows the private individual to proceed in court as though he or she, and not the government, is actually the victim. With this bit of legal fiction, statutes that allow private individuals to sue on behalf of the government, such as the federal False Claims Act, comport with Article III standing requirements; the plaintiff is therefore not barred by the *Lujan* rule.[20] On this basis, Congress would be able to authorize private actors to bring copyfraud claims in both federal and state courts to remedy the public injuries copyfraud causes.

PENALTIES: MAKING COPYFRAUD COSTLY

As penalties for copyfraud are crafted, attention needs to be given to the fact that in addition to inflicting small injuries on many individuals, copyfraud also causes a more general injury to the public as a whole—the infringement of the public domain. Therefore, while individuals should be compensated for their losses, a civil cause of action for copyfraud should allow for penalties broader than any plaintiff's individual injury. Determining the form penalties should take will require careful legislative attention. One possible approach is for Congress to create a system with specified statutory penalties. The system would tie the penalty to various aspects of the defendant's misconduct. For example, the penalty award could take into account the number of publications a publisher has issued with the false copyright notice; misuse of the copyright symbol on a single photograph would thus be penalized less severely than copyfraud in the print run of a hundred thousand books. The size of the penalty might also reflect a judgment about the egregiousness of the copyfraud. Marking an important public document like the Constitution as copyrighted could generate a more serious sanction than asserting copyright in a forgotten poem. Repeat offenders could be subject to greater liability than the defendant in court for the first time. Disgorgement of profits would be a suitable penalty in many instances. This would mean that the defendant who collects fifteen cents per page from people wishing to copy *The Federalist* would lose the benefit of its sales, while the vendor of digitized early newspapers who asserts copyright would forfeit subscription earnings.

Not all the spoils of copyfraud litigation need go to the actual plaintiff who brings the lawsuit. For example, the plaintiff could be entitled to receive some set percentage of the assessed penalty, with the remaining amount payable to the treasury to fund efforts to protect and promote the public domain. In addition to monetary damages, various forms of injunctive relief can be crafted. For instance, the publisher who commits copyfraud could be required to remove the offending publication from the market. A court could direct a losing defendant to issue a public statement retracting the prior claim to copyright or to engage in activities that promote the public domain. An offender might be required to secure court approval before attaching any copyright notice to a future publication. Finally, successful plaintiffs should be entitled to collect attorneys' fees; the availability of attorneys' fees will encourage lawyers to take on copyfraud cases.

USING EXISTING LAWS TO COMBAT COPYFRAUD

Amending the Copyright Act along the lines suggested is the best way to impose liability against those who commit copyfraud. In the absence of such a change, however, existing laws at the federal and state levels could be used to penalize at least some claims of copyright in public domain works.

Civil RICO

Some forms of copyfraud could trigger liability under the federal Racketeer Influenced and Corrupt Organizations Act (RICO), although this is untested. In addition to criminal liability,[21] RICO provides for a civil cause of action in federal and state court in the case of activities

performed as part of an ongoing criminal enterprise. RICO authorizes
"[a]ny person injured in his business or property" because of a RICO
violation to bring a civil action for treble damages.[22] The U.S. attorney
general can also bring civil RICO cases and seek broad equitable relief,
including orders of divestiture, restrictions on future activities, and
dissolution or reorganization of an enterprise.[23] A plaintiff in a civil RICO
case must plead at least two predicate acts and show that the predicate
acts are related, and that they amount to, or pose a threat of, continuing
criminal activity.[24] Predicate acts are "related" for RICO purposes
when they "have the same or similar purposes, results, participants,
victims, or methods of commission, or otherwise are interrelated by
distinguishing characteristics and are not isolated events."[25] Continuing
criminal activity may be demonstrated by either past unlawful conduct
coupled with a threat of future conduct (open-ended continuity) or past
conduct that extended over a substantial period of time (closed-ended
continuity).[26] Important for our purposes are mail fraud and wire fraud,
which are among the various forms of unlawful conduct listed by the
statute that can constitute predicate RICO acts.[27] These offenses refer
to the use of mail and telecommunication devices, respectively, in the
course of committing a fraud, thereby turning fraud (a state law offense)
into an offense that is actionable under federal law. Virtually every act
of copyfraud makes use of mail or of telecommunication devices: books
with false copyright notices, for example, are shipped; invoices to license
public domain works are mailed; orders for falsely marked goods are
placed by telephone; and databases of public domain materials labeled
as copyrighted are accessed electronically. If copyfraud satisfies the
requirements of a state law fraud claim, there is thus the possibility of a
RICO claim.

State Law Causes of Action

Existing state laws might also permit causes of action to deal with
some forms of copyfraud.[28] The most obvious case in which state laws

could provide a cause of action is when someone pays a licensing fee to a licensor who falsely represented ownership of a copyright in a work that is in fact in the public domain. The aggrieved licensee might put forth a claim under state laws of contract for breach of an implied warranty of title, show that an absence of consideration renders the contract void, or make out a claim of unjust enrichment. New York State courts, for instance, have held that if a licensed work later turns out to be in the public domain, the licensee is entitled to recover payments made to the licensor. In one early case, a New York court ordered a music library to refund an opera company more than $50,000 that the opera company had paid for a license to perform *The Merry Widow*, a public domain work. The court held that because the work was in the public domain, the licensor had breached an implied warranty of title and therefore the agreement lacked consideration.[29] A licensee might also have a cause of action based on state law fraud. For example, in *Schlaifer Nance & Co. v. Estate of Andy Warhol*, when a licensing agency that had an agreement with the estate of Andy Warhol to license works by and images of Warhol discovered that many of those works and images covered by the agreement were in the public domain, the agency brought a state law fraud claim against Warhol's estate. Affirming the lower court's ruling in favor of the estate, the U.S. Court of Appeals for the Second Circuit recognized the availability of a state law fraud claim in cases involving the licensing of works wrongly represented as copyrighted.[30] Yet the benefits of these state law causes of action should not be exaggerated. State law claims in contract and fraud might help the individual who has wrongly paid a licensing fee and seeks recovery of the fee; they are, however, less helpful in remedying the more general problem of copyfraud's deterrence of legitimate uses and reproductions.

Copyfraud might also be deemed a form of false advertising under state law. Every state has its own consumer protection laws—modeled on the Uniform Deceptive Trade Practices Act or on the Federal Trade Commission Act—to protect consumers from false advertising. State consumer protection laws provide for relief when the Federal Trade Commission is unable or unwilling to bring a case, and allow private individuals to seek redress rather than depend upon the government to prosecute offenders. These state laws vary in terms of what kind of advertising is unlawful, the type and degree of injury necessary before a party can recover, and the available penalties. In addition to civil penalties, some states impose criminal penalties for false advertising, even if the advertising causes no actual injury.

The possibility of using state false advertising laws to deal with false assertions of copyright remains untested. By their terms, at least, the statutes do not obviously foreclose such actions. In New York, for instance, the Consumer Protection Act prohibits "[f]alse advertising in the conduct of any business, trade or commerce or in the furnishing of any service in this state."[31] Under the statute, false advertising occurs when a statement is "misleading in a material respect."[32] The statute provides for the attorney general to bring an action to recover a civil penalty of up to $5,000 per violation.[33] A private party who has been injured by a violation of the statute may also seek damages and injunctive relief.[34] New York courts have held that a person who is misled or deceived by a materially misleading advertisement suffers an injury within the meaning of the statute.[35] Arguably, a content provider affixing a false copyright notice has, in the conduct of business, made a materially misleading statement about the product being sold. On this logic, an individual who has been injured as a result of the false copyright has a cause of action against the content provider under the state's law.

In turning to state law, we must confront the issue of whether any particular cause of action is preempted by federal law. As we saw in Chapter 5, the Copyright Act contains a preemption clause. It specifies that "all legal or equitable rights that are equivalent to any of the exclusive rights within the general scope of copyright . . . are governed exclusively by this title," and that "no person is entitled to any such right or equivalent right in any such work under the common law or statutes of any State."[36] The act also states that federal preemption does not apply to state law rights with respect to materials beyond the "subject matter" of copyright.[37] Some courts have found that the subject matter of copyright includes works within the *general* subject matter of copyrightable works.[38] On this view, preemption serves to "prevent the states from granting protection to works which Congress has concluded should be in the public domain."[39] That said, there is a strong argument that a state law cause of action with respect to an assertion of copyright in a public domain work is not preempted. Even if public domain material were understood to fall within the general subject of the Copyright Act, the state cause of action would not be equivalent to enforcement of any rights under the act. More significantly, the state cause of action would be consistent with the idea in the preemption analysis that state law should not allow parties to claim copyright-like protections to public domain materials. However, this specific area of law remains undeveloped.[40]

THE BOTTOM LINE

Copyfraud will decline when private citizens are empowered to bring lawsuits to collect monetary penalties against those who falsely claim copyrights in public domain works. By hitting the bottom line, liability for copyfraud can quickly and permanently alter the practices of publishers and other content providers because it is easier for them to make appropriate use of copyright notices than to answer to a lawsuit. Faced with the prospect of a financial penalty, book publishers will use copyright notices that clearly distinguish copyrightable materials from public domain materials. Museums will remove false copyright notices from images of public domain paintings. Archives will stop claiming they own copyrights in everything in their collections. Database providers will remove copyright notices from digitized historical newspapers and other public domain works. Nobody will attach a copyright notice to the Constitution.

Amending the Copyright Act to allow for civil lawsuits against false copyright claims in public domain works is a cost-effective solution to the problem of copyfraud. Few other forms of civil litigation give the same bang for the buck. In most instances, bringing a copyfraud lawsuit will be minimally expensive because it will require little more than identifying the false copyright claim and its maker and then filing a complaint. Courts will be able to efficiently adjudicate the lawsuit without a large commitment of judicial resources. There is little likelihood of either frivolous or drawn-out litigation because most improper uses of copyright notices are easily identifiable, and so liability can be quickly assigned. At the same time, imposing liability for copyfraud will produce large public benefits. When public domain works are freed from copyright notices, using those works will no longer trigger legal threats or demands that uses be licensed. When such threats and demands disappear, people will become less conservative in their use of the public domain and will draw upon it with greater frequency. Gatekeepers will become gateways: publishers, distributors, and others who nowadays block lawful uses of the public domain will facilitate the release of new works that incorporate or draw upon public domain materials.

Imposing liability through civil lawsuits is not the only way to remedy copyfraud. In the coming pages we will see some additional mechanisms for curtailing this and other forms of overreaching. The next chapter shows how to prevent interference with fair use.

CHAPTER 9

DEFENDING
COPYRIGHT FAIR USE

W HILE COPYFRAUD involves a false ownership claim to intellectual property, other forms of overreaching entail overzealous assertions of intellectual property rights. Remedying this kind of overreaching requires the implementation of measures to define clearly the limits of rights and to keep rights within their proper boundaries. A good first step is to change the way our current system handles fair use.

As we saw in Chapter 2, interference with fair use succeeds because fair use law is unpredictable: the fair use provision of the Copyright Act is written in general terms, and court decisions are typically limited to fact-specific cases. In the absence of clear rules, the threat of litigation deters individuals from relying upon fair use and leads gatekeepers to insist that all uses of copyrighted works be licensed.

Previous commentators have sought to remedy these problems and restore fair use to its proper role. Some have recommended that Congress amend the fair use provision of the Copyright Act to more specifically set out uses that are fair. In particular, they urge that Congress adopt statutory safe harbors that specify an amount of copying that is per se fair use; uses beyond the safe harbor amount could qualify as fair use, but only if a court so ruled in a specific case. Gideon Parchomovsky and Kevin Goldman, for example, argue that Congress should specify that for literary works that are at least one hundred words long, either a total of 15 percent or three hundred words, whichever is shorter, may be copied without permission.[1] For audiovisual works, they argue that a total of either 10 percent or thirty seconds, whichever is shorter, may be reproduced, and that "anyone may include in an audiovisual work any architectural, choreographic, or pictorial work, so long as that work is not displayed for more than thirty seconds and provided those thirty seconds comprise no more than ten percent of the new work."[2] Clarity in fair use is desirable. However, Congress is not the best entity for producing it. Congress's slow and deliberate processes are not well suited to generating fair use rules that keep pace with changing circumstances.

Other commentators have offered proposals to adjust the rules of litigation in order to reduce the risk of liability to those who seek to make fair use of copyrighted works. One proposal would eliminate or reduce damage awards against defendants who demonstrate a good-faith but mistaken belief that their use was a fair use.[3] Another proposal advocates making attorneys' fees available to prevailing parties in order to deter copyright owners from bringing weak copyright infringement claims while encouraging defendants to assert fair use defenses.[4] Each of these proposals seeks to reduce the risk that a fair use of a copyrighted work will be the subject of a copyright infringement action. However, by leaving fair use determinations in the hands of courts, these proposals will not lead to clarity in the meaning of fair use, and they will not adequately deter copyright owners from threatening litigation for unlicensed uses of their works.

Rather than adjust fair use law around the edges, we must make some changes more basic in nature to bring predictability to fair use and shield it from litigation. A good first step would be to give the task of regulating fair use to an administrative agency. Agency regulation can resolve many of the problems fair use presents when, as now, it is the province of Congress and the courts. After examining how an agency would perform this regulatory role and the resulting benefits, we will take up some additional mechanisms to protect fair use.

ADMINISTERING FAIR USE

The modern state is an administrative state. For the day-to-day implementation of the law, government relies upon administrative agencies. Agencies are especially important when legal directives are required to guide people's behavior but neither Congress nor the courts are able to regulate with sufficient clarity. Congress often lacks the institutional capacity (or the will) to determine how a statute will apply on the ground and in a variety of contexts. And although courts decide individual issues, it often takes a long time for judicial rulings to form a comprehensive regulatory framework. Administrative agencies fill these voids.

As we have seen in the preceding chapters, in the modern information society, intellectual property laws affect vast numbers of individuals and entities. Virtually every use or creation of information raises questions of intellectual property rights. Intellectual property law also is becoming increasingly complex as new issues of how it applies in specific contexts regularly arise. Under these conditions, it is unrealistic to expect Congress or the courts to provide and update the legal directives that can guide behavior on a daily basis. Although federal agencies play a part in the administration of some aspects of intellectual property law, their role in intellectual property law, compared to those in other areas of federal law, is quite limited. Intellectual property law is well suited to agency governance, and the problems we saw in Chapter 2 with respect to fair use are particularly ripe for agency regulation, yet no agency regulates fair use in the United States.[5]

By contrast, in other nations, agencies play roles in administering copyright law. For example, in 2007, Israel enacted a new copyright statute that took effect in May 2008. The statute adopts the four-factor fair use approach in the U.S. Copyright Act but gives the minister of justice authority to "make regulations prescribing conditions under which a use shall be deemed a fair use."[6] The minister's authorization to issue fair use regulations resulted from a concern that greater precision was needed but neither the legislature nor the courts could supply it. With this statutory authority in place, the minister of justice is now beginning the process of issuing fair use regulations.

We should learn from the Israeli approach. An administrative agency can, and should, regulate fair use in the United States. Agency regulation can combat overreaching by bringing clarity to the law of fair use and keeping copyrights within their proper boundaries.

Agencies Old and New

Before examining how a federal agency should regulate fair use, it is useful to address the question of which federal agency should play this role. There are several options as to where responsibility for the administration of fair use might be assigned. This might be an existing agency or one created solely for this purpose. Alternatively, agency functions could be performed by private entities that are certified or regulated by the government.[7] Should responsibility for regulating fair use be assigned to an existing federal agency, one possible candidate is the Copyright Office, which is part of the Library of Congress, a legislative agency. The Copyright Office currently registers copyrights, provides assistance to Congress (including preparing copyright legislation and legislative reports and providing advice on compliance with multilateral agreements), and administers compulsory and statutory licenses.[8] Other commentators also have proposed a more active role in intellectual property law for the Copyright Office. For example, Mark Lemley and R. Anthony Reese have proposed giving copyright owners the option to bring before an administrative law judge within the Copyright Office infringement actions against consumers who upload copyrighted works on peer-to-peer networks.[9] Joseph Liu argues in favor of giving the Copyright Office increased rulemaking, adjudicatory, and enforcement authority, particularly with respect to complex issues raised by technological change.[10] As Liu notes, however, significant changes would need to be made to the structure and makeup of the Copyright Office to ensure that it possesses the expertise and resources necessary to fulfill these sorts of additional responsibilities.[11] The United States Patent and Trademark Office, which issues patents and registers trademarks, also could be given responsibility for administering fair use. It, however, already is understaffed and would also require additional resources.

The role of the Copyright Office in issuing administrative exemptions to the anti-circumvention provision of the Digital Millennium Copyright Act (DMCA) suggests the possibility of relying upon that office to administer fair use, but also some need for caution. Critics have complained that in performing its role under the DMCA, the Librarian of Congress—and, by extension, the Copyright Office—has unduly favored content owners, particularly by failing to provide exemptions for fair use or for consumers to make backup copies of lawfully purchased media.[12] There also has been criticism that the Librarian (and the Copyright Office) has taken a very narrow view of the exemption provision of the DMCA, imposed unduly high standards for granting an exemption, and granted far fewer exemptions than were warranted. Thus, although the Copyright Office has regulatory experience, Congress would need to consider carefully whether the Copyright Office can be relied upon to administer fair use (and, if so, how)—or whether the task should be assigned to a new agency.

These concerns point to the risk that the agency will be captured by special interest groups, regardless of whether a new agency is created or an existing one assigned responsibility. Given the high stakes involved in regulating fair use, particular care should be taken to ensure that the agency's decision making is balanced. This would be easier today than it was when the fair use provision of copyright law was adopted in 1976, because in addition to advocates for copyright owners, there are now prominent organizations dedicated to protecting the interests of users.[13] Nonetheless, content industries have a stronger starting position.[14]

Agency funding is also an important element of agency independence. Jessica Litman contends that rather than serving the interests of Congress (and, by extension, the general public), "the Copyright Office has tended to view copyright owners as its real constituency" because lawyers representing copyright owners protect the Copyright Office from congressional budget cuts.[15] One way to avoid this problem would be to give the agency responsible for fair use an independent income source. For example, the agency could be funded through fees collected from those who have dealings with the agency, as described in the coming pages, or by a fee imposed upon registration of a copyright with the Copyright Office.

Creating a New Agency for Fair Use: Two Models

Let us assume a new federal agency is created to administer fair use. Two models of agency regulation could effectively resolve the current problems that exist in leaving fair use to Congress and the courts. These models are discussed in turn.

Model 1: The Agency for Fair Use. Under Model 1, Congress would do three things to provide the legal framework for agency action. First, Congress would make it unlawful to interfere with fair uses of copyrighted works and subject offenders to civil penalties. Similar to federal consumer protection laws, a federal fair use protection statute would protect the public from false claims and other practices by copyright owners that limit fair uses of copyrighted works. Second, Congress would create an agency—let us call this Agency for Fair Use (AFU)—whose principal task would be to enforce this statute. AFU would enforce the statute through the usual agency mechanisms of rulemaking and adjudication. Third, Congress would specify that federal fair use law, including

AFU's regulations, preempts state laws of contract that limit fair uses of copyrighted works.

Under Model 1, the agency would generate regulations prohibiting interference with fair uses of copyrighted works. These regulations would specify, consistent with the provisions of section 107 of the Copyright Act, the uses that constitute fair uses of copyrighted works in specific sectors and prohibit interference with those uses. The agency's authority would extend to all types of works, including books, sound recordings, and films. In developing these regulations, AFU would be expected to receive input from copyright owners, those who seek to make use of copyrighted works, representatives from relevant industries and interest groups, copyright law experts, and other interested parties. Most federal agencies use the procedure of notice-and-comment rulemaking provided for under the Administrative Procedure Act: the agency gives the general public notice that a rule is being contemplated, provides the language or a general description of the proposed rule, and invites comments from the public.[16] Prior to notice and comment, some agencies, including the Environmental Protection Agency, use a process of negotiated rulemaking, in which the agency brings together representatives of affected groups to negotiate the terms of the proposed rule.[17] The development of fair use regulations is well suited to the public notice-and-comment procedure and also may be suited to negotiated rulemaking. E-rulemaking, in which members of the public participate online in the comment process, would be a particularly useful method for generating broad input on fair use regulations.[18]

As with other agency regulations, AFU's fair use regulations would have the force of law. Uses of copyrighted materials in accordance with AFU's regulations therefore would be fair use and non-infringing.[19] Conversely, use of materials in ways that AFU's rules do not permit would not be fair use. In accordance with the provisions of the Administrative Procedure Act, judicial review of AFU's regulations would be limited.[20]

In addition to issuing fair use regulations, AFU could bring actions through the adjudicative mechanisms already provided for in the Administrative Procedure Act to enforce the prohibition on interfering with fair use.[21] In the case of a possible violation of the law, AFU would issue a complaint setting forth its charges. The respondent could settle with AFU or contest the charges and proceed to adjudication before an administrative law judge. That judge would issue an initial decision setting forth findings of fact and conclusions of law and the disposition of the case. The administrative law judge could decide in favor of the respondent and dismiss the case or, upon finding that the respondent violated the statute, assess civil penalties, issue an order to cease and desist, or impose other appropriate remedies. The administrative law judge's initial decision would be subject to review within the agency, which would enter a final decision and order. AFU's final orders would be reviewable in the U.S. Court of Appeals. Violations of AFU's final orders would also be subject to separate civil penalties through a suit in federal district court to enforce the agency's order. Once AFU has determined in a litigated administrative adjudicatory proceeding that a practice constitutes an unlawful interference with fair use and has issued a final cease-and-desist order, it would be able to obtain civil penalties from other parties who thereafter violate the standards articulated by AFU. AFU could also be empowered with authority similar to that of the Federal Trade Commission[22] to challenge a practice directly in court without first making a final agency determination that the challenged conduct is unlawful.

Under Model 1, defendants in copyright infringement actions could assert fair use as a defense. In determining whether a particular use is fair and therefore renders the defendant's copying non-infringing, courts would defer to AFU's regulations. Given that those regulations would define fair use with considerable specificity, in most instances it should be clear whether a use is fair well before the defendant's appearance before a judge.

Administrative law experts will recognize that giving AFU power to enforce a prohibition on interfering with fair use may be essential in order for courts to defer to AFU's regulations on what fair use permits. The Supreme Court has indicated that deference is inappropriate when a statute is administered by the courts rather than by the agency itself.[23] It is therefore unlikely that courts would accept an agency's understanding of fair use law if the agency's sole function were to issue interpretive regulations. By contrast, giving AFU enforcement power makes judicial deference on the meaning of fair use appropriate.

Model 2: The Copyright Infringement Review Office. Under Model 2, Congress would give a federal agency more general responsibility in copyright infringement claims. Let us call this agency Copyright Infringement Review Office (CIRO). Like AFU in Model 1, CIRO would have power to issue regulations defining fair use, which would remain a defense to a claim of copyright infringement. CIRO also would have adjudicative authority. A copyright owner alleging infringement would be required to file, prior to going to court, a complaint with CIRO. The respondent then would be given an opportunity to assert a fair use defense. If within some designated time period the respondent failed to assert a fair use defense, the copyright owner would be entitled to proceed with the copyright infringement claim in federal court, where the respondent would be deemed to have waived a fair use defense.[24] If, on the other hand, the respondent asserts a fair use defense, CIRO would conduct an investigation to determine if the allegedly infringing use is a fair use under CIRO's fair use regulations. If CIRO concludes that the use is fair and there was no infringement, it would issue a notice to this effect. The copyright owner then would have a period of time in which to file a lawsuit. If CIRO concludes that no fair use defense is available and therefore the respondent's copying is likely infringing, it could attempt a settlement between the parties or issue a notice authorizing the copyright owner to bring a lawsuit within a designated period of time. In deciding the copyright infringement action, courts would defer to the agency's decision as to whether under the Copyright Act and agency regulations the use at issue is a fair use.

There are existing models for this form of streamlined dispute resolution. The U.S. Equal Employment Opportunity Commission (EEOC) enforces federal laws prohibiting employment discrimination through a charge-processing procedure. Under this procedure, an individual who believes he or she is a victim of employment discrimination files a charge with the EEOC, which then conducts an investigation. The EEOC may dismiss the charge and issue the complaining party a notice to that effect; the complaining party then has ninety days in which to file a lawsuit. If the EEOC determines that discrimination did occur, it will attempt conciliation with the employer to develop a remedy. If conciliation is unsuccessful, the EEOC may bring a lawsuit or close the case and give the employee ninety days to bring suit. In a different context, the Internet Corporation for Assigned Names and Numbers, a nonprofit organization, has established the Uniform Domain-Name Dispute-Resolution Policy to resolve Internet domain name registration disputes.[25] A registrant seeking to register a domain name must represent that the name does not infringe any third party's rights and agree to participate in a mandatory administrative proceedings should a third party assert a claim. Administrative panels formed by approved dispute resolution providers conduct these proceedings. Administrative panels have authority to cancel a domain name registration (or transfer it) if the complainant demonstrates that the registrant's domain name is identical or confusingly similar to a trademark or service mark in which the complainant has rights; the registrant has no rights or legitimate interests in the domain name; and the domain name has been registered and is being used in bad faith, determined through a multifactor test. Although these procedures do not preclude subsequent litigation, they provide a streamlined process for resolving domain name disputes.

Fair Use Regulations

Under both Model 1 and Model 2 an agency would be empowered to issue regulations governing fair use. Although it is not my purpose to set out the specific fair use regulations that such an agency should adopt, it is useful to consider the general form such regulations would take. In the classic formulation, legal directives fall somewhere on a continuum between rules at one end and standards at the other. A rule provides clarity, but it is also rigid; a standard allows for flexibility, but because it depends upon judgment calls, its application also can be unpredictable. An agency would not be able to decide where along this continuum it should situate its fair use regulations until it received input from experts, interested parties, and members of the public. This decision also would probably depend on the types of creative works at issue.

In some cases, when precision is more important than flexibility, a strong rules-based approach—such as numerical limitations on the amount of copying allowed—might be appropriate. In other instances, the agency might conclude that it is too difficult or undesirable to adopt numerical limits or other rules, and that an approach grounded in standards better reflects and protects fair use. Dissatisfaction with the quantitative approach of preexisting guidelines, such as the Classroom Guidelines, discussed in Chapter 2, should not lead one to think that an agency empowered to make legally binding regulations should avoid precision. Likewise, the current shortcomings of the four statutory fair use standards do not indicate that all standards-based approaches should be off the table. Past experiences should inform the process but not limit its options.[26]

That said, the agency should ensure that it does not produce regulations that are so complex that only experts can decipher and apply them. Right now fair use is too vague to guide behavior. The agency needs to be careful that it does not produce the opposite problem by requiring users to work through a thicket of confusing regulations before they can decide whether to make use of a copyrighted work. An open process in which non-experts have an opportunity to play a role in the development of regulations is essential for guarding against this risk.

The agency (or Congress, in empowering the agency) likewise would need to consider how its own regulations would relate to or be informed by past judicial decisions on the meaning of fair use. At a minimum, it would be wise for the agency to take account of how courts have decided fair use issues in cases before them. By examining these cases, the agency could better identify and prepare regulations for the most common disputes that arise under fair use law. In addition, in crafting its own regulations, the agency would benefit from understanding how judges have interpreted and applied the fair use provision of the Copyright Act. On the basis of a close reading of approximately three hundred fair use cases, Pamela Samuelson reports that the cases fall into common patterns or policy-relevant clusters—such as educational uses, news reporting, and parody—and that within such clusters there is a degree of coherence among the cases.[27] She argues that identifying which cluster a case falls into is a helpful tool for determining whether a proposed use would be fair—beyond simply applying the statutory fair use factors.[28] Although Samuelson's target audience is judges (and commentators), her recommendation to "look . . . for common patterns in the fair use case law upon which to build a more predictable body of fair use law" should be useful to the agency as it develops fair use regulations.[29] Nonetheless, it would be undesirable for the agency to be bound by the courts' applications of the fair use provision of the Copyright Act in past cases. The agency would need to be free to develop regulations for future uses that reflect the interests of relevant parties and of the general public. Requiring the agency to adhere to past judicial decisions reached in specific disputes would interfere with this task.

The Benefits of Agency Administration

Agency administration of fair use would offer significant benefits. An agency, which has the flexibility to adopt regulations quickly, is in a better position than Congress to specify the details of uses that are fair, to revise and update its regulations when necessary, and to issue new regulations as industries or technologies evolve, new practices emerge, different uses become prevalent, or new concerns take hold. An agency also has distinct advantages over courts. When courts are responsible for applying fair use, it is hard to predict in advance of a judge's ruling whether a proposed use of a copyrighted work is indeed fair. Fair use regulations issued by an agency would provide predictability at the outset. Individuals would be able to consult the regulations and determine in advance whether a proposed use of a copyrighted work is fair. Accordingly, the risk of litigation would vastly diminish; the current gap between what fair use law allows and what industry norms dictate would close.

Further, an administrative agency could generate fair use regulations that are tailored to individual sectors and contexts but still reflect a uniform body of law. Among other things, an agency would be able to take account of practices and interests in specific industries, assess the economic impact on copyright owners of allowing particular uses as fair, and hear from creators about their needs and interests. An agency could track the success and failings of regulations in one sector in order to inform decisions about regulating in another. Similarly, an agency would be in a strong position to examine broadly the purposes of fair use. Commentators have offered thoughtful proposals for how each of the four fair use factors should be implemented, including ways that protect First Amendment interests,[30] recognize social and cultural practices,[31] and take account of other public interests. An agency could take account of these kinds of concerns in developing its regulations.

Fair use regulations issued by an agency would provide certainty to a large number of users at once. An agency, therefore, offers an advantage over the non-judicial entities other commentators have proposed to make fair use determinations. Michael Carroll has suggested that Congress amend the Copyright Act to create a Fair Use Board within the Copyright Office with power to declare a proposed use of a copyrighted work to be a fair use.[32] Similar to a private letter ruling from the IRS or a no-action letter from the SEC, a favorable opinion from the Fair Use Board would immunize the petitioner from copyright liability for the proposed use. Under Carroll's approach, the copyright owner would receive notice and an opportunity to challenge the petition. Because a favorable ruling by the Fair Use Board would apply only to the party bringing the petition, the copyright owner would remain free to challenge the same or similar uses by other parties. David Nimmer would have Congress authorize a fair use arbitration system.[33] Under Nimmer's approach, the Register of Copyrights would compile a list of qualified arbiters. A user of copyrighted material who is unable to negotiate a license agreement with the copyright owner would be permitted to institute a fair use arbitration, and the copyright owner would have an opportunity to respond. Both parties would be allowed to object to a certain percentage of the available arbiters. The case would be heard before one arbiter to whom neither party objected or, if the case is identified by the parties as a complex matter, before three arbiters to whom neither party objected. The arbiter or arbiters would issue a ruling on whether the use is fair, along with reasons for the decision.

However, neither Carroll's nor Nimmer's model entirely escapes the litigation model of fair use. Under Carroll's approach, the Fair Use Board's rulings would be subject to administrative review in the Copyright Office and to de novo review by the federal courts of appeals. While judicial review would allow the potential user to know in advance whether the proposed use is fair (rather than after making the use and being sued for it), it is likely to slow down fair use determinations and make them expensive. Under Nimmer's approach, the arbiter's ruling would not be binding on a court in an infringement action but would be relevant to the court's determination of damages and attorneys' fees. More generally, although there is much to commend in allowing parties to obtain a determination prior to infringement litigation as to whether a use is fair, both proposals fall short in that they would provide certainty only to the individual user who goes through Carroll's Fair Use Board or Nimmer's arbitration, and the certainty is only with respect to the particular use that is reviewed. Other potential users would not know whether *their* uses are fair use unless they too go through the process. Certainty on a large scale would therefore be impossible. Millions of uses of copyrighted works occur annually. Even if a small portion of these uses were the subject of requests for individual review, they would quickly overwhelm the capacities of the board or the arbiters. Regulations issued by an administrative agency, by contrast, work wholesale. They would apply to all users, giving them virtual certainty as to whether their uses are fair, without the need for individualized adjudication.

Agency regulation is also preferable to relying on contracts and the market to determine which uses of copyrighted works are permissible. As we saw in Chapter 5, the current vagueness of the fair use law allows copyright owners to use contracts to limit fair use. By providing precision, agency regulation would promote uses of copyrighted works that do not require advanced approval by and payment to a copyright owner. Many contracts are highly restrictive. Agency regulation would allow uses beyond those a copyright owner would normally permit. Contracts also allow copyright owners to prevent criticism and stifle other forms of speech they do not favor. Agency regulation would better serve the First Amendment interests that fair use protects. Further, reliance upon contracts means that permissible uses may vary. Different copyright owners have different rules about how their works may be used; contract law is state law, and so the enforceability and interpretation of contractual provisions vary among states. Agency regulation can restore uniformity to fair use.

Preventing New Forms of Overreaching

As we have seen throughout this book, content providers have been highly creative in finding ways to strengthen and protect their own interests. Agency regulation of fair use will succeed only if there are mechanisms to prevent new forms of overreaching that may emerge once the agency takes charge. Each of the two models I have proposed contains some built-in safeguards against this risk.

Model 1 provides for affirmative protections for fair uses of copyrighted works. Recognizing that agency-issued rules are only effective if people abide by them, Model 1 addresses two potential sources of non-compliance. First, copyright owners might continue to assert a more restrictive version of fair use than the law in fact provides—now in the form of agency regulation—and threaten copyright infringement actions against users who comply with the applicable fair use rules. Although clarity in fair use will reduce the likelihood of this problem, there nonetheless remains a risk that copyright owners will continue to interfere with fair use of copyrighted works. Under Model 1, AFU therefore would be empowered to respond to efforts by copyright owners to interfere with fair uses of copyrighted works. Second, fair use regulations will lose their enforcement power if copyright owners continue to condition access to copyrighted works on agreements to forgo fair uses of those works. Having clear fair use rules is meaningless if fair use has been waived. Under Model 1, federal law would therefore preempt state contract law permitting copyright owners and consumers of copyrighted works to contract out of fair use. Agreements in which a consumer gives up a fair use claim or accepts a definition of fair use that is more restrictive than that provided by federal law (including agency regulations) would become unenforceable.

Model 2 reflects the recognition that even when regulations clarify uses that are fair, some disputes over fair use will still occur. Therefore, in addition to issuing regulations, the agency would be empowered to determine fair uses in the first instance in specific cases. In any subsequent lawsuit, the court would defer to those determinations. While this procedure would not prevent copyright owners from bringing infringement lawsuits in federal court even when the use is fair according to the agency's judgment, the procedure would be likely to deter virtually all claims in which the defendant has made use of a work in accordance with the agency's fair use regulations. Under Model 2, a regulation on point combined with agency power to issue a decision in a specific case will shield most fair uses from litigation.

ADDITIONAL FAIR USE PROTECTIONS

Agency administration potentially is fair use law's best partner. By addressing the factors that allow copyright owners to interfere with fair use, an agency can protect the ability of individuals to make fair use of copyrighted works. By anticipating new forms of overreaching, an agency can defend fair use from future threats. Empowering an administrative agency is the best choice for defending fair use. However, Congress might not, of course, take up the proposal I have offered. Three additional ways in which fair use can be protected therefore merit discussion. The first involves a change to how damages are awarded in copyright infringement cases in order to reduce significantly the risk that those who make fair use of copyrighted works will be sued. The second invites state government agencies to challenge interference with fair use. The third involves privately developed fair use guidelines, advance screening and certification by lawyers of proposed uses, and insurance in the event of an infringement lawsuit.

Limiting Statutory Damages to Commercial Infringement

A simple change to how damages are awarded in copyright infringement cases could significantly protect fair use. Section 504 of the Copyright Act gives copyright owners a choice as to the damages they may recover from infringers. The copyright owner is entitled to elect actual damages suffered as a result of the infringement along with any profits earned by the infringer. Alternatively, the copyright owner may opt for statutory damages—an amount provided for by Congress that does not require the copyright owner to demonstrate the size of the injury he or she has suffered or of the gain to the infringer. Under section 504, a court may impose statutory damages ranging from $750 to $30,000 per infringed work ($750 to $150,000 per work in the case of willful infringement). Applying this provision in 2009 in a case involving illegal sharing of thirty copyrighted songs on the peer-to-peer network Kazaa, a Boston jury imposed damages against defendant Joel Tenenbaum, a graduate student, in the amount of $22,500 per song for a total of $675,000.[34]

The reason for statutory damages is the fact that a plaintiff's injuries can be difficult to calculate. In copyright cases, the value of a copyright can be hard to assess, and so figuring out the exact harm caused by infringement can be problematic. Requiring proof of actual injury before a monetary award may be issued puts the copyright owner at a disadvantage. The legislative history of the Copyright Act demonstrates that members of Congress had this concern in mind when they made statutory damages available in copyright cases. Statutory damages ensure the copyright owner a recovery in the case of infringement.

The problem with section 504 is that, aside from different ranges for willful and nonwillful infringement, it does not draw distinctions among different kinds of infringement. In particular, section 504 draws no distinction between infringement of a copyrighted work for personal use and infringement for commercial use: both are subject to statutory damages of up to $30,000 per work or $150,000 in the case of willful infringement. Yet these two types of infringement are likely to have very different impacts on the plaintiff's bottom line. The actual loss to the copyright owner from infringement for personal use is typically very low compared to infringement on a commercial scale. Indeed, without the availability of statutory damages (and on the scale available under section 504), copyright owners would not bring many infringement claims against noncommercial infringers because the amount they could recover would be very small. Statutory damages are meant to approximate actual losses by the plaintiff or gains by the defendant. However, by failing to distinguish among different kinds of infringement, section 504 can allow a copyright owner to recover, particularly in noncommercial cases, an amount that far exceeds the injuries to the copyright owner or profit by the defendant. To be sure, a court is able to award statutory damages at the low end of section 504's stated range. But in every case a defendant faces the risk of an award at the top of the range. Under these circumstances, it is easy to see why the threat of an infringement lawsuit is so powerful.

Congress should amend section 504 to provide for separate statutory damages for commercial and noncommercial infringement. Statutory damages available for noncommercial infringement should be substantially lower than those available for commercial infringement—perhaps by a ratio of 1 to 10. Reducing statutory damages for noncommercial infringement would go a long way in facilitating fair use by users who are willing to assume some risk of liability. Copyright owners would still be able to bring an infringement claim. They could elect actual damages when noncommercial use causes injury that exceeds the amount provided for by statute, and they could still obtain a court order prohibiting the defendant from future acts of infringement. What copyright owners could not do is threaten to sue for an amount that is many multiples of any actual harm to them or benefit to the user. Statutory damages also serve a deterrent effect. I will think twice about infringing a work, even for my own use, if I know that under section 504 I will be on the hook for $150,000. The problem today is that statutory damages over-deter. Once we factor in the expense, hassle, and embarrassment of litigation, reduced statutory damages in noncommercial cases will still provide sufficient deterrence to would-be infringers while liberating many forms of fair use.

Fair Use and the Sword of State Sovereign Immunity

So far, we have considered ways in which the federal government can defend fair use. This should not lead us to underestimate the role state government can play. State government is in a unique position to challenge overreaching. The Supreme Court has interpreted the Eleventh Amendment to the U.S. Constitution to give states, as sovereign entities, broad immunity from lawsuits for money damages.[35] A nonconsenting state is immune from such suits in federal court brought by its own citizens, the citizens of another state, or citizens of foreign countries. Sovereign immunity also prohibits suits for money damages against state government in state court under federal law. The Supreme Court has held that Congress can abrogate a state's sovereign immunity and permit suits against the state, but only in limited circumstances. In particular, Congress may not abrogate state sovereign immunity when it is legislating pursuant to its powers under Article I of the Constitution.[36] Congress may abrogate state sovereign immunity under its authority to enforce the provisions of the Fourteenth Amendment,[37] which, among other things, prohibits a state from "depriv[ing] any person of life, liberty, or property, without due process of law" and from "deny[ing] any person within its jurisdiction the equal protection of the laws."[38] However, a separate line of case law holds that Congress's power under the Fourteenth Amendment is itself limited. Congress may only enact laws pursuant to this power that are "congruent" and "proportional" to remedying or preventing violations of rights that have been recognized by the Court.[39]

Important for our purposes is state sovereign immunity's ability to shield a state from claims that it has violated intellectual property rights. In 1999 in *Florida Prepaid Postsecondary Education Expense Board v. College Savings Bank*, the Supreme Court held that Congress could not abrogate state sovereign immunity and subject a state to a lawsuit for money damages under federal patent law.[40] In that case, the

College Savings Bank, a New Jersey company, had patented a system for students to save money for college. When Florida Prepaid Postsecondary Education Expense Board, an agency of the Florida government, copied the system for use by Florida residents, College Savings Bank sued for patent infringement.

In 1992, Congress had amended the Patent Act to abrogate state sovereign immunity to authorize suits for money damages against state governments for patent infringement. However, in *Florida Prepaid* the Supreme Court held that this amendment was invalid as beyond Congress's authority. Congress could not rely upon its power, in Article I of the Constitution, to pass laws protecting patents because Article I is not a proper basis for abrogating state sovereign immunity. The Court also rejected the government's argument that the 1992 amendment to the Patent Act could be justified as an exercise of Congress's power to enforce the Fourteenth Amendment. While patents are property under the Fourteenth Amendment, the Court reasoned that authorizing suits against state government was not congruent and proportional to any constitutional violation by state government. In enacting the amendment, "Congress identified no pattern of patent infringement by the States, let alone a pattern of constitutional violations" to justify the heavy-handed measure of overriding a state's sovereign immunity.[41] The College Savings Bank therefore could not sue Florida Prepaid for damages for violating its patent.[42]

This brings us to copyright. In section 511 of the Copyright Act, Congress has abrogated state sovereign immunity for copyright violations to make states liable for monetary damages in the same way as any other party that has infringed a copyright.[43] The Supreme Court has not ruled on whether this abrogation of state sovereign immunity is valid. However, the Court's decision in *Florida Prepaid* strongly suggests that it is not. It would be hard to justify this provision of the Copyright Act as congruent and proportional to violations of constitutional rights by state government and thereby a valid exercise of Congress's power under the Fourteenth Amendment. Relying upon *Florida Prepaid*, lower federal courts have therefore held that the abrogation of state sovereign immunity for copyright claims is invalid.[44]

While Eleventh Amendment immunity is generally thought of as a shield protecting the state from a lawsuit, we should view it also as a sword. As we have seen, the threat of liability for infringement leads potential users of copyrighted works to obtain licenses unnecessarily and to refrain from making fair use of copyrighted works. Eleventh Amendment immunity removes the strength of that threat with respect to state government. Agencies of state government should rely upon Eleventh Amendment immunity to fight back against overreaching copyright claims.

In particular, state universities should make aggressive use of the fair use provision of the Copyright Act.[45] In many circumstances, employees of state universities need to use copyrighted works: in their own publications, in the classroom, and in course packets for students. Instead of paying to obtain a license, state universities with a reasonable argument that fair use applies should invoke the fair use doctrine and take comfort that the Eleventh Amendment will protect them from litigation. Other state agencies, such as libraries, archives, and even government offices, should also use Eleventh Amendment immunity as a sword.

The benefits of the sword of state sovereign immunity are likely to extend beyond state government itself. State agencies can undercut the licensing culture. Their reliance upon fair use might embolden other actors also to rely more aggressively on fair use. In addition, if state agencies do not obtain licenses before using copyrighted content, courts might be less inclined to view the existence of a licensing market as a factor weighing against fair use in cases involving other defendants.

One state has shown a willingness to stand up to what it views as improper behavior by copyright owners. In the past few years, the Recording Industry Association of America (RIAA) has subpoenaed

Internet service providers to provide names of users who, it believes, have unlawfully shared copyrighted music. The RIAA has sent many such subpoenas to universities to identify students engaged in allegedly unlawful activity. The RIAA has also enlisted universities to deliver letters offering settlements in the range of $3,000 to students who pay immediately by credit card. Many universities have complied with these subpoenas and requests, and the RIAA has settled with thousands of individual users.

However, in September 2007, when the RIAA subpoenaed the University of Oregon, the Oregon attorney general moved to quash the subpoena. Among other things, the attorney general argued that the subpoena imposed an undue burden because the university could not determine the identity of the students who had allegedly infringed copyrights without conducting investigations, and that the RIAA was seeking disclosure of information that the university was required to keep confidential under state and federal student privacy laws.[46] Other states should follow Oregon's example and stand up for fair use.

While the sword of state sovereign immunity can be a useful tool, some limitations bear mentioning. The Eleventh Amendment does not bar suits against state officers for injunctive relief.[47] A copyright owner therefore can sue a state official to stop future acts of copyright infringement. Yet state agencies should welcome such suits. If the only risk to the state is enjoinment, such cases present an ideal opportunity for the state agency to rebut in court overreaching copyright claims and to strengthen fair use law. However, the Eleventh Amendment does not protect cities, so they cannot take advantage of the approach suggested here. The Eleventh Amendment also does not protect a state against suits brought by other states or by the federal government. A state can therefore be held liable if it infringes copyrights held by a state government or the federal government. Such instances will probably be rare but they might arise. Although federal government works are in the public domain, state government works are protected by copyright.

Federal and state agencies also own copyrights that have passed to them, for example, by gifts to government archives.

Because state sovereign immunity is designed to shield state treasuries, the Eleventh Amendment does not prevent suits against state officers who are sued in their individual capacities and must pay any damages out of their own pockets. There is therefore a risk that a copyright owner may bring a claim against an individual employee of the state agency. However, government officials are shielded by the doctrine of qualified immunity, which bars lawsuits against government officers under certain circumstances.[48]

Ensuring and Insuring Fair Use: The Three-Pillar Approach

Defending fair use should not be solely the province of government. Private actors can also play an important role, as illustrated by a recent strategy to allow documentary filmmakers to rely upon fair use. In 2007, the Fair Use Project at Stanford Law School, intellectual property attorney Michael Donaldson, and insurance company Media/Professional initiated a program to facilitate fair use of copyrighted works by filmmakers. This program builds upon the *Documentary Filmmakers' Statement of Best Practices in Fair Use,* which was developed in 2005 by a consortium of organizations representing documentary filmmakers and the Center for Social Media at American University. The *Statement of Best Practices* sets out what "documentary filmmakers currently regard as a reasonable application of the copyright 'fair use' doctrine."[49] It identifies four classes or types of uses of copyrighted materials that documentary filmmakers commonly wish to make, and, with respect to each class, describes how fair use law applies and applicable limitations. To give effect to these standards, Stanford's Fair Use Project provides free legal services to filmmakers whose films comply with the *Statement of Best Practices.* Lawyers review the film before it is released and, if it meets the applicable standards, are available to defend the filmmaker against subsequent copyright infringement claims. In turn, Media/Professional provides insurance coverage in the event the filmmaker is later found liable. The cost of the fair use insurance coverage ranges from $200 to $2,000, an amount that adds 10 percent to the price of a typical errors-and-omissions policy.

This three-pillar approach—rules, insurance, and legal counsel—has some obvious benefits. The *Statement of Best Practices* was developed by entities with an interest in protecting fair use and allowing filmmakers to be able to make fair use of copyrighted works with confidence that such uses are lawful. The insurance company also has a reliable basis on which to provide coverage and so can adopt a less cautious approach to fair use than it otherwise might. The availability of legal counsel promotes compliance with the law at the outset and allows uses of copyrighted works without fear of the costs of litigation.

These mechanisms have had notable success. Filmmakers who have incorporated copyrighted materials into their films have relied upon the *Statement of Best Practices* to satisfy distributors and broadcasters that these uses are lawful and to avoid hefty licensing fees.[50] Public television and cable companies have also incorporated the statement as part of their business practices.[51] In an interview, filmmaker Gordon Quinn reported that as a result of the *Statement of Best Practices*, "we have really won our rights back."[52] The solution is not, of course, perfect. In particular, paying for insurance coverage is inconsistent with the idea that fair use is meant to be free use. Nonetheless, the costs are smaller than the alternative of obtaining a license, and the outcome preferable to not being able to make use of a copyrighted work at all.

This same approach could be extended to protect fair use in other contexts. For example, it would be possible to develop reliable fair use guidelines for music sampling; lawyers and musicologists could preview works by artists who are not supported by major labels, and insurers could provide coverage for approved recordings. Law school students could lend significant support in such endeavors by reviewing whether a proposed use of a copyrighted work is fair and defending subsequent claims of infringement. In every law school there are large numbers of students who are interested in intellectual property law, as well as clinical programs in which students do pro bono work on behalf of clients (for example, helping convicted criminal defendants prepare appellate briefs, assisting abused spouses by preparing restraining orders, and helping undocumented immigrants with asylum claims) and in the process acquire practical skills and receive academic credit for their work. A few law schools, including Brooklyn Law School, where I teach, have created clinics that handle intellectual property matters, again typically for clients who cannot afford to hire lawyers. Other law schools could create IP clinics in which students provide support to authors and other creators who seek to make fair use of copyrighted works.

FROM USERS TO GATEKEEPERS

Defending fair use requires more than giving creators the tools to make use of copyrighted works. It also depends upon persuading publishers, distributors, and other gatekeepers that they need not insist that every use of copyrighted material be licensed. The proposals set out in this chapter for defending fair use would go a long way in achieving that goal. In particular, agency administration would bring clarity to fair use. Gatekeepers would therefore know in advance how copyrighted works may be used without risking a lawsuit. Likewise, removing the risk of statutory damages would shield fair use in noncommercial works from litigation. As the experience with documentary films shows, collaboration between insurers and lawyers based on well-defined fair use rules can eliminate additional hurdles. Finally, by standing up for fair use, state agencies can alter industry norms that require permission and payment. In each of these ways, creators and gatekeepers alike can rely upon fair use in the way the Copyright Act intends.

In the next chapter, we turn from defending limitations on intellectual property rights to protecting, affirmatively, the public domain.

CHAPTER 10

PUTTING INTELLECTUAL
PROPERTY IN ITS PLACE

I N 1947, when the Marx Brothers were about to begin
production of *A Night in Casablanca,* Warner Brothers
threatened to sue them if they did not change the movie's title. Warner
Brothers said the title infringed their own rights in the 1942 hit *Casablanca* starring Humphrey Bogart and Ingrid Bergman. Groucho Marx
sent Warner Brothers a letter that began,

Dear Warner Brothers,
   Apparently there is more than one way of conquering a city and holding
it as your own. For example, up to the time that we contemplated making
this picture, I had no idea that the city of Casablanca belonged exclusively to
Warner Brothers. However, it was only a few days after our announcement
appeared that we received your long, ominous legal document warning us not
to use the name Casablanca.
   It seems that in 1471, Ferdinand Balboa Warner, your great-great-
grandfather, while looking for a shortcut to the city of Burbank, had stumbled
on the shores of Africa and, raising his alpenstock (which he later turned in
for a hundred shares of common), named it Casablanca.
   I just don't understand your attitude. Even if you plan on re-releasing
your picture, I am sure that the average movie fan could learn in time to

distinguish between Ingrid Bergman and Harpo. I don't know whether I could, but I certainly would like to try.

You claim that you own Casablanca and that no one else can use that name without permission. What about "Warner Brothers"? Do you own that too? You probably have the right to use the name Warner, but what about the name Brothers? Professionally, we were brothers long before you were.[1]

Groucho Marx had it right. Intellectual property needs to be put in its place. This requires more than simply policing the outer boundaries the law sets on intellectual property rights. We must also find ways to protect, affirmatively, the public domain.

DEFINING THE PUBLIC DOMAIN

A robust public domain requires that we do away with the current presumption, which permeates the law and the culture, that every work is protected unless proven otherwise. Copyright is a special right, a privileged exception to free communication, given for a limited time to authors and other creators in recognition of their exertions. Copyright should be treated as the exception to a general rule favoring free exchange. Authors and publishers have strong incentives to protect their own interests. A presumption against copyright will help protect the interests of the public in its domain. The Copyright Act should be modified to include a preamble stating that copyright is an exceptional privilege granted for important public reasons for a limited period. The act should make clear that the starting assumption is that works belong in the public domain, that copyright exists only when a work falls within the parameters set out by the act, and that the rights that attach are limited and circumscribed. So too the Lanham Act should specify at the outset that a trademark represents a privilege rather than an entitlement and that the accompanying rights are limited.

The public domain also deserves a physical existence. There currently exists no centralized place to go to in order to find out which works are in the public domain and available for free use, nor any accepted standard means of identifying works in the public domain as such. Congress could help secure the public domain by creating a searchable online public domain registry that lists works that can be freely used and adds new works once their copyrights expire. Just as the catalog of copyrighted works maintained by the United States Copyright Office provides information about registered copyrighted works, the public domain registry would allow members of the public to determine which works are available for use.

One easy way to generate an instant catalog of public domain works would be to require publishers, as a condition of enforcing future copyright claims, to furnish a list of all their publications that belong in part or in whole in the public domain. The public should also be encouraged to submit titles for inclusion in the registry. If it is not clear whether a work is in fact protected by copyright (a problem that arises with so-called orphan works, for which no copyright owner can be found), the registry could post the work provisionally and allow it to fall into the public domain if no copyright claim is asserted within six months or some other reasonable time period.[2]

In addition to punishing, in the ways described in Chapter 8, publishers and other content providers who attach false copyright notices to works in the public domain, Congress should create a symbol and proper form of notice to designate these works. In the same way that the Copyright Act authorizes the use of the symbol © or the word *Copyright* (or *Copr.*) for copyrighted works, a symbol such as ℗, or simply the label "Public domain," could be specified for designating such works once it has been ascertained that they do indeed belong in the public domain, perhaps followed with the statement "May be freely copied." Publishers and other content providers would be required to attach the notice to any public domain materials of which they make use. Just as © is universally recognized as designating copyright ownership, a public domain symbol would indicate public ownership.

Clearly establishing what does and does not belong in the public domain is just the first step. In the same way that Congress must create and empower a federal agency to administer fair use, as described in Chapter 9, it should likewise delegate responsibility for protecting the public domain. One possibility is to create a Public Domain Bureau within the Department of Justice. It would be charged with monitoring improper claims to ownership over public domain materials and prosecuting offenders, and would also perform a variety of other functions designed to protect a robust public domain. These might include providing guidance to schools and universities on lawful copying practices; preparing bulletins about legitimate and illegitimate forms of copying to be distributed in libraries, copy shops, and other locations; responding to e-mails and telephone calls from members of the public reporting false assertions of copyright; and conducting public relations programs to increase public awareness of copyright and accessibility of public domain works.

The federal government can also use tax laws to prevent nonprofit entities from restricting access to works in the public domain and from disseminating inaccurate information about copyright law that discourages users from making use of such works. As we have seen, many museums and archives wrongly assert copyright in works in their collections, limit fair uses of copyrighted works, and use restrictive contracts. Given that these entities are publicly subsidized, Congress should require them to abandon these practices in order to maintain tax exempt status and make the Public Domain Bureau responsible for monitoring compliance with this requirement. Public schools and private schools that receive government funding should also be required to provide their students with accurate information about intellectual property law. In an age in which virtually everybody is both a consumer and a creator of content, knowing the rules of intellectual property law is nearly as important as knowing the rules of the road. Rather than leave it to interest groups to disseminate skewed information about what intellectual property law prohibits and permits, schools should provide education on the basics of intellectual property in the same way they provide training in other life skills.

THE POWER OF LIBRARIES

Libraries should be at the forefront of efforts to protect the public domain. Libraries are important repositories of public domain works, and some have generous access and copying policies. For example, the Music Department of the Free Library of Philadelphia imposes no restrictions on the ability of its patrons to make copies of public domain sheet music.[3] Seeking to deliver the public domain to the public, the Internet Archive Bookmobile travels around the country and, using a satellite, downloads and prints out public domain books for libraries, schools, and retirement homes along its route.[4] And in a welcome development in 2009, Cornell University Library, which had previously licensed digital reproductions under restrictive conditions, announced that it would no longer require its users to seek permission to publish public domain items from its collections. In announcing the change, a library spokesperson stated, "We decided it was more important to encourage the use of the public domain materials in our holdings than to impose roadblocks."[5] Private efforts of this nature represent an important form of resistance to overreaching, and they should be encouraged.

There are additional activities in which libraries can engage to promote the public domain and combat overreaching. Librarians are already organized into active associations. The largest of these organizations, the American Library Association, has more than sixty thousand members. It is active on copyright issues: its Office of Government Relations closely follows and seeks to influence government policies that affect libraries, including those on virtually every copyright issue.[6] These organizations should put the remedying of overreaching on their agendas. Publishers aggressively market their works to librarians, giving libraries enormous purchasing power. For some publishers, particularly those of specialized works, libraries are the principal customers. Librarians should use their purchasing power to counter overreaching. For example, librarians should purchase editions of public domain works that are clearly marked as such.

A reproduction of *Macbeth* that contains a proper notice specifying that the play is in the public domain should be preferred over an edition with a notice that the play may not be copied. This step would both increase access to public domain works and give publishers an incentive to mark their titles correctly.

The power of librarians to combat copyfraud and other forms of overreaching is greatly enhanced in the digital age. In many libraries, collections are increasingly in the form of electronic resources rather than physical books. Electronic resources are often very expensive; some databases run hundreds of thousands of dollars. Librarians who purchase these resources should insist that providers remain within the limits of copyright law. For example, if the provider of a database of historical newspapers attaches a false copyright notice to the pages of the newspaper, the library should insist that it be removed. If the database provider wants to prohibit all copying of materials from the database, librarians should insist upon mechanisms to protect fair use. Individual consumers might not be able to resist standard-form contracts, but organized librarians can.

There are also more mundane things librarians can do. For example, librarians can provide their visitors with accurate information about the public domain. A simple step would be for every public library to provide basic information—on a notice board, in pamphlets, or on its website—about the contours of copyright protection and the uses that validly can be made of public domain works. Libraries could also provide more specific information about particular works. For instance, works in a library collection that are clearly in the public domain could be labeled as such—say, with a green "PD" sticker on the spine. The library catalog could include, along with the usual information about authorship and publication, an annotation as to whether a work (or part of it) falls in the public domain.

ACCESSING THE PUBLIC DOMAIN

The more people know about copyright law and the easier it is to identify and locate public domain works, the greater the likelihood that we will be able to return copyright to its proper bounds. Government can further reduce the problem of overreaching by making public domain works easily accessible. Indeed, federal governmental agencies already do a great deal to allow members of the public to see and even obtain copies of many government-owned works. For example, the American Memory project (http://memory.loc.gov), operated by the Library of Congress, offers online access to a huge collection of historical materials.[7] State governments and their agencies also provide access to many public domain works. For example, the California Sheet Music Project at the University of California at Berkeley offers public domain sheet music online.[8] This approach should be expanded upon to make even more public domain works easily accessible through the Internet and other sources. The actual work does not have to be carried out by the government. For example, the federal government, through the National Endowment for the Humanities, currently provides funding to a variety of libraries, archives, and other entities to digitize public domain works, including historical newspapers, presidential papers, the writings of Frederick Douglass and Henry David Thoreau, and historical maps.[9]

Government should also support and encourage the efforts of private entities and individuals to counteract copyright overreaching by increasing information about and access to the public domain. For example, Congress could easily and cheaply enact a program making available public domain development grants to support such endeavors. Numerous privately operated websites provide general information about the limits of copyright law and support for protecting the public domain in order to facilitate permissible reproduction and use,[10] while others collect and make available free of charge public domain books and other works. The Avalon Project at Yale Law School (http://avalon.law.yale. edu) makes available the text of historical legal documents. Public domain books are available at Project Gutenberg (http://www.gutenberg.org), the University of Pennsylvania's Online Books Page (http://onlinebooks. library.upenn.edu), and the Universal Digital Library (http://www. ulib.org). Images are available at Public Domain Pictures (http://www. publicdomainpictures.net) and PD Photo (http://www.pdphoto.org). The Incredible Art Department (http://www.incredibleart.org) has links to public domain images of artworks, while the Mutopia Project (http:// www.mutopiaproject.org) offers classical and contemporary music scores. A variety of websites, including Download.com, provide access to public domain computer software. Some sites rely on volunteers to identify appropriate works for inclusion and create electronic versions of them. Project Gutenberg, for example, offers over thirty-two thousand e-books ranging from Victor Hugo's *Les Misérables* to various editions of the Bible, all prepared, proofread, and distributed by thousands of volunteers.

A VIRTUAL LIBRARY FOR THE DIGITAL AGE: BENEFITS AND RISKS

Digitization of public domain works should be encouraged. At the same time, we should ensure that efforts to increase access to the public domain do not lead to new forms of ownership and control. Such oversight is particularly important with respect to large-scale digitization projects such as that undertaken by Google. In 2002, Google began its Library Project, a plan to scan and index millions of books from the collections of university and civic libraries. The books in that project, many of which are out of print, include both public domain works and works that are copyrighted; most of the copyrighted books are orphan works. Members of the public can, at no cost, use Google's search engine to search for and access books that have been scanned. Public domain books can be browsed online at Google Books (originally called Google

Print) or downloaded in their entirety as PDFs, and passages varying in length from copyrighted books can be read online. Through a separate Google project, the Partner Program, in-print copyrighted books that Google receives from publishers are scanned and indexed, and each publisher determines how much of a book the public can access on Google Books.

In 2005, the Authors Guild (an organization that represents writers) and the Association of American Publishers sued Google on the grounds that, by scanning copyrighted books without permission and then displaying portions of those books online, Google was infringing the copyrights in the books. Google contended that its activities constituted permissible fair use. Nonetheless, in October 2008, Google and the plaintiffs agreed upon a proposed settlement.[11] Under the terms of the settlement (which requires approval by the federal district court overseeing the case), Google will pay $45 million to compensate the owners of copyrights that have allegedly been infringed. Google will also spend $30 million to create a Book Rights Registry, which will collect and distribute to copyright owners a portion of Google Books' revenues generated from advertising accompanying the online books, referral links to booksellers, and the sale of individual and institutional subscriptions that will provide access to the full texts of copyrighted works. In return, Google will be released from liability for copyright infringement. Google will also be able to display up to 20 percent of a copyrighted book to users without a subscription. Importantly, the lawsuit that led to this settlement agreement is a class action that represents *all* owners of registered copyrights in books, including foreign authors and publishers who have registered works in the United States. The settlement therefore binds all these copyright owners (unless they individually opt out). It does not, however, bind future authors.

Google's efforts in digitizing public domain books are cause for celebration. By making available the full text of books that are no longer copyrighted and creating new mechanisms for searching through these texts online, Google's Library Project not only provides access to the public domain but also gives us tools to make use of public domain works in unprecedented ways. The project opens up new avenues for research and puts a vast collection of knowledge at our fingertips. Nonetheless, caution is warranted. Given that no other company or organization has the resources and incentive to replicate Google's Library Project, for the foreseeable future Google will be the principal online repository of public domain books. Google will also generate advertising fees and other revenues from making these public domain works available. Accordingly, the public should insist that Google take concrete steps to ensure that public domain books really are available for public use and are accurately marked as such.

To do this, Google must provide accurate copyright and publication information for digitized books. Currently, when a public domain book is downloaded as a PDF file, Google attaches a notice that reads in part, "This is a digital copy of a book that was preserved for generations on library shelves before it was carefully scanned by Google as part of a project to make the world's books discoverable online. It has survived long enough for the copyright to expire and the book to enter the public domain. A public domain book is one that was never subject to copyright or whose legal copyright term has expired." This is a good start. But overall, the copyright information that Google Books provides is far from perfect. Google does not display the public domain notice when a work is viewed online rather than downloaded. In designating works as in the public domain, Google relies upon the publisher's own designation along with the date of publication. This means that Google replicates any phony or overreaching copyright notices that publishers attach to modern books. (It also means that if the publisher says a book is still copyrighted, the book is not part of Google's public domain collection.) What is worse, Google exacerbates the effects of improper copyright notices. As part of the digitization process, Google inserts its own watermark that reads, "Copyrighted material," on each page of works it treats as copyrighted. Because Google defers to a publisher's copyright claim, this watermark appears on every page of some works that are in the public domain. For example, a variety of editions of *The Federalist* show the words of Hamilton, Madison, and Jay with this watermark at the bottom of each page. While it is unlikely that Google means to defraud anybody, its unrestrained use of the "Copyrighted material" watermark ends up being even more misleading than a single copyright notice appearing at the beginning of the printed version of the book.

Google Books also contains a plethora of misdated books, thus compounding problems concerning the provision of accurate information regarding copyright status. According to Google Books, for example, the Bantam mass-market paperback edition of Tom Wolfe's 1987 novel *The Bonfire of the Vanities* was published in 1888.[12] In addition, a search for books published in 1899 turns up a multitude of books that were not published in that year: Google evidently inserts 1899 whenever it cannot easily determine the true year of publication. If the books marked in this way really were all published in 1899, they would no longer be copyrighted, but Google makes many of them available only in snippet view. Getting the date of publication correct should be a high priority because it is essential to determining whether a work is in the public domain or not.

The public should insist that Google accurately and consistently designate public domain works as such. Google should remove from the books it has already digitized incorrect copyright watermarks, and it should avoid making such errors going forward. Furthermore, the public domain notice that currently appears when a book is downloaded should also be displayed when the works is viewed online. Google should also attach a clearly visible "Public domain" watermark to every page of both online and downloaded versions of public domain works.

Beyond ensuring that any copyright and publication information that it itself provides is accurate, Google is in a good position to correct false claims of copyright by book publishers. In digitizing books, it can strip copyright notices from works that are not copyrighted and display those books in full. With respect to books that contain public domain material and copyrighted material, Google can include a notice to that effect, and during scanning it can accurately mark as such public domain portions of books that also contain copyrighted material. Google also should insist that publishers providing books for inclusion in the subscription database provide accurate copyright notices that clearly designate any public domain materials as such. Finally, Google's plans to sell subscriptions should raise some concerns among the public. Given the sheer size of the book database that Google is likely to provide, and in light of the widespread use by other content providers of contract law and technological measures to extinguish fair use and other permissible uses of copyrighted works, we should be very wary of any efforts by Google to restrict or do away with uses that copyright law permits.

LAWYERS AND THE LAW

The law can and should protect the public domain. As the law does so, it needs the cooperation of lawyers. Lawyers play a major role in many of the instances of overreaching we have encountered in this book. Lawyers craft the overreaching copyright notices that are attached to books and DVDs. They issue DMCA takedown notices that result in the disabling of non-infringing works. Lawyers insist that every music sample be cleared. They prepare contracts that restrict the uses of databases, music files, and electronic books. Lawyers threaten consequences when intellectual property law imposes none.

It is time for the legal profession to ask whether overreaching is consistent with the professional obligations of lawyers themselves.[13] Certainly, lawyers have professional obligations as zealous advocates for their clients. However, when it comes to intellectual property law, conscientious representation can easily turn into excessive lawyering.

Every state imposes on its lawyers codes of professional responsibility and disciplinary rules, typically based upon the American Bar Association's Model Rules of Professional Conduct. Lawyers may be sanctioned or disbarred for violating these rules. These provisions are implicated in at least some forms of overreaching. For example, under New York's Rules of Professional Conduct, based on the ABA model, lawyers may not "advance . . . a claim or defense that is unwarranted under existing law" or "knowingly make a false statement of fact or law."[14] Lawyers are also prohibited from threatening criminal prosecution in order to gain an advantage in a civil matter.[15]

The American Bar Association and state bar associations should consider adopting new provisions that deal directly with the problem of overreaching or consider issuing interpretations of existing rules that confront the problem. For example, bar rules should prohibit lawyers from advising clients to claim copyright in works that are in the public domain and should prohibit lawyers from sending out cease-and-desist letters that attempt to prevent fair use. Alternatively, federal law could impose duties of candor on lawyers who practice copyright law. There is a model for this. In the patent context, federal law imposes a duty of candor and good faith upon those filing and prosecuting a patent application with the United States Patent and Trademark Office. Misstatements and omissions of material fact can result in rejection of the patent application and, if the conduct was willful or negligent, the patent being unenforceable. At the same time, it would be a mistake to depend solely on rules that set outer limits of professional legal conduct. Outsiders—government officials, judges, members of the public—with a stake in protecting the balance between intellectual property rights and public interests must also scrutinize the role that lawyers play.

THE STAKE CONTENT PROVIDERS HAVE
IN THE PUBLIC DOMAIN

Content providers should look more closely at what lawyers are doing on their behalf. In many instances, overreaching might be justified by lawyers as zealous advocacy or as a by-product of otherwise good-faith conduct intended to protect the interests of the client. However, an important question when it comes to overreaching in intellectual property law is whether these activities by lawyers, whatever the short-term payoff, are truly in the long-term interests of content providers. Many content providers have not seriously asked themselves this question. Certainly, it is important to protect copyrighted works from infringement. Further, it is understandable that in the digital era, content providers are nervous. Copying is easy and copied works can instantly be shared around the world. The future of traditional industries is uncertain; the recording industry, in particular, has seen dramatic declines in revenues. When lawyers advise content providers that they need to be aggressive in asserting claims and clamp down on every unauthorized use, the advice may be hard to resist. From a long-term business perspective, however, at least some forms of overreaching are of questionable value. Many works that make use of a copyrighted work do not compete with the original. Shutting them down does not enrich the coffers of the owner of the original work. Most takedown notices do not lead to the alleged infringer paying for a license or otherwise covering the costs that go into preparing the notice. Resources spent on trolling the Internet for all unauthorized content could probably be directed to more profitable ends. Preventing educators from cuing up a segment of a DVD to show in class usually means the DVD just isn't used. Using contract law to prohibit a student from printing a page from a database does not obviously serve any long-term interest of the database provider. Getting a video removed from YouTube because it has a copyrighted soundtrack does not increase CD sales.

Content providers should recognize the stake they themselves have in an unfettered public domain. Overreaching angers and alienates customers and may undermine the intellectual property law regime on which content providers depend. Aggressive behavior by content providers has focused public attention on the scope of intellectual property rights and has produced a vocal movement for reform. Many people have come to believe that content owners do not play fair, and that if corporations do not abide by the rules, there is no reason for ordinary people to do so either. If corporations, with their teams of lawyers, cannot distinguish between what is protected and what is free for public use, the argument goes, we cannot expect teenagers with their laptops to grasp the distinction either. If permissible use varies from one product to the next, the average person cannot be expected to respect and abide by intellectual property law. If content owners want private rules to replace the law, users should have a say on what is permissible. Nobody should be surprised, therefore, when consumers fight back by flouting the law themselves. At the end of the day, protecting intellectual property requires acknowledging where private rights end and public rights begin. It is time for content providers to take careful measure of the overreaching that occurs in their names. Their creative future, like that of everyone, depends upon our ability to keep intellectual property in its place and upon a robust public domain.

AFTERWORD

COPYFRAUD and other abuses of intellectual property law now affect, on a daily basis, the way we
live, work, and express ourselves. A good many creative acts—those
long familiar to us as well as those recently made possible by advances
in technology—are impeded by overreaching.

Mariko is a professor of women's studies and film in New York. She
has been invited to deliver a public lecture as part of her university's
anniversary celebrations and has chosen as her topic the depiction of
women drivers in popular movies. Mariko plans to show the audience
a series of short movie clips during her talk. She rents DVDs and asks a
technology specialist at her university to duplicate the clips and place them
in order on a separate disk that she can then play before the audience.
The general counsel of the university gets wind of her request and tells
Mariko that in order to copy the clips, the access-control technologies
on the DVDs would need to be circumvented, which would violate the
Digital Millennium Copyright Act. Mariko is able to find most of the
clips on YouTube, but the university counsel tells her that the university
can't risk liability that might arise from her playing clips of copyrighted

movies posted on the Internet. When she gives her lecture, Mariko has to describe the scenes from the movies instead of showing them.

Beth has written a book manuscript about the history of advertising. She had planned to illustrate the book with screen shots from television ads and reproductions of print ads in order to bring to life the commentary and analysis the book provides, but her publisher has told her that she must obtain permission from the copyright holders to use the ads in her book, and that she is responsible for any associated fees. Beth has concluded that she cannot publish the book with the ads (one copyright holder has quoted a licensing fee of $10,000), but she does not think the book will be as effective without them, and so she has, for now, abandoned the project.

Phil lives in Williamsburg, Brooklyn. A recent law school graduate, Phil works part time at a small law firm in Manhattan that deals mostly with insurance matters. Phil's true passion is music. He works as a DJ every chance he gets. He is often up late at night using his professional audio-sampling equipment to produce recordings that he shares with friends. Phil has generated a substantial fan base in the hip Williamsburg music community. He would like to distribute his recordings more widely and believes that his sampling is permissible fair use, but he does not want to risk being sued for copyright infringement.

Bob, an oceanography student in Florida, started a photo-blog called "Trash Around the World." Readers often e-mail him photos of discarded fast-food containers from Turkey, England, Mexico, China, Russia, and elsewhere, which he posts on his blog. The only commentary on the site is the header line, which says, "Real dishes help the fishes and the oceans and the world. Use real dishes, not plastic or paper." Two fast-food companies, alleging copyright and trademark infringement, demand that Bob remove the images depicting their products. Lawyers for these companies also contact Bob's Internet service provider, resulting in Bob's account being disabled.

For twenty years, Richard and his wife, Peggy, have operated a small hardware store. Two years ago, a branch of a national store that sells a variety of products, including many that Richard and Peggy also sell, opened in town. Richard and Peggy cannot compete with the big chain store on pricing, so they emphasize their customer service. Richard and Peggy hand out fliers with their store name, followed by the words "A sale is just the beginning of our relationship with our customers," and the name of their competitor, followed by the words "The service ends when you hand over your cash." A lawyer for the chain store calls Richard and Peggy and threatens them with trademark infringement for using his client's trademarked name in their flyers.

What all these individuals have in common is that they are victims of overreaching. Mariko should be able to show short film clips as part of her lecture. Beth should be able to include examples of ads in her book. Phil should be able to sample from other artists' recordings in creating his new sounds. Bob should be free to post photographs of trash. Richard and Peggy should be able to refer to their competitor in promoting their own store.

Indeed, the law protects all these activities.

Viewed alone, each incident could seem trivial. Collectively, they are not. Overreaching affects us all. There are millions of people who—along with Mariko, Beth, Phil, Bob, and Richard and Peggy—daily encounter overreaching by owners of intellectual property. Some of these people continue with their activities, undeterred by phony notices, false claims of rights, and lawyers' threats. Many, however, refrain from activities that are lawful or pay to do things that the law deems permissible without charge or anybody's approval.

The effects of overreaching can only increase. Creativity flourishes today on a level unprecedented in human history. We are not all famous authors, renowned photographers, or celebrated songwriters. But virtually everyone today is a creator in one way or another, and our creative works—from political commentary to photo journals to musical remixes—can be instantly shared with the entire world.

Whether as creators or as consumers of creative works, we all have a stake in keeping intellectual property rights within their designated boundaries. Whether we have the power to encourage creativity and be enriched by its results depends on our willingness to claim the protections the law has given us.

REFERENCE MATTER

NOTES

PREFACE

1. U.S. Census Bureau, Statistical Abstract of the United States 2010, 129th ed. (Washington, D.C.: Berman, 2009), Table 351.

CHAPTER 1

1. Terry L. Jordan, *The U.S. Constitution and Fascinating Facts About It*, 7th ed. (Naperville, Ill.: Oak Hill, 1999), 2.

2. U.S. Constitution, art. 1, § 8.

3. *Sony Corp. of America v. Universal City Studios, Inc.*, 464 U.S. 417, 429 (1984).

4. *Twentieth Century Music Corp. v. Aiken*, 422 U.S. 151, 156 (1975).

5. For a useful summary chart, see Peter B. Hirtle, "Copyright Term and the Public Domain in the United States," Cornell Copyright Information Center, http://copyright.cornell.edu/resources/publicdomain.cfm; accessed April 4, 2011.

6. 17 U.S.C. § 102(a) (2006).

7. *Feist Publications, Inc., v. Rural Telephone Service Co.*, 499 U.S. 340, 349 (1991).

8. Ibid., 347.

9. Ibid., 349.

10. Congress has considered legislation that would extend copyright protections to databases and other compilations but has never enacted any such laws (see Chapter 5).

11. 17 U.S.C. § 102(b).

12. *Eldred v. Ashcroft,* 537 U.S. 186, 219 (2003).

13. Willful infringement may also be found where the defendant acted with reckless disregard for whether its conduct infringed the plaintiff's copyright. *Hamil America, Inc., v. GFI,* 193 F.3d 92, 97 (2d Cir. 1999).

14. 17 U.S.C. § 506(e).

15. The numbers of prosecutions cited here were derived from searches in Bureau of Justice Statistics' Federal Criminal Case Processing Statistics database at http://bjs.ojp.usdoj.gov/fjsrc/tsec.cfm.

16. William Shakespeare, *The Life and Death of King John,* ed. A. R. Braunmuller (New York: Oxford University Press, 1989) (blanket copyright notice); William Shakespeare, *Measure for Measure,* ed. Barbara A. Mowat and Paul Werstine (New York: Washington Square Press, 1997) ("All rights reserved including the right to reproduce this book or portions thereof in any form whatsoever."); William Shakespeare, *The Tragedy of Othello the Moor of Venice,* ed. Russ McDonald (New York: Penguin Books, 2001) (blanket copyright notice).

17. Alexander Hamilton, John Jay, and James Madison, *The Federalist: A Commentary on the Constitution of the United States,* ed. Robert Scigliano (New York: Random House, 2000) (copyright claimed by Random House).

18. Charles Dickens, *A Christmas Carol and Other Christmas Stories* (New York: Signet, 1984) (copyright notice plus warning that "no part of this publication may be reproduced . . . in any form . . . without . . . written permission"); Charles Dickens, *A Tale of Two Cities* (New York: Barnes & Noble, 2003) (notice on copyright page stating that the introduction, notes, and suggestions for further reading are copyrighted but also claiming that "[n]o part of this publication may be reproduced . . . without the prior written permission of the publisher").

19. Jane Austen, *Sense and Sensibility,* ed. Claudia L. Johnson (New York: W. W. Norton, 2002) (blanket copyright notice); Jane Austen, *Sense and Sensibility* (New York: Barnes & Noble, 2003) (notice on copyright page that the introduction, explanatory notes, and suggestions for further reading are copyrighted, but also claiming that "[n]o part of this publication may be reproduced . . . without the prior written permission of the publisher").

20. Benjamin Franklin, *Poor Richard's Almanack* (New York: Barnes & Noble, 2004) (stating that the work was originally published in 1733–58, that the introduction and suggested reading are copyrighted by Barnes & Noble, but that "[n]o part of this book may be used or reproduced in any manner whatsoever without written permission of the Publisher").

21. An example is Charles Dickens, *Oliver Twist*, ed. Philip Horne (New York: Penguin Books, 2002) (noting that "[e]ditorial material" is copyrighted, but not making blanket copyright claim, and acknowledging that the work was first published in 1837–38).

22. Richard D. Heffner, *A Documentary History of the United States*, 7th ed. (New York: Signet, 2002).

23. Nick Ragone, *The Everything American Government Book* (Cincinnati, Ohio: Adams Media, 2004), 269–72, 273–90.

24. John Bartlett, *Bartlett's Familiar Quotations*, ed. Justin Kaplin, 17th ed. (New York: Little, Brown, 2002); Robert Andrews, ed., *The New Penguin Dictionary of Modern Quotations,* 3rd ed. (New York: Penguin Books, 2003); Elizabeth Knowles, ed., *The Oxford Dictionary of Quotations,* 6th ed. (New York: Oxford University Press, 2004).

25. Ronald J. Allen, Richard B. Kuhns, and William J. Stuntz, *Constitutional Criminal Procedure,* 3rd ed. (New York: Little, Brown, 1995) (containing copyright notice with warning that "[n]o part of this book may be reproduced . . . without permission in writing from the publisher, except by a reviewer who may quote brief passages in a review").

26. One wrinkle is that effective January 1, 1996, the Uruguay Round Agreements Act, Public Law 103-465, 103d Congress, 2d sess. (Dec. 8, 1994) (codified as amended at 19 U.S.C. §§ 3501–624 (2006)), implementing the Uruguay Round of the General Agreement on Tariffs and Trade (GATT), restored the copyright on certain foreign-published materials previously in the public domain under U.S. law. The change has particular applicability to classical music. GATT restored copyright on a vast body of music first published in the former Soviet Union prior to 1973 (when there were no copyright relations between the Soviet Union and the United States), including works by Shostakovich and Stravinsky.

27. M. William Krasilovsky and Sidney Shemel, *This Business of Music: The Definitive Guide to the Business and Legal Issues of the Music Industry,* 10th ed. (New York: Billboard Books, 2007), 140 ("[Music publishers] claim full originality when they are really only 'finders' of songs in the public domain . . . [and] register copyrights to such songs . . . thereby falsely and unfairly obtaining the benefit of the . . . Copyright Act."); Paul J. Heald, "Reviving the Rhetoric of the Public Interest: Choir Directors, Copy Machines, and New Arrangements of Public Domain Music," *Duke Law Journal* 46, no. 2 (1996): 245 ("Music publishers . . . intimidate the public into buying what they already own by affixing copyright symbols to virtually all public domain music.").

28. J. S. Bach, *The Well-Tempered Clavier*, ed. Willard A. Palmer (Van Nuys, Calif.: Alfred, 2004), 1:5 (noting that "the primary source for the main text . . . is the . . . copy of the first volume, in J. S. Bach's own hand").

29. The Sheet Music Archive, http://www.sheetmusicarchive.net; accessed April 4, 2011.

30. *Woods v. Bourne Co.*, 60 F.3d 978, 991 (2d Cir. 1995).

31. For a proper copyright designation, see Ludwig van Beethoven, *Beethoven Symphonies Nos. 5, 6, and 7 in Full Score* (New York: Dover, 1989) (containing no copyright notice and stating that "[t]his Dover edition, first published in 1989, is a republication of three . . . Symphonies. . . . Lists of instruments and a table of contents have been added.").

32. ProQuest, "ProQuest Historical Newspapers Graphical," http://www.proquest.com/en-US/catalogs/databases/detail/pqhn_graphic_version.shtml; accessed April 4, 2011.

33. Library of Congress, Copyright Office, "Policy Decision on Copyrightability of Digitized Typefaces," *Federal Register* 53, no. 189 (Sept. 29, 1988): 38113.

34. 17 U.S.C. § 105.

35. *President's Commission on the Assassination of President Kennedy: The Warren Commission Report* (1964; repr., New York: Barnes & Noble, 2003).

36. National Commission on Terrorist Attacks, *The 9/11 Commission Report: Final Report of the National Commission on Terrorist Attacks Upon the United States* (Fictionwise eBooks, 2004), http://www.fictionwise.com/ebooks/ebook24549.htm; accessed April 4, 2011.

37. 17 U.S.C. § 504(c)(2).

38. Ibid., §§ 401(d), 402(d). The bar on claiming innocent infringement does not apply to certain activities of nonprofit educational institutions, libraries, archives, and public broadcasting entities.

39. Ibid., § 403.

40. Steven Stanek, "Can Egypt Copyright the Pyramids?" *National Geographic News*, Jan. 15, 2008, http://news.nationalgeographic.com/news/2008/01/080115-egypt-copyright.html.

41. AFP, "Egypt to Copyright Pyramids," *Google News*, Dec. 25, 2007, http://afp.google.com/article/ALeqM5hGhJUxebdPsEOUZ3O5S8f_6VhHww.

42. *Bridgeman Art Library, Ltd., v. Corel Corp.*, 25 F. Supp. 2d 421, 427 (S.D.N.Y. 1998).

43. *Bridgeman Art Library, Ltd., v. Corel Corp.*, 36 F. Supp. 2d 191, 196 (S.D.N.Y. 1999) (internal quotations and citations omitted).

44. Ibid., 197.

45. *Schiffer Publishing, Ltd., v. Chronicle Books, LLC,* 73 U.S.P.Q.2d 1090, 1098 (E.D. 2004).

46. Bridgeman Art Library, "Copyright," http://www.bridgemanart.com/ copyright.aspx; accessed April 4, 2011.

47. Bridgeman Art Library, "Terms & Conditions US," http://www. bridgemanart.com/terms-and-conditions-us; accessed April 4, 2011.

48. Corbis Images, "Corbis Content License Agreement," http://www. corbisimages.com/Content/LicenseInfo/Certified_EULA_US.pdf; accessed April 4, 2011.

49. ARTstor, "Permitted & Prohibited Uses," http://www.artstor.org/our-organization/o-html/permitted-uses.shtml. One of the images available from Art Resource is Vermeer's ca. 1662 *Young Woman with a Water Pitcher,* from the collection of the Metropolitan Museum of Art. A copyright notice reads, "Image copyright © The Metropolitan Museum of Art / Art Resource, NY." Art Resource's website says the following about copyright law: "Photographs and other images are protected under the laws of copyright, and the creators as copyright owners have absolute rights to control the use of their photographs." Nancy E. Wolff, "Copyright Information," Art Resource, 2000, http://www.artres.com/c/htm/StaticPage2.aspx?Page=Copyright.

50. American Antiquarian Society, "Rights and Reproductions," http://www. americanantiquarian.org/reproductions.htm; accessed April 4, 2011.

51. American Antiquarian Society, "License Agreement," http://www. americanantiquarian.org/license.pdf; accessed April 4, 2011. In fairness, when it comes to quoting from materials in its collection, the American Antiquarian Society gives a more balanced view of copyright law. It states, "Permission is not needed to quote from out-of-copyright printed materials in the Society's collections although acknowledgement of the use of such materials is appreciated." American Antiquarian Society, "Requesting Permission to Quote from Manuscripts," http:// www.americanantiquarian.org/msquote.htm; accessed April 4, 2011.

52. Fenimore Art Museum, "The Smith and Telfer Photographic Collection— Conditions of Use," http://www.fenimoreartmuseum.org/node/860; accessed April 4, 2011.

53. Museum of Fine Arts, Boston, "Terms and Conditions," http://www.mfa. org/collections/mfa-images/terms-and-conditions; accessed April 22, 2011 ("The Images are not simple reproductions of the works depicted and are protected by copyright.").

54. Note that a transfer of copyright must be pursuant to a written instrument.

Selling a copy of a copyrighted work or donating it to an archive does not alone transfer the copyright to the archive.

55. Peter B. Hirtle, "Archives or Assets?" Aug. 21, 2003, http://www.archivists.org/governance/presidential/hirtle.asp.

56. Library of Congress, "Legal: About Copyright and the Collections," http://www.loc.gov/homepage/legal.html; accessed April 4, 2011.

57. Gordon Quinn, telephone interview with author, Dec. 16, 2005.

58. Jan Krawitz, e-mail to author, Jan. 18, 2006.

59. Michael C. Donaldson, telephone interview with author, Jan. 7, 2006.

60. Patricia Aufderheide and Peter Jaszi, *Untold Stories: Creative Consequences of the Rights Clearance Culture for Documentary Filmmakers* (Washington, D.C.: Center for Social Media, 2004), 9, http://www.centerforsocialmedia.org/sites/default/files/UNTOLDSTORIES_Report.pdf (discussing the experience of Robert Stone with PBS), 14 (discussing studios' refusals to allow public domain trailers to be used by A&E).

61. Walter J. Coady Jr., "How to Avoid a Lawsuit in Waiting: A Vulnerability to Lawsuits Can Play Havoc with Any Producer's Limited Financial Resources," *MovieMaker*, February 10, 2003, http://www.moviemaker.com/directing/article/how_to_avoid_a_lawsuit_in_waiting_3256.

62. Michael C. Donaldson, *Clearance and Copyright: Everything the Independent Filmmaker Needs to Know*, 2nd ed. (Los Angeles, Calif.: Silman-James Press, 2003), 221.

63. Gunnar Erickson, Mark Halloran, and Harris Tulchin, *The Independent Film Producer's Survival Guide: A Business and Legal Sourcebook*, 3rd ed. (New York: Schirmer Trade Books, 2010), 288.

64. indieProducer, "Legal Issues and Information," http://indieproducer.ning.com/Resources/page/show?id=2029567%3APage%3A18173; accessed April 4, 2011.

65. Fernando Ramirez, "The Many Meanings of 'Fair Use': How and When to Get Permission, Even When It Seems Unnecessary," *The Independent*, Dec. 1, 2005, http://www.independent-magazine.org/node/333.

66. Brandt Goldstein, "Law Professors Help Filmmakers on 'Fair Use,'" *The Wall Street Journal Online*, Jan. 13, 2006, http://nyu.edu/classes/siva/archives/wsjarticle.pdf (quoting law professor Jennifer Jenkins: "[Errors-and-omissions] policies often demand that a filmmaker clear the rights to just about everything in the final version of a film, regardless of what copyright law allows").

67. Matt Dunne, "The Cost of Clearance: The Expense and Complications of Using Copyrighted Materials," *Independent*, April 2005, 30.

68. Goldstein, "Law Professors Help Filmmakers."

69. Aufderheide and Jaszi, *Untold Stories*, 29.

70. Dunne, "The Cost of Clearance," 30–31.

71. Michael Krondl, interview with M. J. Williams (author's research assistant), May 22, 2008.

72. Susan M. Bielstein, *Permissions, A Survival Guide—Blunt Talk About Art as Intellectual Property* (Chicago: University of Chicago Press, 2006), 47–48.

73. *Princeton University Press v. Michigan Document Services, Inc.*, 99 F.3d 1381, 1387 (6th Cir. 1996); *Basic Books, Inc., v. Kinko's Graphics Corp.*, 758 F. Supp. 1522, 1526 (S.D.N.Y. 1991).

74. Jacob Ernest Cooke, ed., *The Federalist* (Middletown, Conn.: Wesleyan University Press, 1961).

75. "Copyrights and Trademarks," pamphlet, available at FedEx Office stores.

76. FedEx Office, "Fedex Office Terms of Use," http://www.fedex.com/us/office/customersupport/terms.html; accessed April 4, 2011.

CHAPTER 2

1. The Boston Globe, "Electronic Reprints: The Boston Globe/Boston.com Copyright & Permissions Rules," http://www.boston.com/help/reprints; accessed April 21, 2011. The "rules" permit making a single copy for "personal noncommercial use."

2. A typical notice reads, "All material is protected by copyright laws of the United States and all countries throughout the world. All rights reserved. Any unauthorized exhibition, distribution, or copying of this film or any part thereof (including soundtrack) is an infringement of the relevant copyright and will subject the infringer to severe civil and criminal penalties."

3. Mike Collett-White, "Prince Moves to Sue Fan Web Sites," *Reuters*, Nov. 7, 2007.

4. Nancy Ramsey, "The Hidden Cost of Documentaries," *New York Times*, Oct. 16, 2005.

5. Katy Chevigny, letter to the editor, *New York Times*, Oct. 30, 2005.

6. *Folsom v. Marsh*, 9 F. Cas. 342, 344 (C.C.D. Mass. 1841).

7. Upham was also named as a defendant in the lawsuit.

8. *Folsom v. Marsh*, 9 F. Cas. 342, 348 (C.C.D. Mass. 1841).

9. Ibid., 348–49.

10. Ibid., 349.

11. "Section 107 is intended to restate the present judicial doctrine of fair use, not to change, narrow, or enlarge it in any way." House Committee on the Judiciary, *General Revision of Copyright Law,* 94th Cong., 2d sess., 1976, H.R. Rep. 94-1476, 66.

12. 17 U.S.C. § 107 (2006).

13. Ibid. The provision also provides that "[t]he fact that a work is unpublished shall not itself bar a finding of fair use if such finding is made upon consideration of all the above factors."

14. House Committee on the Judiciary, *General Revision of Copyright Law*, 94th Cong., 2d sess., 1976, H.R. Rep. 94-1476, 65, 66.

15. In addition, a court is required to remit statutory damages if the infringer "believed and had reasonable grounds for believing that his or her use of the copyrighted work was a fair use" and the infringer is an employee of a school or library or of a public broadcasting entity. 17 U.S.C. § 504(c)(2).

16. Pierre N. Leval, "Toward a Fair Use Standard," *Harvard Law Review* 103, no. 5 (1990): 1106.

17. *Sony Corp. of America v. Universal City Studios, Inc.*, 464 U.S. 417 (1984).

18. *Harper & Row, Publishers, Inc., v. Nation Enterprises*, 471 U.S. 539, 562 (1985).

19. *Campbell v. Acuff-Rose Music, Inc.*, 510 U.S. 569, 585 (1994).

20. *Castle Rock Entertainment, Inc., v. Carol Publishing Group, Inc.*, 150 F.3d 132, 142 (2d Cir. 1998). The court stated that it "[did] not make too much of" the fact that the use at issue was for commercial purposes.

21. *Campbell*, 510 U.S. at 579 ("The central purpose of this investigation is to see . . . whether the new work merely 'supersedes the objects' of the original creation, or instead adds something new, with a further purpose or different character, altering the first with new expression, meaning, or message; it asks, in other words, whether and to what extent the new work is 'transformative.' Although such transformative use is not absolutely necessary for a finding of fair use, the goal of copyright, to promote science and the arts, is generally furthered by the creation of transformative works.") (citations and footnote omitted).

22. *Kelly v. Arriba Soft Corp.*, 336 F.3d 811, 818–19 (9th Cir. 2003).

23. *Elvis Presley Enterprises, Inc., v. Passport Video*, 349 F.3d 622, 629 (9th Cir. 2003).

24. Ibid.

25. *New Era Publications International, ApS, v. Carol Publishing Group*, 904 F.2d 152, 158 (2d Cir. 1990), *cert. denied*, 498 U.S. 921 (1990).

26. *Salinger v. Random House, Inc.*, 811 F.2d 90, 98 (2d Cir. 1987).

27. *Lennon v. Premise Media Corp.*, 556 F. Supp. 2d 310, 325 (S.D.N.Y. 2008).

28. *Harper & Row, Publishers, Inc.*, 471 U.S. at 564–65.

29. *Sony Corp. of America*, 464 U.S. at 442.

30. *Ringgold v. Black Entertainment Television, Inc.*, 126 F.3d 70, 74 (2d Cir. 1997).

31. *Newton v. Diamond*, 388 F.3d 1189, 1190 (9th Cir. 2004).

32. *Sandoval v. New Line Cinema Corp.*, 147 F.3d 215, 217–18 (2d Cir. 1998).

33. *Campbell*, 510 U.S. at 591.

34. The Court did not determine whether, in the final analysis, 2 Live Crew's parody was fair use but remanded the case to the lower court for further development of the record. The parties thereafter settled.

35. *Harper & Row, Publishers, Inc.*, 471 U.S. at 566.

36. *Campbell*, 510 U.S. at 578.

37. R. Polk Wagner, "The Perfect Storm: Intellectual Property and Public Values," *Fordham Law Review* 74, no. 2 (2005): 430–31.

38. Hari Kunzru, *Transmission* (New York: Dutton, 2004).

39. Rick Bragg, *All Over but the Shoutin'* (New York: Vintage, 1997).

40. Frank Rich, *Ghost Light: A Memoir* (New York: Random House, 2000); Anita Shreve, *The Pilot's Wife: A Novel* (New York: Back Bay Books, 1999).

41. Cengage Learning, "Author Guidelines: Copyrights and Permissions," http://college.hmco.com/reviewers_authors/ra_author_guidelines_part03.html; accessed April 4, 2011.

42. University of Virginia Press, "Guide to MS [Manuscript] Preparation," http://www.upress.virginia.edu/authorinfo/msprep2.html; accessed April 4, 2011 ("As author of your MS, you are responsible for obtaining permissions to use material owned by others").

43. *The Chicago Manual of Style*, 15th ed. (Chicago: University of Chicago Press, 2003), 137, 132–33.

44. Penguin Group (USA), Inc., "Permissions FAQ," http://us.penguingroup.com/static/pages/permissions/PermissionsFAQ.html; accessed April 4, 2011.

45. Felicia R. Lee, "A Romance Novelist Is Accused of Copying," *New York Times*, Jan. 12, 2008.

46. 17 U.S.C. § 107.

47. James Gibson, "Risk Aversion and Rights Accretion in Intellectual Property Law," *Yale Law Journal* 116, no. 5 (2007): 882.

48. Ibid., 884.

49. Ibid., 895–98.

50. Ibid., 899.

51. House Committee on the Judiciary, *General Revision of Copyright Law,* 94th Cong., 2d sess., 1976, H.R. Rep. 94-1733, 70. The official name of the Classroom Guidelines is "Agreement on Guidelines for Classroom Copying in Not-for-Profit Educational Institutions."

52. House Committee on the Judiciary, *General Revision of Copyright Law,* 94th Cong., 2d sess., 1976, H.R. Rep. 94-1476, 68.

53. *Princeton University Press v. Michigan Document Services, Inc.,* 99 F.3d 1381, 1390 (6th Cir. 1996); *American Geophysical Union v. Texaco, Inc.,* 60 F.3d 913, 919 n.5 (2d Cir. 1994).

54. *Addison-Wesley Publishing Co., Inc., v. New York University,* 1983 WL 1134, at *2 (S.D.N.Y. May 31, 1983).

55. See, e.g., *Basic Books, Inc., v. Kinko's Graphics Corp.,* 758 F. Supp. 1522, 1535, 1537 (S.D.N.Y. 1991) (noting that "the Classroom Guidelines express a specific prohibition of anthologies," but "refus[ing] to hold that all unconsented anthologies are prohibited without a fair use analysis.").

56. According to one estimate, 80 percent of U.S. universities adhere to the Classroom Guidelines as a fair use ceiling. William W. Fisher and William McGeveran, "The Digital Learning Challenge: Obstacles to Educational Uses of Copyrighted Material in the Digital Age," Berkman Center for Internet & Society, Research Publication No. 2006-09, Aug. 10, 2006, 57, http://cyber.law. harvard.edu/sites/cyber.law.harvard.edu/files/BerkmanWhitePaper_08-10-2006. pdf.

57. *Cambridge University Press, Oxford University Press, Inc., and Sage Publications, Inc., v. Patton,* Amended Complaint No. 1:08-CV-01425-ODE (N.D. Ga. Dec. 15, 2008), para. 28.

58. Copyright Advisory Office, Columbia University, "Fair Use Checklist," http://copyright.columbia.edu/copyright/fair-use/fair-use-checklist; accessed April 4, 2011.

59. Copyright Permissions Center, University of Minnesota, "Copyright Laws & Guidelines," http://www.copyright.umn.edu/laws.html; accessed April 4, 2011.

60. One university states, "When it comes to copyright law, faculty and staff may be personally liable for fines or criminal charges." Marshall University, "Copyright Basics," http://marshall.edu/Muonline/copyrightbasics.asp; accessed April 4, 2011.

61. See Communications & Creative Services, Colorado State University,

"Copyright Guidelines," http://ccs.colostate.edu/course_guidelines.aspx; accessed April 4, 2011 ("[P]hotocopying copyrighted works without obtaining permissions . . . is directly contrary to the academic mission to teach respect for ideas and the intellectual property that expresses those ideas.").

62. Stanford University Libraries, "Copyright & Fair Use," http://fairuse. stanford.edu/Copyright_and_Fair_Use_Overview/chapter9/9-d.html; accessed April 4, 2011. Stanford advises, "Even if you ultimately persuade the court that your use was in fact a fair use, the expense and time involved in litigation may well outweigh any benefit of using the material in the first place."

63. Georgia Harper, "Managing the Risk of Copyright Infringement Liability," Office of General Counsel, University of Texas System, http://www.utsystem.edu/ OGC/IntellectualProperty/riskmgt.htm; accessed April 4, 2011.

64. *Shloss v. Sweeney*, 515 F. Supp. 2d 1068, 1073 (N.D. Cal. 2007).

65. Subsequently, the court ruled that Shloss, as the prevailing party in her lawsuit, was entitled to recover attorneys' fees from the estate. *Shloss v. Sweeney*, 515 F. Supp. 2d 1083, 1086 (N.D. Cal. 2007).

66. Carol Loeb Shloss, *Lucia Joyce: Supplemental Material*, http://lucia-the-authors-cut.info/index.html; access April 4, 2011.

67. Andy Peters, "Agreement to Sell MLK's Papers Fails to Quell Copyright Debate," *Law.com*, June 28, 2006, http://www.law.com/jsp/article.jsp?id=1151399127954.

68. Dinitia Smith, "A Portrait of the Artist's Troubled Daughter," *New York Times*, Nov. 22, 2003; Anne Whitehouse, "Bios Shine a Light into Sylvia Plath's Dark Corners," *Atlanta Constitution*, Nov. 3, 1991.

69. Frederick Nolan, "Obituary: Dorothy Hart," *The Independent*, April 25, 2006.

70. Carol Armstrong, "Biology, Destiny, Photography: Difference According to Diane Arbus," *October* 66 (Fall 1993): 29.

71. Friends of Active Copyright Education, The Copyright Society of the U.S.A., "Moving Images: Frequently Asked Questions," http://www.csusa.org/face/movim/ index.htm; accessed April 4, 2011 (follow "Moving Images FAQs" hyperlink).

72. Friends of Active Copyright Education, The Copyright Society of the U.S.A., "Words: Copyright Basics," http://www.csusa.org/face/words/index.htm; accessed April 4, 2011 (follow "Words Copyright Basics" hyperlink).

73. Ibid. (follow "Words FAQs" hyperlink).

74. Music Publishers Association of the United States, "Copyright Resource Center: Frequently Asked Questions," http://www.mpa.org/copyright/faq.html; accessed April 4, 2011.

75. Copyright Alliance Education Foundation, "Library of Classroom Curricula," http://www.copyrightfoundation.org/library_of_classroom_curricula.

76. Music Rules! "MusicRules! True Music Fans Play by the Rules," 2009, http://www.music-rules.com/pdf/MusicRulesPoster.pdf.

77. Music Rules! "Music Rules! Elementary Activities," 2010, http://www.music-rules.com/pdf/MusicRulesElemActivities.pdf.

78. Ibid.

79. Ibid.

80. Music Rules! "Music Rules! Teacher Guide," 2010, http://www.music-rules.com/pdf/MusicRulesTeacherGuide.pdf.

81. B4U Copy, "Become Copyright Smart! Know the Risks & Make the Right Choice," 2007, http://www.b4ucopy.com/teens.

82. Copyright Alliance Education Foundation, "Curriculum Detail: Lucky & Flo: Crime-Fighting Canines," 2009, http://www.copyrightfoundation.org/library/11/lucky__flo_crime_fighting_canines.

83. Seeking to counteract these pro-industry educational efforts, in June 2009 the Electronic Frontier Foundation launched its own curriculum, titled "Teaching Copyright." It tells students, "Fair use allows people other than the copyright owner to copy part or, in some circumstances, all of a copyrighted work, even where the copyright holder has not given permission or objects." Teaching Copyright, "Fair Use Frequently Asked Questions," http://www.teachingcopyright.org/handout/fair-use-faq; accessed April 5, 2010.

CHAPTER 3

1. Kembrew McLeod, "How Copyright Law Changed Hip Hop: An Interview with Public Enemy's Chuck D and Hank Shocklee," *Stay Free!* Fall 2002, http://www.stayfreemagazine.org/archives/20/public_enemy.html.

2. Ibid.

3. *Grand Upright Music, Ltd., v. Warner Brothers Records, Inc.*, 780 F. Supp. 182, 183 (S.D.N.Y. 1991).

4. *Bridgeport Music, Inc., v. Dimension Films*, 410 F.3d 792 (6th Cir. 2005).

5. Ibid., 801.

6. The Sixth Circuit panel reached its result on the basis of its reading of sections 106(2) and 114(b) of the Copyright Act. Section 106(2) gives the copyright holder the exclusive right to prepare derivative works based upon the copyrighted work. In the case of sound recordings, section 114(b) limits that right to "a derivative work in which the actual sounds fixed in the sound recording are rearranged,

remixed, or otherwise altered in sequence or quality." Section 114(b) also provides that the rights of sound recording copyright holders "do not extend to the making or duplication of another sound recording that consists entirely of an independent fixation of other sounds, even though such sounds imitate or simulate those in the copyrighted sound recording." 17 U.S.C. § 114(b) (2006). Together, the Sixth Circuit panel concluded, these provisions mean that the owner of a copyright in a sound recording has the exclusive right to sample the recording because a sample from the recording is a derivative work of the recording. *Bridgeport Music, Inc.*, 410 F.3d at 800–801. An artist who wishes to use the sounds from a prior recording therefore needs permission from the copyright owner to sample or must independently create the sounds. According to the Sixth Circuit panel, the doctrine of de minimis copying applies to musical compositions, but the language of the Copyright Act precludes the application of the doctrine to sound recordings (798–801).

7. Inconsistent with its desire to announce a "bright-line rule," the Sixth Circuit ducked the question of whether sampling even a single note was infringement. Because, the court said, the case before it concerned a three-note sample, there was no need to provide a definitive answer to the question of whether the same prohibition extends to one note. But the court also suggested that a one-note sample might be permissible because "under the Copyright Act, the sound recording must 'result from the fixation of a series of musical, spoken, or other *sounds* . . . .' 17 U.S.C. § 101 (definition of 'sound recording')." *Bridgeport Music, Inc.*, 410 F.3d at 800 n. 9 (emphasis added).

8. Although the court rejected the application of the de minimis doctrine to sampling, it stated that if it were to apply that doctrine, it would agree with the trial judge's quantitative and qualitative analysis and find that the copying at issue was de minimis. Ibid., 798 n. 4. Yet the court never explains why a sample that, in the court's own view, is trivial and unrecognizable to the listener is at the same time a derivative work, which, in the language of section 114(b), rearranges, remixes, or otherwise alters in sequence or quality the actual sounds fixed in the original recording. Section 101 of the Copyright Act defines a derivative work as "a work based upon one or more preexisting works, such as a translation, musical arrangement, dramatization, fictionalization, motion picture version, sound recording, art reproduction, abridgment, condensation, or any other form in which a work may be recast, transformed, or adapted." 17 U.S.C. § 101. The Sixth Circuit was required, then, to explain why a sample is a derivative work within the meaning of the Copyright Act in the first place. Section 101, which includes in its set of examples of derivative works an "abridgement" or "condensation" of

an earlier work, plainly contemplates that a derivative work might be shorter than the original. Yet that still leaves the question of why a copy of a protected work that both the trial judge and the appellate court understood to be de minimis falls within section 101's definition of a derivative work, particularly when courts have recognized other de minimis works not to be derivative. Section 114(b) does not create new categories of derivative works (and it says, "the actual sounds," not "any of the actual sounds"). Arguably, a three-note sequence is not a derivative work at all under section 101, and therefore not a use of "the actual sounds" under section 114(b), any more than use of a few words from a book is a derivative work of the book.

9. *Bridgeport Music, Inc.*, 410 F.3d at 802.

10. Ibid.

11. Admittedly, borrowing four seconds from some songs, because they repeat or otherwise emphasize a single phrase, could be tantamount to taking the whole song.

12. *Bridgeport Music, Inc.*, 410 F.3d at 801, 804.

13. Ibid., 804.

14. Jon Healey and Richard Cromelin, "When Copyright Law Meets the 'Mash-Up,'" *Los Angeles Times*, March 21, 2004.

15. *Bridgeport Music, Inc.*, 410 F.3d at 801.

16. *Brief for Sony BMG Music Entertainment, UMG Recordings, Inc., and Warner Music, Inc., in Support of Defendant-Appellee's Petition for Hearing En Banc*, No. 02-6521 (6th Cir. June 17, 2005).

17. *Bridgeport Music, Inc.*, 410 F.3d at 805.

18. Such rights include the right to prepare derivative works in sound recordings, which the Sixth Circuit relied upon.

19. "Philo," e-mail to David Wheatley (author's research assistant), July 8, 2008.

20. Leah Collins, "For Rapper Buck 65, Songwriting No Longer a Daily Grind," *Ottawa Citizen*, Nov. 1, 2007.

21. Edwin F. McPherson, "Pick Me! Pick Me! The New Copyright Lottery," *Entertainment and Sports Lawyer* 24, no. 2 (2006): 14. These rates are for samples that are cleared before release of the new recording. A copyright owner who claims infringement once the recording is on the market will normally demand considerably more to settle the case.

22. Roger Friedman, "Is Diddy's 'Vote or Die' Dead or Just Sleeping?" *Fox News*, April 25, 2006, http://www.foxnews.com/story/0,2933,192954,00.html.

23. "Fight for Your Right to Sample? Why the Beasties' Best Album Could Never Happen Today," *Entertainment Weekly*, Nov. 19, 2004, 40.

24. McLeod, "How Copyright Law Changed Hip Hop."

25. Lyndsey Parker, "Dust to Dust," *Yahoo! Music*, March 1, 2006.

26. Morgan Page, online conversation with David Wheatley (author's research assistant), May 21, 2008.

27. Nate Patrin, "Pitchfork Interviews: Steinski," *Pitchfork Media*, Aug. 26, 2008, http://pitchfork.com/features/interviews/7149-steinski.

28. McLeod, "How Copyright Law Changed Hip Hop."

29. Rob Walker, "Mash-Up Model," *New York Times*, July 20, 2008; Ryan Dombal, "Pitchfork Interviews: Girl Talk," *Pitchfork Media*, Aug. 30, 2006, http://pitchfork.com/features/interviews/6415-girl-talk.

30. Dombal, "Pitchfork Interviews: Girl Talk."

31. *Bridgeport Music, Inc., v. Justin Combs Publishing*, 507 F.3d 470 (6th Cir. 2007).

32. Anthony Falzone, "Diddy Could Save Sampling: Why Hasn't He or Any Other Big-Name Rapper Even Tried?" *Slate*, Nov. 2, 2007, http://www.slate.com/id/2177238.

33. Sony Music Entertainment, one of the largest record companies in the world and the parent to more than a dozen separate labels, is also a subsidiary of the Sony Corporation of America.

34. Corey Moss, "*Grey Album* Producer Danger Mouse Explains How He Did It," *MTV News*, March 11, 2004, http://www.mtv.com/news/articles/1485693/20040311/danger_mouse.jhtml.

CHAPTER 4

1. 17 U.S.C. § 512(c) (2006).

2. Ibid., § 512(c)(3).

3. Ibid., § 512(c)(1).

4. To be eligible to use the safe harbor, the online service provider must first meet two criteria: it must implement and inform its account holders of a policy under which accounts that repeatedly infringe copyright are terminated, and it must accommodate technical measures used by copyright owners to identify or protect copyrighted works. Ibid., § 512(i).

5. 17 U.S.C. § 512(g)(1).

6. Ibid. § 512(f). Likewise, there is liability under this section for sending a false counter-notice.

7. Ibid., § 512(g)(3).

8. Ibid., § 512(g)(2)(C).

9. Brian McWilliams, "Big Retailers Squeeze FatWallet," *Wired*, Nov. 20, 2002, http://www.wired.com/techbiz/media/news/2002/11/56504.

10. Ibid.

11. However, when Wal-Mart invoked the subpoena provision of section 512(h) of the DMCA to force FatWallet to identify the individual who posted Wal-Mart sales information, FatWallet decided to fight back. Represented by the Samuelson Law, Technology and Public Policy Clinic at the University of California, Berkeley, FatWallet demanded that Wal-Mart withdraw the subpoena and sought damages against all the retailers under section 512(f). When Wal-Mart withdrew its subpoena, the matter was dropped. Tim Storm, e-mail to author, May 21, 2009. For further information, see Declan McCullagh, "Wal-Mart Backs Away from DMCA Claim," *CNET News*, Dec. 5, 2002, http://news.cnet.com/2100-1023-976296.html.

12. Chilling Effects, "Macy's Wants Site to Pull Black Friday Ads," Oct. 30, 2007, http://www.chillingeffects.org/tradesecret/notice.cgi?NoticeID=16067.

13. Declan McCullagh, "RIAA Apologizes for Threatening Letter," *CNET News*, May 12, 2003, http://news.cnet.com/2100-1025_3-1001095.html.

14. Nikolaus Gebhardt, "Viacom Claims Copyright on Irrlicht Video," Irrlicht3d.org, Feb. 5, 2007, http://www.irrlicht3d.org/pivot/entry.php?id=451.

15. Chilling Effects, "Universal Studios Stumbles on Internet Archive's Public Domain Films," Feb. 27, 2003, http://www.chillingeffects.org/notice.cgi?NoticeID=595.

16. Dan Frosch, "Enforcing Copyrights Online, for a Profit," *New York Times*, May 3, 2011.

17. Jennifer M. Urban and Laura Quilter, "Efficient Process or 'Chilling Effects'? Takedown Notices Under Section 512 of the Digital Millennium Copyright Act," *Santa Clara Computer and High Technology Law Journal* 22, no. 4 (2006): 651, 667.

18. Electronic Frontier Foundation, "Wiki Operator Sues Apple Over Bogus Legal Threats," April 27, 2009, http://www.eff.org/press/archives/2009/04/27.

19. Katharine Mieszkowski, "No Free Speech for Animal Rights Web Sites," *Salon.com,* Aug. 31, 2001, http://www.salon.com/technology/log/2001/08/31/dmca_animals.

20. Matt Loney and Evan Hansen, "Google Pulls Anti-Scientology Links," *CNET News*, March 21, 2002, http://news.cnet.com/2100-1023-865936.html.

21. Lee's website is http://alsolikelife.com/shooting. Nate Anderson, "What

Fair Use? Three Strikes and You're Out . . . of YouTube," *Ars Technica*, Jan. 15, 2009, http://arstechnica.com/tech-policy/news/2009/01/what-fair-use-three-strikes-and-youre-out-of-youtube.ars.

22. *Lenz v. Universal Music Corp.*, 572 F. Supp. 2d 1150, 1154–55 (N.D. Cal. 2008).

23. *Savage v. Council on American-Islamic Relations, Inc.*, 87 U.S.P.Q.2d 1730, 2008 WL 2951281 (N.D. Cal. 2008).

24. Brave New Films claimed Savage had directed Original Talk Radio to send the takedown notice.

25. *Brave New Films 501(C)(4) v. Weiner*, 2009 WL 1622385 (N.D. Cal. 2009). "Michael Savage" is the on-air name of Michael Weiner.

26. Eduardo Moisés Peñalver and Sonia K. Katyal, *Property Outlaws: How Squatters, Pirates, and Protesters Improve the Law of Ownership* (New Haven, Conn.: Yale University Press, 2010), 114.

27. *Online Policy Group v. Diebold, Inc.*, 337 F. Supp. 2d 1195, 1203 (N.D. Cal. 2004).

28. Ibid., 1204.

29. Ibid., 1204–6.

30. Trevor Potter (general counsel, McCain-Palin 2008) to Chad Hurley (CEO, YouTube) and Zahavah Levine (chief counsel, YouTube), Oct. 13, 2008, http://www.publicknowledge.org/pdf/mccain-letter-20081013.pdf.

31. Zahavah Levine (chief counsel, YouTube) to Trevor Potter (general counsel, McCain-Palin 2008), Oct. 14, 2008, http://www.publicknowledge.org/pdf/youtube-letter-20080514.pdf.

32. Richard Perez-Pena, "A.P. Cracks Down on Unpaid Use of Articles on Web," *New York Times*, July 23, 2009.

33. MacWorld, "iTunes Store and DRM-Free Music: What You Need to Know," Jan. 7, 2009, http://www.macworld.com/article/138000/2009/01/drm_faq.html.

34. 17 U.S.C. § 1201(a)(1)(A).

35. Ibid., § 1201(a)(2), (b)(1). The statute defines "[to] circumvent a technological measure" as meaning "to descramble a scrambled work, to decrypt an encrypted work, or otherwise to avoid, bypass, remove, deactivate, or impair a technological measure, without the authority of the copyright owner," and it defines a technological measure that "effectively controls access to a work" as a measure that "in the ordinary course of its operation, requires the application of information, or a process or a treatment, with the authority of the copyright owner, to gain access to the work." Ibid., § 1201(a)(3)(A)–(B).

36. The statute provides a cause of action in federal court for any person "injured by a violation" of the anti-circumvention measures. An injured party may elect to receive actual damages, plus the defendant's profits, or statutory damages. Ibid., § 1203(a)–(c).

37. In criminal cases, there is an available penalty of up to a maximum of a $500,000 fine and five-year imprisonment; this penalty is doubled for a second such violation. Ibid., § 1204(a).

38. 17 U.S.C. § 1201(d)–(g).

39. Ibid., § 1201(a)(1)(B)–(D).

40. The exemptions issued in July 2010, the most recent rulemaking cycle, are outlined by James H. Billington, "Statement of the Librarian of Congress Relating to Section 1201 Rulemaking," July 26, 2010, http://www.copyright.gov/1201/2010/Librarian-of-Congress-1201-Statement.html.

41. 17 U.S.C. § 1201(c)(1).

42. These bills include the Digital Media Consumers' Rights Act of 2002, the Benefit Authors Without Limiting Advancement or Net Consumer Expectations Act of 2003, and the Freedom and Innovation Revitalizing U.S. Entrepreneurship Act of 2007.

43. *Universal City Studios, Inc., v. Reimerdes*, 111 F. Supp. 2d 294 (S.D.N.Y. 2000), *aff'd*, *Universal City Studios, Inc., v. Carley*, 273 F.3d 429 (2d Cir. 2001).

44. *Reimerdes*, 111 F. Supp. 2d at 304.

45. *Sony Corp. of America v. Universal City Studios, Inc.*, 464 U.S. 417 (1984). This case is discussed in Chapter 2.

46. *Reimerdes*, 111 F. Supp. 2d at 323. The court stated, "By prohibiting the provision of circumvention technology, the DMCA fundamentally altered the landscape. A given device or piece of technology might have a substantial noninfringing use, and hence be immune from attack under *Sony's* construction of the Copyright Act—but nonetheless still be subject to suppression under Section 1201 [of the DMCA]" (internal quotations omitted).

47. William W. Fisher and William McGeveran, "The Digital Learning Challenge: Obstacles to Educational Uses of Copyrighted Material in the Digital Age," Berkman Center for Internet & Society, Research Publication No. 2006-09, Aug. 10, 2006, 23–26, http://cyber.law.harvard.edu/sites/cyber.law.harvard.edu/files/BerkmanWhitePaper_08-10-2006.pdf.

48. Library of Congress, "Rulemaking Hearing: Section 1201," May 7, 2009 (statement of Francesca Coppa), http://www.copyright.gov/1201/hearings/2009/transcripts/1201-5-7-09.txt.

49. For a collection of fan fictional works, see http://www.fanfiction.net.

50. Billington, "Statement of the Librarian of Congress."

51. *Metro-Goldwyn-Mayer Studios, Inc., v. Grokster, Ltd.*, 545 U.S. 913 (2005).

52. *Chamberlain Group, Inc., v. Skylink Technologies, Inc.*, 381 F.3d 1178 (Fed. Cir. 2004).

53. 17 U.S.C. § 1201(a)(3).

54. *Chamberlain Group, Inc.*, 381 F.3d at 1202.

55. The plaintiff in the case did not allege any copyright infringement.

56. Ibid.

57. Ibid., 1200 n. 14.

CHAPTER 5

1. Mark Twain, *The Adventures of Huckleberry Finn* (New York: Harper & Brothers, 1912), vii.

2. Rights and Reproductions Information Network, "AAM Member Museums Rights and Reproduction Survey 2003/4 Results" (n.p.: Registrars Committee of the American Association of Museums, May 2004), 37–39. The survey reports that thirty-one out of eighty-one responding museums used forms drawn up by or reviewed by an attorney.

3. E. J. Graff, "The Schlesinger Library: Documenting Women's History," *Radcliffe Quarterly*, Summer 2005 (quoting Nancy F. Cott, director, Schlesinger Library).

4. Schlesinger Library, "Services and Policies," http://www.radcliffe.edu/schles/services.aspx; accessed April 5, 2011.

5. Columbia University Libraries, "The Papers of John Jay: Copyright and Use," http://www.columbia.edu/cu/lweb/digital/jay/copyright.html; accessed April 5, 2011.

6. The Historical Society of Pennsylvania, "Permission to Quote Form," http://www.hsp.org/files/HSP_PermissiontoQuoteform.pdf; accessed April 5, 2011.

7. The Massachusetts Historical Society, "Rights & Reproductions," http://www.masshist.org/legal/rights.cfm; accessed April 5, 2011.

8. American Library Association and Society of American Archivists, "ALA-SAA Joint Statement of Access: Guidelines for Access to Original Research Materials (August 1994)," revised Aug. 2009, http://www.archivists.org/statements/alasaa.asp.

9. Complaint for Declaratory Relief, *Schwartz v. Berkeley Historical Society*, No. 05-CV-1551 (N.D. Cal., filed April 15, 2005).

10. Ibid., paras. 7, 11.

11. Ibid., paras. 8–9.

12. Ibid., paras. 10–12.

13. Ibid., paras. 14–15.

14. Stipulation of Dismissal, *Schwartz v. Berkeley Historical Society*, No. 05-CV-1551 (N.D. Cal., entered Sept. 9, 2005).

15. *Salinger v. Random House, Inc.*, 650 F. Supp. 413 (S.D.N.Y. 1986).

16. Ibid., 416–17.

17. In ruling on Salinger's application for a preliminary injunction against publication, the district court found that the excerpts were fair use or did not otherwise infringe any of Salinger's copyrights. Ibid., 426. The court also rejected Salinger's claim that Hamilton had violated his rights as a third-party beneficiary under the access agreements because it construed the agreements to prohibit only copying that would infringe copyright (427). On appeal, the United States Court of Appeals for the Second Circuit disagreed with the trial court's fair use analysis and reversed, but it did not consider Salinger's breach-of-contract claim. *Salinger v. Random House, Inc.*, 811 F.2d 90 (2d Cir. 1987).

18. *Saturday Evening Post Co. v. Rumbleseat Press, Inc.*, 816 F.2d 1191 (7th Cir. 1987).

19. Ibid., 1199–2000. Posner reasoned that enforcing the contractual provision posed little danger of a monopoly because if it were indeed the case that the *Post* did not own valid copyrights, it could not prevent others from making porcelain dolls in the future, and would-be licensees would look into the validity of any asserted copyright.

20. Minor League Baseball, "Terms and Conditions of Credentials for Minor League Baseball Events," § 2, http://web.minorleaguebaseball.com/documents/2009/09/23/7116698/1/2010MediaCredential.pdf ; accessed April 27, 2011.

21. Ibid., § 3.

22. Ibid., §§ 4, 6.

23. Associated Press, "The Associated Press Terms and Conditions of Use," para. 1, http://www.ap.org/pages/about/terms.html; accessed April 5, 2011.

24. *U.S. News & World Report*, "Terms and Conditions," Mar. 15, 2011, http://www.usnews.com/usnews/usinfo/terms.htm.

25. CBS Interactive, "Terms of Use," May 24, 2010, http://cbsitou.custhelp.com/app/answers/detail/a_id/1320.

26. OCLC, "WorldCat Resource Sharing Terms: The First Search/Electronic Collections Online Service Terms," § 2, http://firstsearch.oclc.org/help/en/fslegal.html; accessed April 5, 2011.

27. YouTube, "Terms of Service," § 5(B), http://www.youtube.com/t/terms; accessed April 5, 2011.

28. For example, at NYTimes.com, in the terms of service, the *Times* disclaims "warranties of any kind," including the implied warranties of merchantability and fitness for a particular purpose. *New York Times*, "Terms of Service," § 5.2, http://www.nytimes.com/ref/membercenter/help/agree.html; accessed April 5, 2011.

29. Facebook's clickwrap agreement provides, "[Y[ou grant us a non-exclusive, transferable, sub-licensable, royalty-free, worldwide license to use any IP content that you post on or in connection with Facebook." Facebook, "Statement of Rights and Responsibilities," http://www.facebook.com/terms.php; accessed April 5, 2011.

30. *Video Pipeline, Inc., v. Buena Vista Home Entertainment, Inc.*, 342 F.3d 191, 203 (2003).

31. Microsoft, "Microsoft Easy Assist Pre-Release (Beta) Service Agreement," § 4, http://office.microsoft.com/en-us/help/microsoft-software-license-terms-HA010253792.aspx; accessed April 5, 2011.

32. Symantec, "Terms and Conditions," § 16.3, https://www4.symantec.com/Vrt/offer?a_id=38693; accessed April 5, 2011.

33. *Sony Computer Entertainment, Inc., v. Connectix Corp.*, 203 F.3d 596, 599 (9th Cir. 2000).

34. 17 U.S.C. § 1201(f) (2006).

35. Apple, "iTunes Store Terms and Conditions," http://www.apple.com/legal/itunes/us/terms.html#SERVICE; accessed April 5, 2011. This includes DMCA exemptions issued by the Library of Congress (see Chapter 4).

36. Amazon.com, "Amazon Kindle: License Agreement and Terms of Use," http://www.amazon.com/gp/help/customer/display.html?nodeId=200144530; accessed April 5, 2011.

37. Novell, "SUSE LINUX Enterprise Server (SLES 10): Novell Software License Agreement," http://www.novell.com/licensing/eula/sles_10/sles_10_english.pdf; accessed April 5, 2011.

38. U.S. Constitution, art. 6, § 2.

39. 17 U.S.C. § 301(a).

40. Ibid., § 301(b)(1).

41. *Vault Corp. v. Quaid Software, Ltd.*, 847 F.2d 255, 270 (5th Cir. 1988).

42. *Altera Corp. v. Clear Logic, Inc.*, 424 F.3d 1079, 1082 (9th Cir. 2005).

43. Ibid., 1089–90.

44. *ProCD, Inc., v. Zeidenberg*, 86 F.3d 1447 (7th Cir. 1996).

45. *Feist Publications, Inc., v. Rural Telephone Service Co.,* 449 U.S. 340 (1991). See Chapter 1 for further discussion of this case.

46. *ProCD, Inc.,* 86 F.3d at 1453.

47. Ibid., 1454.

48. Ibid., 1455.

49. Ibid.

50. For example, in *Bowers v. Baystate Technologies,* the Federal Circuit held that section 301 of the Copyright Act did not preempt a shrinkwrap provision that barred reverse engineering. *Bowers v. Baystate Technologies, Inc.,* 320 F.3d 1317, 1323 (Fed. Cir. 2003). The court found that the mutual assent and consideration that underlie a contract make a breach-of-contract claim qualitatively different from a copyright claim.

51. *Compco Corp. v. Day-Brite Lighting, Inc.,* 376 U.S. 234, 237 (1964). See also *Sears, Roebuck & Co. v. Stiffel Co.,* 376 U.S. 225, 232–33 (1964). The *Sears* case invalidated a state unfair-competition law that prevented copying of unpatented work, holding that "a State may not, when the article is unpatented and uncopyrighted, prohibit the copying of the article itself or award damages for such copying."

52. *Bonito Boats, Inc., v. Thunder Craft Boats, Inc.,* 489 U.S. 141 (1989).

53. Raymond T. Nimmer, "Breaking Barriers: The Relation Between Contract and Intellectual Property Law," *Berkeley Technology Law Journal* 13 (Fall 1998): 829.

54. Ibid., 829, 841–43.

55. Mark A. Lemley, "Intellectual Property and Shrinkwrap Licenses," *Southern California Law Review* 68, no. 5 (1995): 1264; Michael J. Madison, "Legal-Ware: Contract and Copyright in the Digital Age," *Fordham Law Review* 67, no. 3 (1998): 1134, 1139; David Nimmer, Elliot Brown, and Gary N. Frischling, "The Metamorphosis of Contract into Expand," *California Law Review* 87, no. 1 (1999): 76.

56. In this respect, the licenses offered by Creative Commons and other forms of private ordering that *increase* the rights of users beyond those allowed by copyright law are also not without costs. Private ordering, even when intended to enhance the rights of users, can create confusion about what uses are actually permissible and can inadvertently spill over to materials that are not even protected by copyright law. Séverine Dusollier, "Sharing Access to Intellectual Property Through Private Ordering," *Chicago-Kent Law Review* 82, no. 3 (2007): 1413, 1417–18, 1425–26.

57. Such a provision cannot, however, apply to the question of whether the user has assented to the license itself, and so the resolution of that issue will remain subject to variation.

58. Robert W. Gomulkiewicz and Mary L. Williamson, "A Brief Defense of Mass Market Software License Agreements," *Rutgers Computer and Technology Law Journal* 22, no. 2 (1996): 342.

59. In some instances courts have refused to enforce a license where they have concluded that the user did not consent to the terms because these were hidden. One example is *Specht v. Netscape Communications Corporation*, which held unenforceable a license that was viewable only if the visitor scrolled to the bottom of the webpage. *Specht v. Netscape Communications Corp.*, 306 F.3d 17 (2d Cir. 2002).

60. Christina Bohannan, "Copyright Preemption of Contracts," *Maryland Law Review* 67, no. 3 (2008): 619–20.

61. Ibid., 620.

62. Ibid.

63. Ibid., 652.

64. Ibid., 654–55.

65. Ibid., 651.

66. The European Union's Computer Software Directive bars contractual provisions prohibiting the reverse engineering of software in order to develop interoperable products. Council Directive 91/250/CEE, arts. 5(3), 6(1), 9(1), 1991 O.J. (L 122) 42. The directive also provides that "the making of a back-up copy by a person having a right to use the computer program may not be prevented by contract insofar as it is necessary for that use" (art. 5(2)).

67. The American Law Institute's *Principles of the Law of Software Contracts* (Philadelphia: American Law Institute, 2010), which set limits on the use of contracts that give software manufacturers stronger rights than intellectual property law confers, is also instructive. Under section 1.09(b), "[a] term of an agreement is unenforceable if it . . . conflicts impermissibly with the purposes and policies of federal intellectual property law." The commentary identifies four particular terms that, while not necessarily invalid, demand careful scrutiny: terms that preclude making fair use of the software, ban or limit reverse engineering, restrict copying or dissemination of factual information, or forbid subsequent transfer of the software.

68. For databases containing a mix of public domain and copyrighted materials, the database right would extend only to the public domain portions of the database; copyright law would protect the copyrighted portions.

69. Council Directive 96/9/EC, 1996 O.J. (L 77) 20.

70. Ibid., art. 7(4). Because the right is separate from copyright, the owner of a copyright in the database does not lose remedies available under copyright law.

71. Ibid., art. 10(1), (2).

72. Ibid., art. 7(1).

73. Ibid., art. 7(1), (2). Extraction is defined as "the permanent or temporary transfer of all or a substantial part of the contents of a database to another medium by any means or in any form" (art. 7(2)(a)). Reutilization is defined as "any form of making available to the public all or a substantial part of the contents of a database by the distribution of copies, by renting, by on-line or other forms of transmission," excluding the first sale of a lawful copy (art. 7(2)(b)).

74. Ibid., art. 8(2). To head off the possibility of a user taking all of a database in small amounts over time, there is liability for repeated and systematic extractions and reutilization of insubstantial parts of a database (art. 7(5)). Member states have the option of imposing additional restrictions on the database maker's rights in certain circumstances (art. 6(2)).

75. Whereas in the European Union a user is entitled to extract an "insubstantial" portion of a database, for our purposes, it would be better to set numerical limitations on permissible copying from the database.

CHAPTER 6

1. Brad Stone, "Amazon Erases Orwell Books from Kindle," *New York Times*, July 17, 2009; Miguel Helft, "Amazon.com Offers to Replace Copies of Orwell Book," *New York Times*, Sept. 4, 2009.

2. Nicholson Baker, "A New Page: Can the Kindle Really Improve on the Book?" *New Yorker*, Aug. 3, 2009, 27.

3. *Bobbs-Merrill Co. v. Straus*, 210 U.S. 339 (1908).

4. Ibid., 341.

5. Ibid., 342.

6. Ibid., 349. The publisher had argued in the lower court that the downstream purchaser was contractually bound by the price restriction but dropped that claim by the time the case reached the Supreme Court.

7. Ibid., 351.

8. *Independent News Co. v. Williams*, 293 F.2d 510 (3d Cir. 1961).

9. Ibid., 517–18.

10. Ibid., 518 n. 4.

11. Ibid., 517.

12. 17 U.S.C. § 106(3) (2006) (giving the copyright owner the exclusive right "to distribute copies or phonorecords of the copyrighted work to the public by sale or other transfer of ownership, or by rental, lease, or lending").

13. Ibid., § 109(a).

14. Ibid., § 109(b)(1)(A). The ban does not apply to nonprofit activities of nonprofit libraries and educational institutions.

15. 17 U.S.C. § 109(d).

16. Ibid., § 109(b)(2)(A). The restriction does not apply to the lending of software by nonprofit libraries so long as they attach a copyright warning notice to the software.

17. TurboTax, "TurboTax Desktop Software: Tax Year 2010 End User License Agreement," § B.3, http://turbotax.intuit.com/corp/desktoplicense.jsp; accessed April 5, 2011.

18. Ibid., § A.2.C.

19. *SoftMan Products Co., LLC, v. Adobe Systems, Inc.*, 171 F. Supp. 2d 1075 (C.D. Cal. 2001).

20. Ibid., 1083 n. 8.

21. Moreover, the court noted, SoftMan was not bound by any contractual restrictions because it was not a party to the distributorship licensing agreement and it had not accepted the provisions of the end user license agreement by installing the software on a computer.

22. *Adobe Systems, Inc., v. One Stop Micro, Inc.*, 84 F. Supp. 2d 1086 (N.D. Cal. 2000).

23. Ibid., 1088.

24. Ibid., 1090–93.

25. 17 U.S.C. § 117(a)(1).

26. *Krause v. Titleserv, Inc.*, 402 F.3d 119 (2d Cir. 2005).

27. Ibid., 124.

28. Ibid.

29. *Vernor v. Autodesk, Inc.*, 621 F.3d 1102 (9th Cir. 2010).

30. *Vernor v. Autodesk, Inc.*, 555 F. Supp. 2d 1164, 1166 (W.D. Wash. 2008).

31. Ibid.

32. Autodesk could, however, pursue a claim for breach of the license agreement.

33. *Vernor v. Autodesk, Inc.*, 621 F.3d 1102, 1111 (9th Cir. 2010).

34. Ibid., 1116.

35. Adobe Systems, "End-User License Agreement," § 5, http://www.adobe.com/products/eulas/players/shockwave; accessed April 5, 2011.

36. *MDY Industries, LLC v. Blizzard Entertainment, Inc.*, 629 F.3d 928, 942 (9th Cir. 2010).

37. Ibid., 938.

38. Ibid., 938.

39. Ibid., 941.

40. Ibid., 941.

41. Ibid., 941.

42. *NEBG, LLC, v. Weinstein Co. Holdings*, 490 F. Supp. 2d 89 (D. Mass. 2007).

43. Ibid., 96–97.

44. Randall Stross, "First It Was Song Downloads. Now It's Organic Chemistry," *New York Times*, July 27, 2008.

45. Jefferson Graham, "Firestorm Rages Over Lockdown on Digital Music," *USA Today*, Nov. 13, 2005. Chapter 4 discusses the recording industry's use of technological protection measures.

46. Rhapsody, "Rhapsody Service Terms of Use" § 6, http://www.rhapsody.com/terms_of_use; accessed April 5, 2011.

47. Ibid.

48. Ibid., § 2(p).

49. Ibid., § 7.

50. Ibid., § 3(b).

51. Kaplan PMBR, "Enrollment Form," http://www.kaptest.com/pmbr/download/Enrollment-Form-Post-April-18.pdf; accessed April 5, 2011.

CHAPTER 7

1. Complaint, *Hell's Angels Motorcycle Corp. v. Walt Disney Motion Pictures Group, Inc.*, No. CV-06-1459 (C.D. Cal. March 6, 2006).

2. *In re Trade-Mark Cases*, 100 U.S. 82, 94 (1879).

3. U.S. Constitution, art. 1, § 8.

4. Ibid.

5. 15 U.S.C. § 1127 (2006). A service mark is a trademark used in connection with services rather than goods.

6. *Wal-Mart Stores, Inc., v. Samara Brothers, Inc.*, 529 U.S. 205, 209 (2000). Trade dress protection does not extend to "functional" designs. "In general terms, a product feature is functional, and cannot serve as a trademark, if it is essential to the use or purpose of the article or if it affects the cost or quality of the article." *TrafFix Devices, Inc., v. Marketing Displays, Inc.*, 532 U.S. 23, 32 (2001) (quotations omitted).

7. U.S. Trademark No. 3,365,816 (issued Jan. 8, 2008).

8. A building's design can also be protected under the related category of trade

dress. *Taco Cabana International, Inc., v. Two Pesos, Inc.*, 932 F.2d 1113 (5th Cir. 1991) (recognizing trade dress in the design of a Mexican restaurant), *aff'd*, 505 U.S. 763 (1992).

9. *Two Pesos, Inc., v. Taco Cabana, Inc.*, 505 U.S. 763, 768 (1992).

10. *KP Permanent Make-Up, Inc., v. Lasting Impression I, Inc.*, 543 U.S. 111, 122 (2004).

11. 15 U.S.C. §§ 1057, 1072.

12. Ibid., §§ 1057, 1072, 1117, 1121.

13. The ^SM symbol is used for an unregistered service mark.

14. 15 U.S.C. § 1125(a)(1)(A).

15. See *KP Permanent Make-Up, Inc.*, 543 U.S. at 122. For incontestable marks, the Lanham Act recognizes the defense. 15 U.S.C. § 1115(b)(4). For non-incontestable marks, the defense is a judge-made doctrine.

16. *Sunmark, Inc., v. Ocean Spray Cranberries, Inc.*, 64 F.3d 1055, 1058 (7th Cir. 1995).

17. For marks that are incontestable under 15 U.S.C. § 1065, the Lanham Act recognizes nominative fair use. 15 U.S.C. § 1115(b)(4). For non-incontestable marks, nominative fair use is a creation of the courts.

18. In contrast to descriptive fair use, nominative fair use is not ordinarily a defense to infringement but rather goes to the analysis of whether there is a likelihood of confusion (and therefore infringement in the first place). However, in the Third Circuit, nominative fair use is a defense. *Century 21 Real Estate Corp. v. Lendingtree, Inc.*, 425 F.3d 211, 228 (3d Cir. 2005).

19. *New Kids on the Block v. News America Publishing, Inc.*, 971 F.2d 302 (9th Cir. 1992).

20. Ibid., 308.

21. Typically, this is not a traditional defense in the sense that a defendant raises it after being found liable for infringement. Rather, the court generally considers the First Amendment issue in determining whether there is any likelihood of confusion.

22. *Rogers v. Grimaldi*, 875 F.2d 994, 999 (2d Cir. 1989).

23. *Twin Peaks Productions, Inc., v. Publications International, Ltd.*, 996 F.2d 1366, 1379 (2d Cir. 1993).

24. As one court has explained, "When businesses seek the national spotlight, part of the territory includes accepting a certain amount of ridicule. The First Amendment . . . allows such ridicule in the form of parody." *Nike, Inc., v. "Just Did It" Enterprises*, 6 F.3d 1225, 1227 (7th Cir. 1993).

25. *Louis Vuitton Malletier S.A. v. Haute Diggity Dog, LLC*, 507 F.3d 252, 263 (4th Cir. 2007).

26. *Hormel Foods Corp. v. Jim Henson Productions, Inc.*, 73 F.3d 497 (2d Cir. 1996).

27. *Coca-Cola Co. v. Gemini Rising, Inc.*, 346 F. Supp. 1183 (E.D.N.Y. 1972).

28. Ibid., 1189 and n. 9.

29. See Federal Trademark Dilution Act of 1995, Pub. L. No. 104-98, §4, 109 Stat. 985 (codified as 15 U.S.C. § 1127 (2000)) (superseded in part by Trademark Dilution Revision Act of 2006, Pub. L. No. 109-312 §2, 120 Stat. 1730 (codified as 15 U.S.C. § 1125 (2006))).

30. The Lanham Act provides for injunctive relief where there is a likelihood of dilution, so that the owner of the trademark can prevent the defendant from using the mark. 15 U.S.C. § 1125(c)(1). Damages are only available in a dilution action if the defendant willfully intended to trade on the recognition of the plaintiff's mark (blurring) or willfully intended to harm the reputation of the plaintiff's mark (tarnishment). Ibid., § 1125(c)(5)(B).

31. 15 U.S.C. § 1125(c)(2)(B).

32. *Tiffany & Co. v. Boston Club, Inc.*, 231 F. Supp. 836, 843 (D. Mass. 1964); *Eli Lilly & Co. v. Natural Answers, Inc.*, 233 F.3d 456, 467–69 (7th Cir. 2000).

33. 15 U.S.C. § 1125(c)(2)(C).

34. *Archdiocese of St. Louis v. Internet Entertainment Group*, 34 F. Supp. 2d 1145, 1146 (E.D. Mo. 1999); *Hasbro, Inc., v. Internet Entertainment Group, Ltd.*, No. C96-130WD, 1996 WL 84853, *1 (W.D. Wash. Feb. 9, 1996).

35. 15 U.S.C. § 1125(c)(2)(A).

36. *7-Eleven, Inc., v. Lawrence I. Wechsler*, 83 U.S.P.Q.2d 1715, 1721–22, 2007 WL 1431084, *6–7 (T.T.A.B. May 15, 2007); *Pepsico, Inc., v. #1 Wholesale, LLC*, 84 U.S.P.Q.2d 1040, 2007 WL 2142294 (N.D. Ga. July 20, 2007).

37. 15 U.S.C. § 1125(c)(3)(A).

38. Ibid.

39. Ibid., § 1125(c)(3)(B), (C).

40. *MasterCard International, Inc., v. Nader 2000 Primary Committee, Inc.*, 70 U.S.P.Q.2d 1046, 2004 WL 434404 (S.D.N.Y. March 8, 2004).

41. Fox sought also to prevent Franken from using a photo of Fox commentator Bill O'Reilly on the book's cover on the ground that the photo suggested that O'Reilly was endorsing the book.

42. Complaint, *Fox News Network, LLC, v. Penguin Group (USA), Inc.*, No. 602514/2003 (Sup. Ct. N.Y. Aug. 7, 2003), para. 77.

43. Bench Opinion, *Fox News Network, LLC, v. Penguin Group (USA), Inc.*, No. 03-CV- 6162 (S.D.N.Y. Aug. 22, 2003).

44. The infringement section of the Lanham Act states that any person who "use[s] in commerce any reproduction, counterfeit, copy, or colorable imitation of a registered mark in connection with the sale, offering for sale, distribution, or advertising of any goods or services on or in connection with which such use is likely to cause confusion, or to cause mistake, or to deceive" is liable for such use. 15 U.S.C. § 1114(1)(a).

45. *Bosley Medical Institute, Inc., v. Kremer*, 403 F.3d 672, 676, 680 (9th Cir. 2005) (emphasis added).

46. Lisa Bannon, "Barrister Barbie? Mattel Plays Rough," *Wall Street Journal*, Jan. 6, 1998.

47. Ibid.

48. *Mattel, Inc., v. MCA Records, Inc.*, 296 F.3d 894, 903–4, 907 (9th Cir. 2002).

49. *Mattel, Inc., v. Walking Mountain Productions*, 353 F.3d 792, 807, 812 (9th Cir. 2003).

50. Complaint, *Frankel v. Lyons Partnership, LP,* No. 06-CV-6413 (S.D.N.Y. Aug. 23, 2006).

51. Settlement Agreement, *Frankel v. Lyons Partnership, LP*, No. 06-CV-6413 (S.D.N.Y. Nov. 21, 2006).

52. *Caterpillar, Inc., v. Walt Disney Co.*, 287 F. Supp. 2d 913, 919–20 (C.D. Ill. 2003).

53. Ibid., 923.

54. Complaint, *Emerson Electric Co. v. NBC Universal Television Studios, Inc.*, No. 06-CV-01454 (E.D. Mo. Oct. 2, 2006).

55. Maureen Dowd, "Sultan of Swagger," *New York Times*, July 13, 2010.

56. Patricia Aufderheide and Peter Jaszi, *Untold Stories: Creative Consequences of the Rights Clearance Culture for Documentary Filmmakers* (Washington, D.C.: Center for Social Media, 2004), 9–10, http://www.centerforsocialmedia.org/sites/default/files/UNTOLDSTORIES_Report.pdf.

57. Blurring may also result from a filmmaker's desire not to give free publicity to a particular product.

58. *Rock and Roll Hall of Fame and Museum, Inc., v. Gentile Productions*, 134 F.3d 749, 754 (6th Cir. 1998) ("[W]hen we view the photograph in Gentile's poster, we do not readily recognize the design of the Museum's building as an indicator of source or sponsorship. What we see, rather, is a photograph of an accessible, well-known, public landmark.").

59. Dismissing the case, the court asked rhetorically, "[A]s between whom was any purchasing decision affected?" *Sherwood 48 Associates v. Sony Corp. of America*, 213 F. Supp. 2d 376, 377 (S.D.N.Y. 2002).

60. Misuse of the registered trademark symbol can lead to a later denial of registration or other consequences. J. Thomas McCarthy, *McCarthy on Trademarks and Unfair Competition*, 4th ed., vol. 3 (Eagan, Minn.: West, 2010), 19:146.

61. *Comedy III Productions, Inc., v. New Line Cinema*, 200 F.3d 593, 595 (9th Cir. 2000).

62. A. Michael Froomkin, "ICANN's 'Uniform Dispute Resolution Policy'— Causes and (Partial) Cures," *Brooklyn Law Review* 67, no. 3 (2002): 629–30.

63. 15 U.S.C. § 1125(d).

64. Ibid., § 1125(d)(1)(A). The statute provides a series of factors for courts to consider in determining whether the requisite intent exists. Ibid., § 1125(d)(1)(B).

65. Jacqueline D. Lipton, "Commerce Versus Commentary: Gripe Sites, Parody, and the First Amendment in Cyberspace," *Washington University Law Review* 84, no. 6 (2006): 1327.

66. *Lamparello v. Falwell*, 420 F.3d 309, 320 (4th Cir. 2005) (quotations omitted).

67. 15 U.S.C. §§ 1069, 1127.

68. Tracy Gruen, "Concert Planner Agrees to Drop 'Mc'; After Challenge from McDonald's, Benefit to Go on with New Name," *Chicago Tribune*, Aug. 4, 2010.

69. Amanda Cantrell, "Branson Trademark Suit Sparks Debate," *CNNMoney. com*, June 29, 2005, http://money.cnn.com/2005/06/29/news/newsmakers/branson_ suit/index.htm.

70. By contrast, see *Virgin Enterprises, Ltd., v. Nawab*, 335 F.3d 141, 146 (2d Cir. 2003) (finding likelihood that the defendant's use of the name "Virgin Wireless" would create confusion, when the plaintiff also markets a variety of electronic products).

71. Steve Stecklow, "The Scariest Monster of All Sues for Trademark Infringement," *Wall Street Journal*, April 4, 2009.

72. Ibid.

73. Michael Perelman, "The Political Economy of Intellectual Property," *Monthly Review* 54, no. 8 (2003): 29.

74. Corynne McSherry, "Cyberlaw and Cyberlawgs," Electronic Frontier Foundation, Jan. 18, 2008, http://www.eff.org/deeplinks/2008/01/cyberlaw-and-cyberlawgs.

75. U.S. Patent and Trademark Office, No. 77/341910, Office Action, March 13, 2008.

76. Denying *Playboy*'s motion for a preliminary injunction, the district court found that because Welles used the Playmate mark to describe and identify herself, her use was protected by the fair use provision of trademark law and in any event there was no likelihood of consumer confusion. *Playboy Enterprises, Inc., v. Welles*, 7 F. Supp. 2d 1098, 1103–5 (S.D. Cal. 1998).

77. Craig S. Mende, "On Watching the Big Game," *Forbes.com*, Feb. 1, 2008, http://www.forbes.com/2008/01/31/superbowl-nfl-trademark-oped-cx_csm_0201superbowl.html.

78. *Central Manufacturing Co. v. Pure Fishing, Inc.*, No. 05-CV-00725, 2005 WL 3090988 (N.D. Ill. Nov. 16, 2005); *Central Manufacturing, Inc., v. Brett*, 492 F.3d 876 (7th Cir. 2007).

79. Executive Committee Order, *In the Matter of Leo Stoller*, No. 07-C-1435 (N.D. Ill. March 8, 2007), http://home.comcast.net/~jlw28129/Stoller_Exec_Comm_Order.pdf.

80. For a collection of relevant correspondence, see the materials submitted by Columbia as part of its lawsuit against Stoller. Complaint, *Columbia Pictures Industries, Inc., v. Stoller*, No. 05C 2052 (N.D. Ill. April 7, 2005), http://home.comcast.net/~jlw28129/05_C_2052.pdf.

81. Trade Marks Act, 1994, ch. 26, § 21(1) (UK). The rights of trademark owners under U.K. law are similar but not identical to those of trademark owners under U.S. law, as discussed in Chapter 7. Under U.K. law, trademark infringement occurs in three circumstances. First, "A person infringes a registered trade mark if he uses in the course of trade a sign which is identical with the trade mark in relation to goods or services which are identical with those for which it is registered." Ibid., § 10(1). No showing of consumer confusion is required under these conditions. Second, there is infringement when "a likelihood of confusion on the part of the public" results from the use of a sign that "is identical with the trade mark and is used in relation to goods or services similar to those for which the trade mark is registered" or is "similar to the trade mark and is used in relation to goods or services identical with or similar to those for which the trade mark is registered." Ibid., § 10(2). Third, similar to the U.S. law of dilution of famous marks, there is infringement under U.K. law when a person "uses in the course of trade a sign" that is "identical with or similar to the trade mark" and "used in relation to goods or services which are not similar to those for which the trade mark is registered" where "the trade mark has a reputation in the United Kingdom and the use of the sign, being without due cause, takes unfair advantage of, or is detrimental to, the distinctive character or the repute of the trade mark." Ibid., § 10(3).

82. Ibid., § 21(1), (2).

83. *L'Oréal (UK), Ltd., v. Johnson & Johnson* [2000] E.T.M.R. 691, 698–99.

84. Trade Marks Act, § 21(2).

85. Ibid., § 21(1).

86. Similar to the American law of trademark fair use, U.K. law specifically allows certain uses of registered marks, including a use to identify somebody else's goods or services, as occurs in comparative advertising. Ibid., § 10(6).

87. Because it may be hard to prove actual damages, and actual damages might not be high enough to act as a sufficient deterrence, statutory damages should be available.

88. This is not to suggest that licensing does not occur. But when it does, it usually takes the form of a mutually beneficial marketing arrangement, for example, when cartoon characters are licensed to an apparel company for use on T-shirts.

CHAPTER 8

1. Mark Twain, *The Signet Classic Book of Mark Twain's Short Stories*, ed. Justin Kaplan (New York: Signet, 1985).

2. Frederick Douglass, *Narrative of the Life of Frederick Douglass* (New York: Signet, 1997).

3. *Restatement (Second) of Torts* (Philadelphia: American Law Institute, 1977), § 525.

4. 35 U.S.C. § 292(a) (2006).

5. Section 292(a) provides for a maximum fine of $500 for "every . . . offense" of false marking. Each item marked constitutes a single offense. *Forest Group v. Bon Tool Co.*, 590 F.3d 1295, 1300–1301 (Fed. Cir. 2009).

6. See *Boyd v. Schildkraut Giftware Corp.*, 936 F.2d 76, 79 (2d Cir. 1991).

7. Such actions are known as *qui tam* claims. 35 U.S.C. § 292 (b).

8. *Clontech Laboratories, Inc., v. Invitrogen Corp.*, 406 F.3d 1347, 1352 (Fed. Cir. 2005).

9. Under Supreme Court doctrine, Congress could not constitutionally *require* state governmental agencies to enforce a federal copyfraud law. See *Printz v. United States*, 521 U.S. 898, 923–24, 933, 935 (1997) (invalidating provisions of the Brady Handgun Violence Prevention Act because the Constitution prohibits Congress from commandeering state executive officials to enforce federal law).

10. Trevor W. Morrison, "Private Attorneys General and the First Amendment," *Michigan Law Review* 103, no. 4 (2005): 590.

11. 35 U.S.C. § 292(a).

12. Ibid., § 292(b).

13. See *Vermont Agency of Natural Resources v. United States* ex rel. *Stevens*, 529 U.S. 768, 774–77 (2000) (discussing the history of *qui tam* actions).

14. 31 U.S.C. § 3730(b).

15. Ibid., § 3730(d)(1)–(2). This section provides private claimants with reasonable expenses and attorneys' fees, in addition to a percentage of penalties and damages.

16. *Kowalski v. Tesmer*, 543 U.S. 125, 129 n. 2 (2004).

17. *Whitmore v. Arkansas*, 495 U.S. 149, 155 (1990).

18. *Lujan v. Defenders of Wildlife*, 504 U.S. 555 (1992).

19. *Asarco, Inc., v. Kadish*, 490 U.S. 605, 617 (1989).

20. *Vermont Agency of Natural Resources*, 529 U.S. at 773–74 (holding that a private party had Article III standing to bring an action under the False Claims Act).

21. 18 U.S.C. § 1963.

22. Ibid., § 1964(c).

23. Ibid., § 1964 (a)–(b).

24. *H. J., Inc., v. Northwestern Bell Telephone Co.*, 492 U.S. 229, 239 (1989).

25. Ibid., 240 (internal quotations omitted).

26. *Schlaifer Nance & Co. v. Estate of Andy Warhol*, 119 F.3d 91, 97 (2d Cir. 1997).

27. 18 U.S.C. § 1961(1) (defining predicate offenses). See also section 1341 (prohibiting the use of the U.S. Postal Service or private interstate carrier in committing fraud) and section 1343 (prohibiting the use of wire, radio, or television in interstate fraud).

28. See Paul J. Heald, "Payment Demands for Spurious Copyrights: Four Causes of Action," *Journal of Intellectual Property Law* 1, no. 2 (1994): 259.

29. *Tams-Witmark Music Library, Inc., v. New Opera Co.*, 81 N.E.2d 70, 74–75 (N.Y. 1948).

30. *Schlaifer Nance & Co.*, 119 F.3d at 98–102. However, the court found that the licensing agency could not make out a fraud claim because the agency had sufficient information about the status of the works and images at the time at which it entered the licensing agreement that any reliance on the defendant's misrepresentations was unreasonable, and therefore this could not be the basis for recovery.

31. *McKinney's Consolidated Laws of New York Annotated* § 350 (West 2004).

32. Ibid., § 350-a.

33. Ibid., § 350-d.

34. Ibid., § 350-e.

35. See *Geismar v. Abraham & Strauss*, 439 N.Y.S.2d 1005, 1008 (N.Y. Dist. Ct. 1981).

36. 17 U.S.C. § 301(a).

37. Ibid., § 301(b).

38. See *Baltimore Orioles, Inc., v. Major League Baseball Players Association*, 805 F.2d 663, 676 (7th Cir. 1986) ("Congress contemplated that as long as a work fits within one of the general subject matter categories of section 102 and 103, . . . [section 301(a)] prevents the States from protecting it even if it fails to achieve Federal copyright because it is too minimal or lacking in originality to qualify.") (internal quotations omitted).

39. Ibid., 676 n. 23.

40. As for federal consumer protection law itself, section 5 of the Federal Trade Commission Act prohibits "unfair or deceptive acts or practices in or affecting commerce." 15 U.S.C. § 45(a)(1) (2006). However, courts have held that there is no private right of action under this provision. See *Holloway v. Bristol-Myers Corp.*, 485 F.2d 986, 988–89, 997 (D.C. Cir. 1973). Section 43(a) of the federal Lanham Act allows people injured or likely to be injured by a deceptive or confusing advertisement to sue the offending business. 15 U.S.C. § 1125(a). Yet it is not clear the provision extends to false copyright designation. In 2007, the Federal Trade Commission declined to pursue action against media companies that, according to allegations in a complaint made by the Computer & Communications Industry Association (a trade organization), had violated the consumer protection provisions of section 5 of the Federal Trade Commission Act by misrepresenting the scope of claimed copyrights. Mary K. Engle, "Letter to Computer & Communications Industry Association," Federal Trade Commission, Division of Advertising Practices, Dec. 6, 2007, http://www.ftc.gov/os/closings/staff/071206ccia.pdf.

CHAPTER 9

1. Gideon Parchomovsky and Kevin A. Goldman, "Fair Use Harbors," *Virginia Law Review* 93, no. 6 (2007): 1511–12.

2. Ibid., 1514–17.

3. Michael W. Carroll, "Fixing Fair Use," *North Carolina Law Review* 85 (2007): 1122–43.

4. Thomas F. Cotter, "Fair Use and Copyright Overenforcement," *Iowa Law Review* 93, no. 4 (2008): 1301–8.

5. In Finland, the Copyright Council, part of the Ministry of Education and Culture, issues opinions on the application of that nation's Copyright Act.

Ministry of Education and Culture, "Copyright in Finland," http://www.minedu.
fi/OPM/Tekijaenoikeus/?lang=en; accessed April 5, 2011. The council comprises
representatives of major rights holders and users of protected works and academic
professionals. Although the council's opinions are not binding, courts give them
deference. Ministry of Education and Culture, "Copyright Council," http://www.
minedu.fi/OPM/Tekijaenoikeus/tekijaenoikeusneuvosto/?lang=en; accessed April 5,
2011.

6. Minister of Justice, trans., *Israel: Copyright Act, 2007*, http://www.tau.ac.il/
law/members/birnhack/IsraeliCopyrightAct2007.pdf; accessed April 5, 2011.

7. Michael Abramowicz and John F. Duffy's proposal for privatizing the patent
examination process provides a useful discussion of the benefits of privatization.
Michael Abramowicz and John F. Duffy, "Ending the Patent Monopoly," *University
of Pennsylvania Law Review* 157, no. 6 (2009): 1541.

8. However, because the Copyright Office is part of a legislative agency rather
than an executive agency, there may be constitutional problems in assigning the
Copyright Office increased regulatory functions. See *Freytag v. Commissioner of
Internal Revenue*, 501 U.S. 868 (1991); *Immigration and Naturalization Service v.
Chadha*, 462 U.S. 919 (1983).

9. Mark A. Lemley and R. Anthony Reese, "Reducing Digital Copyright
Infringement Without Restricting Innovation," *Stanford Law Review* 56 (2004):
1413.

10. Joseph P. Liu, "Regulatory Copyright," *North Carolina Law Review* 83, no.
1 (2004): 148–56. In a suggestion that resonates with the themes of this chapter, Liu
writes that "rather than enacting specific industry exemptions to copyright liability,
Congress could delegate to the Copyright Office the authority to promulgate
additional exemptions via regulation," such that "exemption through regulation
could perhaps usefully fill a gap currently left by the relative lack of guidance from
fair use doctrine, and provide additional guidance and certainty to industries that
routinely encounter difficult fair use issues" (151–52).

11. Ibid., 156–57.

12. See, e.g., Electronic Frontier Foundation, *DMCA Triennial Rulemaking:
Failing the Digital Consumer*, Dec. 1, 2005, 2, http://www.eff.org/IP/DMCA/
copyrightoffice/DMCA_rulemaking_broken.pdf ("The   DMCA   triennial
rulemaking has failed to protect lawful consumer activities").

13. James Boyle, *The Public Domain: Enclosing the Commons of the Mind* (New
Haven, Conn.: Yale University Press, 2008), 243–44.

14. As Joseph Liu explains, "A narrow group of interests—namely the movie,

music, publishing, and software industries—stands to benefit from the expansion of intellectual property protection. They have the resources and incentives to lobby for such expansion . . . . Although . . . [consumers] bear much of the cost of expansions, and such costs may be significant in the aggregate, each consumer bears only a miniscule share, spread out over time. Thus, as public choice theorists predict, consumers do not band together in sufficient numbers to oppose efforts by the copyright industries to expand protection." Joseph P. Liu, "Copyright and Time: A Proposal," *Michigan Law Review* 101, no. 2 (2002): 448–49 (footnotes omitted).

15. Jessica Litman, *Digital Copyright: Protecting Intellectual Property on the Internet* (Amherst, N.Y.: Prometheus Books, 2001), 74.

16. 5 U.S.C. § 553 (2006).

17. Ibid., §§ 561–70.

18. Beth Simone Noveck, "The Electronic Revolution in Rulemaking," *Emory Law Journal* 53, no. 2 (2004): 480–92.

19. As is normally true of agency rules, AFU's rules would have only prospective effect. 5 U.S.C. § 551(4) (defining a rule as "an agency statement of general or particular applicability and future effect"); *Bowen v. Georgetown University Hospital*, 488 U.S. 204, 216 (1988) (Scalia, J., concurring) ("The only plausible reading of th[is] . . . phrase is that rules have legal consequences only for the future.").

20. 5 U.S.C. § 706 (providing that the reviewing court shall "compel agency action unlawfully withheld or unreasonably delayed" and "hold unlawful and set aside agency action" that violates a statute, the Constitution, or a procedure established by law or is "arbitrary, capricious, an abuse of discretion, or otherwise not in accordance with law."). In *Chevron USA v. Natural Resources Defense Council*, the Supreme Court set out the standard of judicial review of an agency's interpretation of a statute. If Congress's intent in the statute is clear, then agencies and courts alike are required to "give effect to the unambiguously expressed intent of Congress" and a court must reject an agency's construction of a statute that is "contrary to clear congressional intent." *Chevron USA, Inc., v. Natural Resources Defense Council, Inc.*, 467 U.S. 837, 843, and n. 9 (1984). Where, however, the statute is silent or ambiguous on the precise issue presented, a court may not "simply impose its own construction on the statute"; rather, "the question for the court is whether the agency's answer is based on a permissible construction of the statute" (843–44). *Chevron* further provides that if Congress has explicitly given an agency authority to fill a gap in a statute or elucidate a provision of the statute by regulation then courts must give the agency's regulations "controlling weight unless they are arbitrary, capricious, or manifestly

contrary to the statute" (844). In cases where legislative delegation to an agency is implicit, rather than explicit, *Chevron* instructs that "a court may not substitute its own construction of a statutory provision for a reasonable interpretation made by the administrator of an agency" (844).

21. 5 U.S.C. §§ 554, 556–57.

22. 15 U.S.C. § 53(b) (authorizing the Federal Trade Commission to seek preliminary and permanent injunctions in district court to remedy violations of "any provision of law enforced by the Federal Trade Commission"). Courts have construed this provision to also permit equitable monetary relief. See, e.g., *FTC v. World Travel Vacation Brokers, Inc.*, 861 F.2d 1020, 1024–28 (7th Cir. 1988).

23. See *Adams Fruit Co. v. Barrett*, 494 U.S. 638, 649 (1990) ("Congress has expressly established the Judiciary and not the Department of Labor as the adjudicator of private rights of action arising under the statute. A precondition to deference under Chevron is a congressional delegation of administrative authority.").

24. There would be a procedure for expedited review by CIRO in cases in which the plaintiff seeks a preliminary injunction.

25. Internet Corporation for Assigned Names and Numbers, "Uniform Domain-Name Dispute-Resolution Policy," http://www.icann.org/en/udrp/udrp.htm; accessed April 5, 2011.

26. Kenneth Crews, while critical of guidelines that are inconsistent with the flexible nature of fair use, offers several recommendations for developing guidelines that may be applicable here. Kenneth D. Crews, "The Law of Fair Use and the Illusion of Fair-Use Guidelines," *Ohio State Law Journal* 62, no. 2 (2001): 696–700. He suggests that guidelines should begin with the four statutory fair use factors (696). They should be flexible in their definition of fair use and in how the statutory factors may be met (697). Finally, the guidelines also should be developed through a process that is open to the public and in which parties staking out positions are required to provide legal justifications for those positions (698–700).

27. Pamela Samuelson, "Unbundling Fair Use," *Fordham Law Review* 77, no. 5 (2009): 2541–42.

28. Ibid., 2542.

29. Ibid., 2621.

30. See Rebecca Tushnet, "Copy This Essay: How Fair Use Doctrine Harms Free Speech and How Copying Serves It," *Yale Law Journal* 114, no. 3 (2004): 587 (advocating "tinker[ing] with the elements in the standard fair use test, in particular the purpose of the use and the amount used," in order to accommodate free speech concerns).

31. See Michael J. Madison, "A Pattern-Oriented Approach to Fair Use," *William and Mary Law Review* 45, no. 4 (2004): 1623, 1642–44 (advocating that the fair use factors be applied with a view to whether the use is fair "in the context of a recognized social or cultural pattern"); Lloyd L. Weinreb, "Fair Use," *Fordham Law Review* 67, no. 4 (1999): 1296, 1301, 1306–10 (suggesting that societal acceptance of what is a fair use should inform fair use analysis).

32. See Carroll, "Fixing Fair Use," 1087.

33. David Nimmer, "A Modest Proposal to Streamline Fair Use Determinations," *Cardozo Arts and Entertainment Law Journal* 24, no. 1 (2006): 11.

34. Jonathan Saltzman, "Student Must Pay $675k for Songs," *Boston Globe,* Aug. 1, 2009.

35. The Eleventh Amendment provides, "The Judicial power of the United States shall not be construed to extend to any suit in law or equity, commenced or prosecuted against one of the United States by Citizens of another State, or by Citizens or Subjects of any Foreign State."

36. *Seminole Tribe of Florida v. Florida,* 517 U.S. 44, 72–73 (1996).

37. *Fitzpatrick v. Bitzer,* 427 U.S. 445, 456 (1976).

38. U.S. Constitution, amend. XIV, § 1.

39. *City of Boerne v. Flores,* 521 U.S. 507 (1997).

40. *Florida Prepaid Postsecondary Education Expense Board v. College Savings Bank,* 527 U.S. 627 (1999).

41. Ibid., 640.

42. In a related decision in the same litigation, the Supreme Court held that Congress also could not abrogate state sovereign immunity and subject a state to a lawsuit for false advertising under the Lanham Act. *College Savings Bank v. Florida Prepaid Postsecondary Education Expense Board,* 537 U.S. 666, 672–75 (1999). Abrogation was invalid because the Fourteenth Amendment does not protect a right to be free from a competitor's false advertising or a more general right to be secure in one's business interests.

43. Section 511(a) provides, "Any State, any instrumentality of a State, and any officer or employee of a State or instrumentality of a State acting in his or her official capacity, shall not be immune, under the Eleventh Amendment of the Constitution of the United States or under any other doctrine of sovereign immunity, from suit in Federal court by any person, including any governmental or nongovernmental entity, for a violation of any of the exclusive rights of a copyright owner." 17 U.S.C. § 511(a) (2006).

44. See *Chavez v. Arte Publico Press,* 204 F.3d 601 (5th Cir. 2000).

45. Determining whether a particular entity is a state agency that is protected by sovereign immunity is not always easy. However, the Supreme Court has applied state sovereign immunity to a state university. See *Regents of the University of California v. Doe*, 519 U.S. 425 (1997).

46. Memorandum Pursuant to FRCP 45B(3)(A) by the University of Oregon in Support of Motion to Quash Subpoena, 1–17, *Arista Records v. Does*, No. 07-CV-6197 (D. Ore. Oct. 31, 2007).

47. *Ex Parte Young*, 209 U.S. 123 (1908).

48. Qualified immunity exists when state officers act within the scope of their discretionary authority and their conduct does not violate clearly established law. See *Hope v. Pelzer*, 536 U.S. 730, 739 (2002). Whether a state officer is entitled to the defense in a copyright infringement action may depend upon the circumstances of the case. Courts have reached different decisions on this issue in the cases before them. See *Marketing Information Masters, Inc., v. Board of Trustees of the California State University System*, 552 F. Supp. 2d 1088, 1094 (S.D. Cal. 2008) (holding that while a state agency cannot be sued for copyright infringement, a claim against the individual who did the actual copying for the state could proceed); *Chavez v. Arte Publico Press*, 59 F.3d 539, 547–48 (5th Cir. 1995) (granting qualified immunity where the defendant's actions did not violate clearly established law); *Richard Anderson Photography v. Brown*, 852 F.2d 114, 122–23 (4th Cir. 1988) (denying qualified immunity to an employee of a state university). Employees of state government will not avoid liability for clear acts of copyright infringement. See *National Association of Boards of Pharmacy v. Board of Regents of University System of Georgia*, No. 07-CV-84, 2008 WL 1805439, *22–23 (M.D. Ga. April 18, 2008) (rejecting a claim of qualified immunity where the defendant copied and sold a large number of the plaintiff's test questions because the activity clearly violated the law and could not be fair use). But they nonetheless occupy a unique position to invoke fair use and other protections the Copyright Act confers. Indeed, with respect to fair use, the current *ambiguity* in the law works in favor of a claim of qualified immunity: the lack of clear guidance on what constitutes fair use will weigh against a finding that the use violates clearly established law.

49. Association of Independent Video and Filmmakers et al., *Documentary Filmmakers' Statement of Best Practices in Fair Use*, Nov. 18, 2005, http://www.centerforsocialmedia.org/sites/default/files/fair_use_final.pdf.

50. Pat Aufderheide, "How Documentary Filmmakers Overcame Their Fear of Quoting and Learned to Employ Fair Use: A Tale of Scholarship in Action," *International Journal of Communication* 1 (2007): 33.

51. Pat Aufderheide and Peter Jaszi, "Fair Use and Best Practices: Surprising Success," *Intellectual Property Today* 14, no. 10 (2007): 26–27.

52. NPR, "Truth and Consequences," *On the Media*, May 8, 2009, http:// www.onthemedia.org/transcripts/2009/05/08/03. The remaining hitch, Quinn noted, is the anti-circumvention provision of the DMCA, which allows content owners to control access to copyrighted works: "[E]veryone knows how to break this encryption . . . [but] [w]e don't want to have this vulnerability of having broken this strange piece of the law." For additional discussion of this issue, see also U.S. Copyright Office, "§ 1201 Rulemaking Hearings Podcasts," http://www.copyright. gov/1201/hearings/2009/transcripts; accessed April 5, 2011.

CHAPTER 10

1. Groucho Marx, *The Groucho Letters: Letters from and to Groucho Marx* (New York: Simon & Schuster, 1967), 14–15.

2. This proposal would, however, need to comply with the Berne Convention, which requires member nations (including the United States) to provide for a minimum copyright term of fifty years after the author's death for most works by individual authors and prohibits formalities that affect the "enjoyment and exercise" of copyright. United Nations Treaty Series, "Berne Convention for the Protection of Literary and Artistic Works," arts. 5(2), 7(1) (Sept. 9, 1886), as revised, Paris, July 24, 1971, U.N.T.S. 1161, no. 18338, 30.

3. Free Library of Philadelphia, "Sheet Music Collection," http://libwww. library.phila.gov/collections/collectionDetail.cfm?id=15; accessed April 5, 2011.

4. Internet Archive, "Internet Archive Bookmobile," http://www.archive.org/ texts/bookmobile.php; accessed April 5, 2011.

5. Cornell University Library, "Cornell University Library Removes All Restrictions on Use of Public Domain Reproductions," press release, http://www. library.cornell.edu/node/1333; accessed April 5, 2011.

6. In addition to the ALA, there exist a variety of other organizations of librarians with common interests. For example, the American Association of Law Libraries is a five-thousand-member organization of librarians who work in law firms, courts, and corporate departments. The Music Library Association is an organization of librarians and archivists who collect and maintain musical works.

7. Other notable examples include the NASA Image Exchange (http://nix.nasa. gov), which offers downloadable photographs; the National Audiovisual Center (http://www.ntis.gov/products/nac.aspx), which provides copies of informational films produced by the federal government; and the National Archives and Records

Administration (http://www.archives.gov/public), which offers millions of public domain photographs, films, sound recordings, maps, and other items and from which electronic records are accessible online. Visitors to the National Archives in Maryland can use on-site video equipment to make copies of archival film material for their personal use; high-quality reproductions can be obtained through an approved video service.

8. California Sheet Music Project, "19th-Century California Sheet Music," http://people.ischool.berkeley.edu/~mkduggan/neh.html; accessed April 5, 2011.

9. National Endowment for the Humanities, "NEH Projects," http://www.neh.gov/projects/index.html; accessed April 5, 2011.

10. See Chilling Effects (http://www.chillingeffects.org), the Electronic Frontier Foundation (http://www.eff.org), and Public Knowledge (http://www.publicknowledge.org).

11. For an insightful analysis of the settlement, see James Grimmelmann, "How to Fix the Google Book Search Settlement," *Journal of Internet Law* 12, no. 10 (2009): 10–20.

12. Google Books, "The Bonfire of the Vanities," http://books.google.com/books?id=cAe6AwoVsqQC&dq=bonfire+of+the+vanities++1888&hl=en&ei=rmzUT K3dGoL4sAOUg5GNCw&sa=X&oi=book_result&ct=result&resnum=1&ved=0C CgQ6AEwAA; accessed April 5, 2011.

13. Lawyers who practice in federal court are bound by Rule 11 of the Federal Rules of Civil Procedure. Under this rule, every claim or other representation to a court must have a basis in the law. Courts may sanction attorneys who fail to comply with Rule 11. Many of the examples of overreaching we have seen do not involve representations to courts and so would not be subject to Rule 11 sanctions.

14. New York State Unified Court System, *Rules of Professional Conduct*, April 1, 2009, §§ 3.1(b)(1), 4.1.

15. Ibid., § 3.4.

ACKNOWLEDGMENTS

Like most books, this one was a collaborative endeavor. Brooklyn Law School provided me with generous research funding; I am grateful to Joan Wexler, Larry Solan, Michael Gerber, and Michael Cahill for their support and counsel throughout the project. I thank my research assistants: Kristie LaSalle, Max McCann, Justin Musumeci, Meghan Overgaard, Carmela Romeo, Aimée Scala, Ryan Varnum, Tom Volper, David Wheatley, M. J. Williams, and Maayan Zach. Three reviewers for Stanford University Press gave exceedingly helpful comments on the manuscript. I have presented the ideas in this book in many settings, including to groups of lawyers, judges, librarians, law professors, students, media professionals, teachers, and librarians. I am grateful for the questions and feedback I received in each of these settings. I thank also the many colleagues around the country and abroad who answered my questions about intellectual property law and provided valuable commentary and criticism. I gratefully acknowledge the editorial assistance of Sonia Fulop. Michael Melcher and Matthew Moore provided welcome comments on a late draft. Working with Kate Wahl and the editorial team at Stanford University Press has been a pleasure. The library staff at Brooklyn Law School helped to track down sources. My assistant, Bobbi Bullock, helped in numerous ways from the beginning of the project. Portions of Chapters 1 and 8 previously appeared in the *New York University Law Review*. Portions of Chapters 2 and 9 previously appeared in the *William and Mary Law Review*. I am grateful to the editors of those two publications.

INDEX